Securing the State and its Citizens

Securing the State and its Citizens

*National Security Councils from
Around the World*

Edited by
Paul O'Neill

BLOOMSBURY ACADEMIC
LONDON • NEW YORK • OXFORD • NEW DELHI • SYDNEY

BLOOMSBURY ACADEMIC
Bloomsbury Publishing Plc
50 Bedford Square, London, WC1B 3DP, UK
1385 Broadway, New York, NY 10018, USA
29 Earlsfort Terrace, Dublin 2, Ireland

BLOOMSBURY, BLOOMSBURY ACADEMIC and the Diana logo are
trademarks of Bloomsbury Publishing Plc

First published in Great Britain 2022

Cover design by Toby Way
Cover image © hakule/iStock

A catalogue record for this book is available from the British Library.

A catalog record for this book is available from the Library of Congress.

ISBN: HB: 978-0-7556-4201-4
       PB: 978-0-7556-4200-7
       ePDF: 978-0-7556-4203-8
       eBook: 978-0-7556-4202-1

Typeset by RefineCatch Limited, Bungay, Suffolk

To find out more about our authors and books visit www.bloomsbury.com
and sign up for our newsletters.

Contents

Foreword

Lord Mark Sedwill

Global security is becoming both more complex and more contested with profound implications for all nations, especially those with a global perspective like the UK. If National Security 1.0 was the defence of the realm, and National Security 2.0 added protecting the safety of the citizen from terrorist and criminal threats, National Security 3.0 must also encompass economic, environmental and human security. Governments cannot choose between these challenges but must face all of them. That requires them to bring together the national security, economic and social policy communities in a shared national endeavour.

Or at least it does for countries, like the UK, which aspire to a global role but cannot match the weight of the superpowers. The test is simply whether the whole is more or less than the sum of the parts. For the United States and China, the defence ministries of which have budgets bigger than most national economies, central coordination is necessary just to ensure that their foreign, defence, interior and economic ministries, plus their intelligence and security agencies, are acting to implement the leadership's priorities rather than their own. That tendency – '*departmentalitis*' as it is sometimes known in the UK – is present in all governments but is inevitably correlated with scale. The second tier of countries are big enough to have to contend with those centrifugal pressures but some, like the UK, also have national security establishments with sufficient institutional coherence that they can be overcome. The key is culture. And trust.

In the UK, the National Security Council was established by the Cameron Government in 2010 and Peter Ricketts became the first National Security Adviser. I was the fourth. Notwithstanding the publicity, this was evolution not a break with previous practice. Gordon Brown had established the National Security and International Development (NSID) Committee as one of the primary Cabinet committees. Under Tony Blair, David Manning combined for the first time the roles of the Prime Minister's Foreign Policy Adviser and the Head of the Cabinet Office's Overseas and Defence Secretariat: coincidentally but crucially he was on his familiarization visit to Washington on 9/11. For Theresa May, national security began with the security of the nation, and so domestic security issues had more prominence on the NSC agenda.

Prime Ministers as far back as Churchill and Lloyd George appointed officials with similar responsibilities and international counterparts. But national security is as old as the nation state. I kept a portrait in my office of Sir Francis Walsingham, often described (including by the intelligence agencies) as Elizabeth I's 'spymaster' but, with his executive responsibility for both the overseas and domestic security of the Tudor regime, was in reality the national security adviser of his day and arguably the first to integrate all the responsibilities we now expect in that job. Recognizing that effective strategy is ends, ways and means not just policy, my refinement to the systems I inherited was called the 'Fusion Doctrine', designed to create the integrated professional machinery to implement the political decisions of the NSC.

Overseas, the story is also rarely of straight paths or fixed models. In the United States, the role of Special Assistant to the President for National Security Affairs was established by Eisenhower. The clue to the job's authority is in its full title. Impact has varied widely since according to the personalities of the NSAs and the requirements of their presidents. When they start, most now say they want to follow the model of Brent Scowcroft, National Security Adviser in the Ford and Bush 41 presidencies, of the quiet inter-agency facilitator, the model which we recognize in the UK where the distinction between professionals/ advisers and politicians/deciders is constitutionally entrenched. But the Kissinger example, of the roving diplomatic trouble-shooter, able to operate as an alternate Secretary of State, is always a temptation and sometimes vital. And Kissinger's NSC staff of under 100 people is a reminder that strong central structures need not be large and bureaucratic to be effective. Quite the contrary. I was not the only British NSA to struggle to prune ours back.

How nations organise their central governance structures to achieve the coordination and, at its best, genuine coherence will, of course, vary according to their differing political traditions, constitutional systems and national security priorities. However, we can all learn from the experiences of others. In considering and comparing those experiences, this book should be an invaluable source for both national security practitioners and academics studying the field, as they wrestle with the ever more complex and dynamic global security issues of the early- to mid-twenty-first century.

Introduction

Paul O'Neill

> improved coordination of [...] government effort is vital in current conditions. Not only are security threats and hazards more diverse but government itself needs to integrate a wide range of policy instruments to be effective in response. To strengthen strategic coordination of the national security effort and to break down departmental stovepipes [...] the government should develop [...] a National Security Council.[1]

While the world has always been in a state of flux, there is an emerging sense that we are reaching an inflexion point for global security,[2] in which the nature and distribution of global power is changing.[3] Historically, such eras bring heightened risks of conflict as normal competition between states turns to more aggressive forms of contestation, and even war. The natural world is also becoming a greater security concern for most states as a result of climate change and its associated challenges of natural disasters and pandemics. National security systems need to keep pace with the proliferation of threats and keep ahead of the risks and opportunities.

There is no single authoritative definition of national security, and nations interpret it in light of their own circumstances. Traditionally it involved the ability to protect the state itself, its territory and its people from external threats and required the ability to direct the armed forces. Increasingly, it includes consideration of internal threats and natural hazards, for which a wider range of actors is needed. The broadening understanding of security,[4] a complex and deteriorating global

---

1   Paddy Ashdown, George Robertson et al. (2009). 'Shared Responsibilities: A national security strategy for the United Kingdom. Final report of the IPPR Commission on national security in the 21st Century'. *Institute of Public Policy Research*, 22.

2   White House (March 2021). *Interim National Security Strategic Guidance*, 3.

3   HM Government (March 2021). *Competitive Britain in a Global Age: The Integrated Review of Security, Defence, Development and Foreign Policy*, 24.

4   Typically moving from security viewed as primarily for military and police forces towards a wider conceptualization – see Barry Buzan, Ole Wæver and Jaap de Wilde (1997). *Security: A New Framework for Analysis* (Boulder, CO: Lynne Rienner).

security situation involving threats from human actors and nature have reinforced the need for centralized coordination of national security.[5] Thus, the ability to harness activity across different parts of government to safeguard a nation's national security is a critical capability for most states. However, although the desire to reform national security is often driven by exogenous shocks, to be successful it also requires an endogenous desire for change.[6] As a subjective construct, perceptions of security are as important as objective reality and governments increasingly face popular demands for more effective management of multi-faceted and interconnected security problems. This typically involves developing means for coordinating across central, and often local or regional, government, but there is no universal template. National security systems and their coordination are shaped by how nations interpret the threats, risks, and opportunities. And while effective coordination across government is necessary, it is insufficient.[7] COVID-19 in particular has highlighted how governments must work with the private sector across multiple industries, domestically and internationally, in response to today's national security challenges and those likely in the future.

The importance of coordinating diverse actors in response to a broad range of security challenges, and public (and elite) demands for action has led to greater interest in NSCs as a 'whole-of-government' approach. Consequently, recent decades have seen an acceleration in the formation or adaptation of NSCs, or their equivalents, for managing security activity at home. It has also led to the concept of having a NSC being exported as a staple of Security Sector Reform.[8] Countries, particularly in Africa, have it demanded of, or imposed on, them by well-meaning nations for whom a whole-of-government approach, despite the cost and effort of coordinating highly diversified and diffuse ecosystems,[9] is essential.

---

[5] While many states deliver security centrally, not all have formally established permanent organizations for doing so. This book focuses on nations with permanent coordinating structures, often called NSCs or a variation thereof, but this need not always be the case; the case studies reveal many different names. Here, the term NSC is used generically to describe the permanent body tasked with security coordination.

[6] Bryan Mabee (2011). 'Historical Institutionalism and Foreign Policy Analysis: The Origins of the National Security Council Revisited'. *Foreign Policy Analysis*, vol. 7, 27–44.

[7] Bertelsmann Stiftung ed. (2020). *Europe's Coherence Gap in External Crisis and Conflict Management: Political Rhetoric and Institutional Practices in the EU and Member States* (Guetersloh: Verlag Bertelsmann Stiftung), 411.

[8] Western European governments have typically initiated whole-of-government approaches to address external security threats; however, recognition is growing that such approaches could be equally, if not more, important for addressing internal security issues. The NSC, depending on how it is constituted and its role, could be viewed as a mechanism for achieving a whole-of-government approach.

[9] Charles Dunlap Jnr. 'A Whole Lot of Substance or a Whole Lot of Rhetoric? A Perspective on a Whole of Government Approach to Security Challenges', in Volker D. Franke & Robin Dorff eds. (2012). *Conflict Management and 'Whole of Government': Useful Tools for U.S. National Security Strategy?* (Carlisle, PA: Strategic Studies Institute), 198.

An early adopter, the United States, created its NSC in 1947 drawing on its experience of Great Britain's wartime Committee of Imperial Defence.[10] The Council's role was to enhance national security by integrating domestic, foreign and military policies, and enable more effective cross-government cooperation.[11] While pressure to coordinate national levers of power to ensure national security often originated in wartime emergencies, it now covers periods when countries are not at war, even if they cannot be said to be at 'peace' either, and increasingly considers domestic security coordination.

At the highest level, the NSC's purpose is to improve strategic decision-making and responses to complex and multi-dimensional threats to a nation's security. Effective responses require collective effort; no one organization controls all the levers. Actors need to be coordinated and their activity integrated. NSCs, therefore, seek to provide horizontal mechanisms for coordinating and overseeing, sometimes even controlling, what are typically vertical levers of national power. To achieve this, NSCs act across a spectrum of security management activity, involving horizon scanning, strategic planning, and preparation for, response to, and recovery from emergencies. However, responsibility for implementing NSC decisions typically remains with the relevant executive bodies (departments and agencies, national and federal). This can cause friction and NSCs may struggle to overcome domestic frictions that marginalize and undermine them. It is especially true where NSCs oversee, performance-manage and judge the impact of departmental delivery. NSCs must also respond quickly to a complex and changing environment in which new and unique problems are continuously generated. They must balance speed and thoroughness. Adequately understanding the problem requires a plurality of views but hearing and making sense of the diversity of perspectives takes time.

Overview of national security systems

Providing national security is a classic 'wicked problem': it involves choices, but the problem is not 'solved' by them. Furthermore, there is no fixed point at which a nation can be said to be secure – what Horst Rittel and Melvin Webber describe as a 'no stopping rule'.[12] Security is a question of risk, where nations seek solutions

---

[10] Franklyn Johnson (1961). 'The British Committee of Imperial Defence: Prototype of U.S. Security Organisation'. *The Journal of Politics*, vol. 23(2), 231–261.
[11] National Security Act 1947, amended by the National Security Act Amendments 1949.
[12] Horst Rittel and Melvin Webber (1973). 'Dilemmas in a General Theory of Planning'. *Policy Sciences*, vol. 4, 155–169.

that are good enough – 'satisficing' in Herbert Simon's words.[13] Realistically, therefore, NSCs need to bring security threats and/or their effects below the requirement for coordinated inter-agency action at the highest levels of government. The response, however, changes the nature of the 'problem' within a system where emergent behaviour results from how the components interact.[14] The resultant complexity is a function of the number of actors and the number of interactions, both of which are large in the context of national security. The NSC provides a guiding mind for responding to the adaptive consequences of action in a permanent evolution of cause and effect. NSCs, therefore, focus on managing response mechanisms because they cannot control the outcomes, except where problems are static and bounded ('tame' in Rittel and Webber's terms). Consequently, there is no universal design for an NSC. Even where nations are facing identical threats, the system's interactions will be different. And even NSCs perfectly suited to a nation's needs at that time must still be able to adapt because they exist and must evolve within a fluid environment that is in perpetual motion.

The broad range of threats and risks in the security environment has tended to promote greater centralization of power within the Executive. Perversely, however, these problems require a diffuse range of actors that goes beyond central government, making centralization more difficult. A further manifestation of 'wickedness' is how creating a NSC in response to one problem generates new ones. Arthur Chan describes three broad challenges arising from the creation of an NSC: it usurps authority from other parts of government, becoming an additional layer of bureaucracy that slows decision-making and potentially reduces its quality; it becomes a tool for the authoritarian consolidation of power, a danger magnified when the priority is crisis management for which the need for rapid action is used to justify reduced accountability; and it takes resources (funding and talent) from other areas of government, which weakens the overall system's capacity.[15]

Deciding whether to create a NSC, its purpose and structure, all involve weighing the costs and benefits against the impact on the security environment and the problems it generates within government. The NSC, therefore, is an

---

[13] Herbert Simon (1969). *The Sciences of the Artificial* (Cambridge, MA: MIT Press).

[14] Alexander Siegenfeld and Yaneer Bar-Yam (2020). 'An Introduction to Complex Systems Science and Its Applications'. *Complexity*, at https://necsi.edu/an-introduction-to-complex-systems-science-and-its-applications, accessed 30 August 2021.

[15] Arthur Chan (2018). *Overcoming Challenges Arising from the Creation of National Security Councils: a Framework and Lessons from Sub-Saharan Africa*. RAND.

embodiment of how a nation chooses to manage the tensions. The choices are conditioned against three axes: threat; national security system; and role.

- **Threat**. First is whether the severity and complexity of the threat(s) and risks[16] require a national body to coordinate the response(s). Sometimes, doing nothing can be the right answer; knowing when not to react or escalate to a national level is an important but difficult skill for governments. Where action is justified, nations must guard against feeling they require new structures for each problem and consider whether their existing systems can cope, with or without adaptation. While threats typically dominate the thinking, nations should also consider opportunities through which their national security can be enhanced, but few do because government systems become 'fixed' with the problems they face.
- **National security system**. NSCs cannot be considered in isolation; this axis considers the nature of the polity and how the NSC fits within the broader national security system. It includes considerations of how centralized or decentralized the nation is, and thus the authority a central body has or needs over other actors. The nature of the polity also dictates how open or closed it is to engaging others from outside its ranks.
- **Role**. The NSC's role and accountabilities need to be clear,[17] both internally and in its relationships with the rest of the system. This helps determine how much resource the NSC needs itself, such as a staff, and how much it can call on resources elsewhere in the system. An important question is whether the NSC will be the default body for coordination of all security challenges, or whether bespoke arrangements will be used for novel problems. There is also a choice about how far the NSC's central coordination function should extend into delivery.

Purpose of this book

This work sought to understand the factors influencing the need for, and the size, shape and evolution of how countries respond to their national security

---

[16] For the purposes of this book, risk refers to a combination of the likelihood that something will occur in the future, and its consequences. These factors allow governments to make policy proposals for risk management, or accept the risk without treatment. See Mikkel Vedby Rasmussen (2006). *The Risk Society at War: Terror, Technology and Strategy in the Twenty-First Century* (Cambridge: Cambridge University Press), 4.

[17] Chan, op. cit., 4.

challenges. Despite the importance of NSCs, the literature available in English is dominated by the United States, the United Kingdom, or examples of capacity building in fragile states.[18] It is rare to find comparative studies. Notable exceptions are a 2018 RAND report into three sub-Saharan African countries,[19] and another study considering how European Union (EU) nations and the EU have approached cross-government coordination.[20] The EU study covers similar whole-of-government themes, but principally in relation to external crisis and conflict management approaches; nevertheless, it offers interesting insights and themes concerning how NSCs operate in different cultural and legal contexts.

To plug the gap in the literature, this book draws on multiple case studies to explore how nations have approached the challenge of coordinating their national security. Not all countries have something called an 'NSC', and while structures for coordinating national security are analogous, they are not necessarily the same. Some are separate bodies, others integrated into functional departments and others result from the interaction of multiple actors in a network. For our purposes, NSCs/equivalents must have oversight of responses to external security threats and authority to shape the use of diplomatic and military levers of a nation's power, even if they remain largely domestically focused. This comparative view offers a reference for security professionals and scholars interested in the choices facing non-authoritarian governments in developing national security decision-making apparatus, either at home or undertaking security sector reform efforts internationally.

Hypothesis

There is no universal structural solution to how a NSC should look; its design should reflect the unique mix of threats, risks and opportunities a nation faces, the wider national security system in which responses are generated and delivered and the role it is given. Form must follow function; the NSC and its ecosystem will continually evolve as the threats change. Using an organizational design lens offers essential insights for making sense of the choices nations face.

---

[18] OECD (2006). 'Whole of Government Approaches to Fragile States'. *DAC Guidelines and Reference Series.*
[19] Chan, op. cit., examines Sierra Leone, Côte d'Ivoire, and Mozambique.
[20] Bertelsmann Stiftung, op. cit.

It helps policy makers consider the options for responding to the wicked problem of delivering national security and enables others to make sense of the myriad choices facing nations as their security needs change over time.

Methodology

This book takes an inductive approach, drawing general principles from different countries' practises. Chapters were sought from country experts, mostly in-country practitioners or academics, exploring how nations have approached the challenge of coordinating responses to complex and diverse national security threats. All chapters, but particularly those in African nations and the Middle East, were affected by sensitivities to fundamental questions about their national security. This work is therefore focused on learning from the organizational and structural choices nations have made about national security coordination rather than the security decisions themselves, which has allowed a wider range of chapters to be included.

The eighteen chapters cover six continents: Asia (Japan, India, Iraq, Israel); Europe (France, Georgia, Norway, Ukraine, United Kingdom); North America (Canada, United States), Oceania (New Zealand); and South America (Argentina, Colombia). The sixth continent, Africa, is covered by three country-specific studies (Ghana, Kenya and South Africa), but with fifty-four countries, it is particularly complex. Consequently, another chapter draws conclusions on the different approaches adopted more widely in Africa, including through security sector reform activity, often following decolonization and/or conflict. Its author drew on her extensive experience advising on NSCs across Africa, including for the African Union. With the 2018 RAND study, and wider security sector reform literature, this work contributes further valuable insights to the sum of our knowledge about NSCs in Africa.[21]

Generic lessons were derived from the case studies using the factors in Jay Galbraith's Star Model, which offers an organizational design lens on national

---

[21] Chan op.cit.; Paul Jackson (2018). 'Second-Generation Security Sector Reform'. *Journal of Intervention and Statebuilding*, vol. 12(1), 1–10; Ann Fitz-Gerald, Paula MacPhee and Ian Westerman, 'African Militaries, Security Sector Reform and Peace Dividends', in David Francis (2017). *African Peace Militaries* (London: Routledge); African Union (2014). *SSR Trends and Challenges in Africa: a Partners' Summary of the first Africa Forum on SSR*, at https://issat.dcaf.ch/download/73225/1245531/ SSR%20Trends%20and%20Challenges%20in%20Africa%20-%20Partners%20Summary%20of%20 the%20first%20Africa%20Forum%20on%20SSR.pdf, accessed 30 August 2021.

security systems.[22] The five factors are: **Strategy,** determining direction; **Structure,** determining where decision-making power resides; **Processes** affecting coordination; **People,** their mindsets and skills; and **Reward** systems that set the right authorities, motivations and behaviours.[23]

Key considerations for NSCs were:

- **Strategy.** The nature of the threat and risk(s) for which the NSC was shaped: whether it was internal or external; dealing with a human actor amenable to psychological influence (deterrence, coercion) or not, e.g. pandemic, natural disaster and climate change. Strategy also determines whether the NSC should be optimized for crisis management or long-term security challenges that require sustained activity over years or decades, and the degree to which it sets direction and/or ensures its decisions are implemented, almost invariably by others.

- **Structure.** The size, shape and composition of the Council and its supporting staff, on which decision-makers depend for relevant, accurate and timely advice. The structure also reflects other aspects of the national security system within which the NSC sits. Inevitably, the formal structure is a result of institutional politics and compromise, and the shadow structures that often reflect where real power resides in a system or organization.

- **Process.** How the NSC works as its own system, and how it fits in with the rest of the national political and security ecosystem.

- **People.** The degree to which the people, their skills, capacity and credibility support or undermine desired outcomes. A crucial appointment is that of the person charged with leading the coordination, often a National Security Advisor (NSA) or equivalent, and the nature of their role, responsibilities and the degree to which these are formalized or open to change through personality of the head of government or the NSA themselves.

- **Rewards.** How working and cooperating with the NSC was incentivized, reflecting perceived value of cooperation in terms of outcomes, and

---

[22] Organizational design is defined as the process of aligning the structure of an organization with its objectives, with the ultimate aim of improving efficiency and effectiveness. It involves intervening in its processes, structure and culture; there is a strong emphasis on organizational behaviour, human resource development and organizational change. See, for example, University of Southampton 'Organisational Development & Design Explained' at www.southampton.ac.uk/hr/services/od-explained/index.page, accessed 30 August 2021.

[23] Jay Galbraith (2014). *Designing Organizations: Strategy, Structure and Processes at the Business Unit and Enterprise Levels* (San Francisco: Jossey-Bass).

individual incentives in terms of career benefit. It also considers the power systems through which the NSC gains authority over other actors; whether formal authority in a hierarchical sense, from controlling resources, including information or access to key individuals, and its dependence on sponsorship or patronage, although this can be ephemeral in democracies.

The five factors above exist in relationship, so as well as being individually important they must be in organizational harmony (within the NSC) and externally coherent with the nation's security ecosystem. All are tempered by culture, both of the NSC itself and of the other actors (individual, institutional and constitutional) in the wider national security system.

While this volume takes an organizational design perspective on NSCs, it draws on other relevant bodies of literature, notably whole-of-government approaches (typically looking into a nation's own system), and security sector reform, which usually refers to developing the capacity of other's security systems. Management studies offers a third oeuvre. While an imperfect analogy, NSCs operating within broader national security systems can be seen as having similarities with commercial joint ventures. Both comprise more or less independent actors who see shared value in collaborating within defined parameters (e.g. to meet a specific threat) but who retain independence beyond the joint venture's bounds in 'correlated' but not identical behaviours.[24] Rosabeth Moss Kanter's work on joint ventures offers useful insights for thinking about national security collaborations, describing eight compatibility requirements for successful business alliances:[25]

1. Individual Excellence. Partners bring value to, and recognize positive benefits from, the alliance.
2. Importance. The relationship is of strategic importance/value to all partners; not merely one partner bending others to its objectives.
3. Interdependence. Partners need each other, bringing complementary skills, e.g. different perspectives on a problem's wickedness.
4. Investment. Partners invest in the alliance, including assigning good people.
5. Information. Communication must be reasonably open to ensure enough information is shared to make the relationship work.

---

[24] Siegenfeld and Bar-Yam, op. cit., 2.
[25] Rosabeth Moss Kanter (July–August 1994). 'Collaborative Advantage: The Art of Alliances'. *Harvard Business Review*, 99–103.

6. Integration. Linkages and shared ways of working are developed at multiple levels with people trusted to engage directly with their equivalents across organizations rather than passing information upwards before it moves across to other partners.
7. Institutionalized. The relationship is formalized with clear responsibilities and decision-making processes.
8. Integrity. Partners behave honourably towards, and develop trust in, each other's commitment to mutually beneficial outcomes. Appointing an independent chairman (e.g. a NSA) builds trust and reassures partners that the alliance is not a take-over.

Case studies

The choice of case studies was deliberately broad and moved beyond the 'usual suspects'. They all involve bodies that consider external as well as internal security threats and that exercise oversight of diplomatic and military activity as well as domestic policy coordination and strategic planning. We have deliberately focused on countries with a degree of democratic accountability to their populations, as this requires them to respond to the subjective nature of security and the polity is answerable, to a greater or lesser extent, to the people. Authoritarian regimes too must coordinate national security, perhaps even more than democracies because they are acutely sensitive to threats to their authority and invest more in controlling their population. This can be through oppression or by being seen to provide security against threats, real or manufactured, that create conditions for permanent security crises that they hope validate the centralization of power. However, their coordination of national security is not readily comparable with how non-authoritarian governments operate. Answering explicitly to the people creates a very different social contract, and it is to nations for which the people are, or should be, at the heart of their security thinking that this book is focused.

While the case studies do not represent every possible approach, they are individually and collectively interesting, and the differences offer insights into general lessons about the effective coordination of national security. The countries have markedly different security backstories. A global power (United States); regional power (India); post-colonial government (Ghana); those facing immediate military threats from another state (Ukraine, Georgia); those dealing with insurgencies (either domestic e.g. Colombia, or a combination of domestic and international, like Iraq); others where internal threats have been the driving force, and those for whom resource scarcity is significant (many countries in Africa). They cover those for whom military leadership of security is problematic (Japan) and others where the military is seen as crucial to state survival (Israel). Others consider countries for whom human or environmental security is of a high priority (e.g. Canada, New Zealand). Cases include highly centralized systems (France), those with strongly federal structures (Argentina); those for whom bureaucratic siloes are strongly independent (Norway), and countries whose informal processes are powerful but with an emerging tradition of cooperation (United Kingdom). They also include those subject to security sector reform to reflect new independence (Kenya) and where such reform reflected the absence of trust in formerly oppressive state security institutions (South Africa) that continues to shape the granting of power. All face a multiplicity of threats, unique in composition and do so with very different approaches. The case studies are accurate to October 2021.

The case study authors reflect on how nations approached COVID-19. At the time of writing, the pandemic was still underway, and nations and international institutions were learning and adapting to the challenges reflecting a complex web of concerns involving public health, the economy, society and traditional security spheres where armed groups have sought to exploit the use of militaries in pandemic responses. Thus, analysis focused on whether existing NSCs structures were used, or new ones set up, and the lessons to be drawn from that. However, the ongoing and evolving nature of the pandemic made it impossible to draw definitive conclusions about the success or otherwise of national COVID-19 responses.

In short case studies it was impossible to describe all aspects impacting on the development of NSCs, which for many nations goes back decades while for others it was more recent, but tumultuous. This was true for Colombia, which changed focus from countering a large and violent insurgency to considering wider threats to national security. It also applied to Ukraine which evolved rapidly when faced with the opposite pressure, from considering national security through a broad lens to a more traditional focus on national defence for which the fighting capabilities of a nation's armed forces were paramount. Sometimes, the change in security focus was ideological, e.g. South Africa's embrace of human security to mark a firm shift in focus after years of oppression in a militarized society under the apartheid regime. While the function across NSCs may be analogous, their form is not. All nations face a proliferation of threats, but the threats are different, in time and nature, or in different combinations and severities of common threats, e.g. climate change. Equally, how nations organize to deal with these threats is shaped by their constitution, culture and traditions, and governance structures, all of which impact on the perception of threats and how actors work together. Inevitably, this is reflected in bespoke national arrangements that respond to the threats in a manner congruent with how the polity works at the system-level. NSCs are bespoke and evolving.

The case studies allow us to draw general principles to help those looking to optimize their own approaches to coordinating national security, or are advising others on the subject, by highlighting how others have done it, their lessons and successes. The key questions surround issues of how congruent, capable and credible the means of coordination are with their environment. However, even where the questions posed are the same, national answers are, to a greater or lesser extent, unique.

1

National security structures in Africa

Ann M. Fitz-Gerald

Introduction

It is challenging to discuss approaches to national security in the context of the African continent. Such a small chapter cannot do justice to either the good practices adopted by national security institutions across the continent, nor can it fully represent the countries that require further support in this area. It can, however, expose some of the continental-specific realities underpinning national security structures and practices, hence this chapter takes a broad look at trends concerning African national security structures, functions and representation.[1]

National Security Councils in Africa

National Security Councils (NSCs) across the continent have tended to focus on both internal and external issues. Based on, what has been described as, limitations on the transferability of concepts and principles of civil–military relations to Africa,[2] NSCs in their original post-colonial form tended to be either non-existent or develop into cross-government mechanisms for bringing the harder security sector actors together to discuss a range of issues. In addition to the office of the head of state, actors would normally include intelligence, defence, gendarme and police functions.

---

[1] For further reading, see: Geneva Centre for Security Sector Governance (DCAF) (November 2014). *SSR Trends and Challenges in Africa: A Partner's Summary of the First Africa Forum on SSR*; Paul Jackson (2014). 'State-building through security sector reform: the UK intervention in Sierra Leone', *Peacebuilding*, vol. 2(1), 83–99; Paul Nantulya (February 2016). *More than a technocratic exercise: National Security Strategy Development in Africa*, Africa Centre for Strategic Studies.

[2] Rocky Williams (1998). 'Towards The Creation of an African Civil Military Tradition'. *African Journal of Political Science*, vol. 3(1), 20–41.

Very few national security offices have been well-staffed or well-resourced. Experience across the continent has tended to see these offices situated in the Prime Minister's office under the direction of a National Security Adviser (NSA) with, in the case of the better-resourced national security functions, a small team of analysts. The analysts tend to map trends and issues concerning direct security threats to near borders and internal instability. In the context of the latter, and particularly in larger African states with federalist arrangements and regional states, this team is responsible for liaising with their counterpart offices in the regions. Beyond this, the analysts' primary function is to support the NSA and NSC meetings, which are normally chaired by the head of state, with the NSA as 'secretary'. Whereas the better resourced NSA offices outsource administration and logistics supporting the NSC to the team of analysts and administrators, where the NSA office is staffed only by the NSA, the Adviser him/herself becomes entangled in administrative work, e.g. Malawi in 2011 or Somalia. As such, the Adviser has tended not to be a leader with strong onward career prospects.

Some NSA offices work in support of a national security strategy (NSS) or a national security policy (NSP) document. Relatively few African countries produced NSS or NSPs as these offices were formed and have tended to lack the capacity necessary to develop meaningful macro-strategic documents. Representatives from some African countries in this research, particularly north African, suggested that, while a NSS existed, it was classified and not in the public domain. For countries falling within this category, it suggests that national security direction has not benefited from input from civil society.[3] Consequently, some of these documents may lack robust research bases or are not developed following good research practice and principles. In some cases, they may project the fixed views of the government administration, so the benefactor of national security efforts becomes the political party in office rather than the people. This issue goes against the principles of security institutions being institutions for the people and not vanguard institutions for the party in power; it also undermines key tenets of the concept of 'human security'[4] which call for the individual person to be the key referent object of national security.

---

[3] Based on interviews concerning the approach taken towards crafting national security policy in Algeria.

[4] Definition of human security from the UN Trust Fund for Human Security at www.un.org/humansecurity/what-is-human-security/, accessed 30 August 2021.

Developing a wider understanding of 'national security' in Africa

NSPs and NSS are a fairly new phenomenon in many African countries. The leading framework for the continent was, until recently, donor-funded national development strategies. Throughout the 1990s, these took the form of poverty reduction strategy programmes (PRSPs) under the guidance of the United Nations Development Programme and World Bank.[5] The rationale behind PRSPs was that support would be given for countries to produce their own national PRSP and commit to producing such documents every few years until the countries could lead in a strategic and nationally resourced and 'owned' process (frequently titled something other than a 'PRSP'). In many countries, the focus on development strategies alongside the growth of NSCs staffed by more traditional security actors has, arguably, created two competing security systems – one with a 'harder' focus and one with a more human focus.

The increasingly connected and mutually reinforcing interface between security and development issues heralded in 'whole-of-government approaches', 'cross-government security planning' and, over time, security-relevant considerations in what had traditionally been national development dialogue processes. This was reinforced by research commissioned by the international development community, indicating that the highest levels of poverty in Africa were found in the most conflict-affected countries.[6] As a result, development organizations in most donor countries focused on the concept of security and began operating more akin to a department of state than autonomous aid organizations that focused primarily on multilateral humanitarian and development partners.

The implication for African countries was that development-focused strategy papers like the PRSP exposed security-related objectives such as 'conflict resolution' and 'security sector governance'.[7] These developments intersected with donor thinking on 'security sector reform' which encouraged security sector programme activities to be better informed by clear and concise national security objectives.[8] This focus encouraged a wider institutional fabric to support security

---

[5] David Craig and Douglas Porter (2003). 'Poverty Reduction Strategy Papers: A New Convergence?', *World Development*, vol. 31(1), 53–69.

[6] Brigitte Rohwerder (14 July 2014). *The Impact of Poverty on Conflict.* GRDSC Applied Knowledge Services.

[7] E.g., evolution of Uganda's PRSP process between 2002 and 2007, at www.imf.org/en/Publications/CR/Issues/2016/12/31/Uganda-Poverty-Reduction-Strategy-Paper-23894, accessed 30 August 2021.

[8] Experience in Sierra Leone between 2007 and 2010, based on interviews in May 2012 with members of the Office of National Security, Freetown, Sierra Leone.

policy – one that went beyond hard areas of security and embraced more people-oriented security policy organizations. This included ministries such as justice, economic, labour, women and youth, borders and immigration among others.

These international developments across donor organizations impacted on African countries in two distinct ways. First, the pre-requisite for countries wishing to benefit from development of their security sectors to have the 'right' kind of framework of actors to progress with policy development exercises in this area. This included involvement of civil society; something which, as a result of years of contested civilian leadership across many African countries, and military leaders emerging as freedom fighters and subsequently holding office, was often associated with mistrust and dissent. Indeed, for the twenty-eight-year rule of the Ethiopian People's Revolutionary Democratic Front (EPRDF), civil society organizations in Ethiopia with an interest in security, justice or human rights were not legally permitted to organize and operate.[9]

Second, more recently, donor 'defence engagement' funding has been added. This development within the international donor community saw a softer form of security sector engagement which, for some donors, could be classified as 'ODA-able' (counted under Overseas Development Assistance) and thus supported by multi-year (versus annual) funding commitments. But some defence engagement-funded support encouraged approaches akin to Western-style security reviews which could not be sustained in recipient countries without being propped up by external actors. These interventions could, in some cases, also produce sub-optimal outcomes, e.g. Burundi.[10] The result tended to be intense donor-funded efforts to encourage a range of strange bedfellows to discuss and strategize around security, only to produce national security documents – such as reviews, strategies, policies and even concept papers – which were left on the shelf unimplemented. In many African countries, the lack of resources and limited authority vested within the office of the NSA meant this broader security sector architecture often rolled NSCs back to the hard security formations that pre-dated donor-funded interventions.

[9] Contributor (16 February 2019). 'Does the Revised Civil Society Proclamation deliver on the Promise of Reform', *The Reporter*.

[10] Ann Fitz-Gerald (2012). *SSR and Peacebuilding: Thematic Review of SSR and Peacebuilding and the Role of the Peacebuilding Fund*. United Nations.

Strategic national security policy outputs

Strategic security policy outputs tended to be classified in four different groups.

1. Countries that produced a 'homegrown' NSP or NSS;
2. Countries that produced a post-conflict donor-assisted NSP or NSS;
3. Countries that produced a national security document which, given limitations in legislative and policy processes, was not formally adopted as a policy;
4. Countries basing their national security planning on another related-type of document, e.g. Defence White Paper, Defence and Security Policy, Cyber Security Strategy, Food Security Strategy, etc. Ironically, while these documents take a wide approach to the strategic analytical context, they inevitably become narrower in scope, aspiration and intent than regular NSS.

The first category includes countries where the impetus for the NSP process came as a result of a broader vision for reform and/or government desire to support decision-making in response to complex environmental trends, the latter requiring delegated authority for this process. Such was the case for Ethiopia in 2002 following the end of the war with Eritrea in 2000. The challenge with this 'homegrown' effort was that because the document was authored by the Prime Minister himself, it has not been updated since his death in 2012. Other national security developments have come by way of processes heavily influenced by defence institutions.

Other post-conflict countries supported by widespread donor-funded SSR programmes developed NSP processes and legislative amendments as part of wider peace processes and security/peacebuilding engagement (e.g. Burundi, Liberia). Other processes, e.g. The Gambia, were fuelled by donor support to political transitions which, based on past history, require priority to be given to security governance processes. The Gambia in 2017, following the ousting of President Jammeh who had initially refused to recognize the outcome of the election,[11] prioritized a 'security sector assessment', followed by a 'security sector reform strategy' (2019) and a NSS in 2020 through their NSC and NSA.[12]

---

[11] President Jammeh remained in Office for almost eight weeks until a final 16 January deadline was issued and Senegalese forces were deployed to The Gambia to assist with the peaceful ousting of the President and to facilitate the inauguration of the newly elected President Adama Barrow.

[12] Momodou Jawo (26 October 2020). 'Gov't Makes Great Progress on Security Sector Reforms', *The Point.*

Often 'national security-type documents' do not become formally adopted as government policy. These include papers that characterize new strategic security contexts, security policy frameworks, policy 'statements' and NSP drafts. Work undertaken on initial post-conflict attempts at producing a NSS for Sierra Leone saw the development of a policy document that could then not be debated or discussed in Parliament due to a lack of parliamentary capacity to support security discussions.[13] Although another NSP was produced in 2017, its adoption has been delayed due to other priorities.[14] The same experience befell the Government of Malawi in 2010. Other 'national security-type' documents can emerge from formal defence review and defence reform processes, albeit recognizing the wider national security context in which defence is situated (South Africa, Senegal). Research indicates a strong appetite in these countries to take forward an NSP process.

Countries basing their national security planning on different types of 'security-related' policy document can be divided into two sub-groups:

1. countries that develop defence, internal security or related national security-type documents with little experience in supporting development of a NSP or NSS;
2. countries with legislative or constitutional provisions supporting national security but without pre-existing security-related policy or strategy documents.

While the Government of Botswana has an old national security document through the National Security Act[15] (passed in 1986), and the Intelligence and Security Services Act[16] and the Corruption and Economic Crime Act,[17] there is no recently developed policy or strategy document. This is despite efforts between 2007 and 2009 to form a coordinating national security secretariat and facilitate country-wide discussion on national security.[18] In the absence of a NSS, Botswana relies heavily on legislative instruments in the form of respective Acts of Parliament pertaining to defence, public safety, justice, and intelligence.[19]

[13] Interviews with members of the Government of Sierra Leone's Office of National Security, May 2012.
[14] Interviews with members of the Government of Sierra Leone's Office of the National Security, 4 March 2021.
[15] Republic of Botswana. National Security Act 1986.
[16] Republic of Botswana. Intelligence and Security Services Act 2008.
[17] Republic of Botswana. Corruption and Economic Crime Act 1994.
[18] The author was involved in the facilitation of the discussions and worked with the National Security Secretariat.
[19] Brig. Gen.(Ret.) Gaseikanngwe Peke (March 2019). *National Security Strategy Development: Botswana Case Study.* Working Paper. Africa Center for Strategic Studies.

Other countries, such as Mozambique, saw the 1997 adoption of a Defence and Security White Paper.[20] Although Senegal has not formalized an NSP in the form of a comprehensive document, it has discussed defence in the context of national security since 2001 and, through the direction of its NSC, sees the concept of national security supported by its bona fide defence policy and other contributing institutions.[21] Similarly, Zambia published an anti-money laundering and terrorism finance strategy[22] and Botswana produced a National Cyber Security Strategy.[23] As authorized by its NSC, Zimbabwe produced a National Social Security Annual Report in 2011.[24]

Although the second group of countries have national security-related legislation, this research was unable to identify any related documents. This includes Chad, Angola, Mauritius, Cape Verde, Central African Republic and Djibouti, for which no publicly accessible information on national security documents or related legislation could be found. This may be because some countries feel their defence-related policy or White Papers are sufficient; or there may be less political appetite to develop a dedicated NSP. It also indicates that some African countries see a reasonably strong link between related strategy/ policy papers (such as those on counter-terrorism, food security, and cyber security) and external actors providing funding support for these types of activities. It is not surprising therefore that these thematic areas tend to be prioritized over the development of comprehensive national security documents, particularly in the absence of a 'post-conflict' environment where external actors are more likely to encourage an NSP process to bring coherency to numerous security reform programmes.

Arguably, there is scope and incentive for these countries to become more proactive in developing NSP documents and national security legislation. This good practice has been consolidated by the African Union and shared with the continent's regional organizations, regional mechanisms and individual member states. It comprises 'operational guidance' that member states with an interest in these issues can follow, and includes support for evolving national security

---

[20] For more information on Mozambique's national security and defence architecture see Anicia Lala. 'Mozambique' in Gavin Cawthra, Andre du Pisani and Abillah Omari eds. (2007). *Security and Democracy in Southern Africa* (Johannesburg: Wits University Press), Chapter 7.

[21] DCAF (20–21 October 2011). *Developing a Guinean National Security Policy Conference Report*, 41.

[22] Republic of Zambia (April 2010). *Anti-Money Laundering and the Combatting of Financing of Terrorism Country Strategy Paper.*

[23] Republic of Botswana (October 2020). *National Cybersecurity Strategy.*

[24] Government of Zimbabwe (2011). *National Social Security Annual Report.*

legislation, which for some countries on the continent requires updating to align with current laws.[25]

Conclusion

Drawing precise conclusions about the national security structures of fifty-four countries – each with their own political cultures, rich history, traditions and resource bases – is impossible. However, based on the post-colonial nature of most African countries, their past and present poverty challenges, recent conflict history and relatively low capacity of independent civil society and oversight bodies, some trends can be drawn. And these are not limited to African countries but are of broader relevance.

The recent history of military rule and military-led liberation movements, means the 'hard' security actors across the security sector are, in many cases, still dominant voices in national security structures and planning. Civilian ministers who oversee roles such as defence, foreign affairs and national security in some African countries often have a weaker voice than their uniformed counterparts. Consequently, NSCs tend to focus on harder (military intervention, counter-terrorism, policing) rather than softer human security issues (immigration, trade and land rights). In this context, while the NSA is a senior post supporting high-level administration and coordination of national security planning meetings, it often lacks human resource capacity and relative authority with the cabinet. For this reason, intelligence agencies play a prominent role in producing national security analysis. Despite this, NSCs remain a fairly common structure for African governments.

In relation to the policy followed by NSCs, experiences appear to group into four: 'homegrown' efforts to produce NSP documents; NSP documents that became a requirement for, and outcome of, donor-funded post-conflict interventions; national security papers that were not formally ratified through a lack of parliamentary oversight and/or civil society capacity and, lastly; security framework documents from a specific branch of security, e.g. counter-terrorism, defence, cyber or food security. In some of these cases, national security documents do exist, but their closed-source nature implies they may not have reviewed critically and thus may lack a solid evidence base.

---

[25] The author was involved in the production of operational guidance notes for the Harmonization of National Security Policy and Legislative approaches. The project was commissioned in 2014 by the African Union and coordinated by the African Security Sector Network.

A growing number of recent experiences offer some good practice that could be considered by both African and non-African countries keen to take forward some form of security policy pathway. Nigeria's 2019 development of a NSS through the NSA's Office included a wider group of government actors that brought a human security 'lens' to both the analysis and response. The Gambia's 2019–2020 experience saw a logical, sequenced and politically-supported security sector assessment, followed by a security sector reform strategy, NSS and, at the time of writing, an inaugural defence policy process. These highlight the benefits of even modest donor funding combined with low-level technical support. Notwithstanding the challenges in having policy formally adopted, Sierra Leone's inclusive approach – in terms of non-traditional security actors (agriculture, finance, etc.) and traditional leaders – is also valuable.

2

Argentina and the long quest for a National Security Council

Martin Verrier

Political instability and the search for a National Security Council

There are good geopolitical reasons for Argentina to have a National Security Council: it is a member of the G20 and the eighth largest country in the world. Despite this, Argentina currently lacks a comprehensive National Security Council. Political instability, the legacy of the broader politics of the Cold War in South America and domestic difficulty in integrating security and defence concepts has made it difficult for Argentina to develop a comprehensive National Security Council. Instead, it has a cluster of diverse national entities that address different missions traditionally assigned to National Security Councils. Nevertheless, Argentina used to have such a Council.

The first and only formal National Security Council was introduced by de facto President Ongania in 1966 as a forum to debate the Argentine national grand strategy.[1] It was not a defence-centred council, but an open one that sought to improve national security by integrating domestic, external, economic and defence policies. In 1973, amid growing concern over the activity of Marxist guerrillas, President Juan Peron enacted a new defence law that formally separated domestic from external security and created a Defence Council. His successor, Maria Estela Peron, then formed a distinct Internal Security Council to direct national efforts against the subversive internal menace.[2] However,

---

[1] Ley de Defensa Nacional, 16.970 [National Defense Law 16.970] 1966.
[2] Ley de Ministerios, 20524 [Ministries Law 20524] 1973, and Decreto de Constitución del Consejo de Seguridad Interna 2770/1975 [Internal Security Council Constitution Decree 2770/1975].

political instability led to a coup in 1976 with a military junta ruling until 1983, which effectively placed all security under military control.

Following the harsh defeat suffered in the Malvinas conflict with the United Kingdom in 1982, there were widespread popular demands for free elections that took place in 1983. Consequently, unlike the progressive democratic transition that occurred in other countries in the region, the transition from military rule occurred almost instantly.[3] The rapid transition also prevented the development of mature democratic institutions, from which Argentina is still recovering.

Despite the junta's abrupt end in 1982, the military remained a powerful political actor. Between 1987 and 1990, some military units rebelled against democratic rule.[4] While unsuccessful, the continuous threat they posed to the democratic order during the late 1980s curtailed the development of democratic security and defence laws.

Fear of the military's power in the late 1980 and early 1990s led parliament to reintroduce a categorical division between domestic security and defence based on geographical grounds.[5] This system placed internal threats under the legal framework and institutions for homeland security and external threats under the national defence legislative framework.

In April 1988, a new Defence Law 23.554[6] introduced a National Defense Council as the leading forum for advising the President on defence matters. The second article of the Law states that 'Defence consists in the integration and coordinated action of all the forces of the Nation for the resolution of conflicts that require the use of the Armed Forces, through deterrence or effectively to deal with foreign aggressions'. The National Defense Council is responsible for designing defence strategies and coordinating armed responses against a military attack. The fourth article specifically differentiated defence from homeland security. The presidential operationalization of this law in 2006 limited even further the nature of the potential threats that could be met using the military. According to this decree, the definition of external aggression is strictly confined to attacks from other countries, ruling the military out of responding to non-state actors.

---

[3] Guillermo O'Donnell and Philippe Schmitter (1986). *Transitions from Authoritarian Rule: Tentative Conclusions about Uncertain Democracies* (Baltimore, MD: John Hopkins University Press), 34.

[4] LT10 (24 May 2019). 'A 32 años del primer levantamiento carapintada', at: https://lt10.com.ar/noticia/241412--a-32-anos-del-primer-levantamiento-carapintada-, accessed 30 August 2021.

[5] Horacio Jaunarena, 'La Seguridad Y La Defensa En La Argentina Del Siglo XXI', at: www.ancmyp.org.ar/user/14-%20HORACIO%20JAUNARENA.pdf, accessed 30 August 2021.

[6] Ley de Defensa Nacional, 23.554 [National Defence Law, 23.554] 1988.

In 1992 the corresponding Homeland Security Law was approved.[7] This law does not rigidly define potential security threats. Instead, it describes security as 'the factual and rightful situation based on the law in which the freedom, life and wealth of the inhabitants, their rights and guarantees and the full authority of the institutions of the representative, republican and federal system established by the National Constitution are guaranteed'. Under this institutional arrangement, an internal security council was adopted. This law, still in force in Argentina, introduced a Homeland Security Council (HSC). It could be defined as a 'crippled' National Security Council, as it is mainly focused on the coordination of national crime prevention strategies and integrated responses to non-military threats. The HSC's primary mission is to advise the security minister on domestic security policies and the development and execution of plans to guarantee domestic security.[8]

The Homeland Security Law allows the use of military forces in domestic matters, either through logistics support to law enforcement agencies or through the authorization of the Crisis Committee. This makes the HSC broader than the Defence Council and the closest to a comprehensive National Security Council.

Both defence and homeland security laws were products of their own time. While they were useful in limiting the use of military forces for domestic purposes, they are inappropriate for addressing current threats such as terrorism, narco-insurgency and serious organized crime.

The HSC as a de facto National Security Council

The path to creating a single, integrated National Security Council has been full of obstacles that have prevented Argentina from reaching the goal. The HSC is the closest Argentina has. In evaluating its effectiveness in this role, three factors are considered most relevant: how effectively *roles and authorities* are defined, including in legislation and through political support; the *level of civilian involvement and accountability* and finally an *assessment of the level of resources*.[9]

7　Ley de Seguridad Interior, 24.059 [Homeland Security Law, 24.059] 1992.
8　Homeland Security Law, op. cit., Article 9.
9　Arthur Chan (2018). *Overcoming Challenges Arising from the Creation of National Security Councils. A Framework and lessons from Sub-Saharan Africa*. RAND, 2.

In terms of roles, the HSC meets some of the conditions to be considered effective. Its roles are clearly defined by the Homeland Security Law and its regulations. The Council coordinates forensics, policing doctrine and operations, criminal intelligence sharing, supervision of the Argentine Police Convention, police training, coordination with the Defence Council and police equipment. Its authority is also laid down in law. The Council sits under the Security Minister, who in Argentina has a higher status than the Defence Minister, with the Security Secretary (also known as the Security Vice-minister, or formerly the Homeland Security Undersecretary) having operational control of the HSC and federal law enforcement agencies.[10] However, it is an imperfect and limited solution as a comprehensive National Security Council because of the rigid separation of defence and security matters, even though there is provision for some control of the military when they are deployed domestically. And while depending heavily on Executive support gives the Council flexibility and authority, this depends on the degree of interest the Executive has in using it and it can affect the Council's capacity to develop an agenda independent of political direction.

In terms of membership, the Council has a predominantly civilian composition with regular input from law enforcement chiefs and the extraordinary participation of military chiefs of staff in cases where the Crisis Committee is called. The membership includes: the Security Minister as President; the Minister of Justice, the Drug Demand Reduction Secretary, Security Minister and the Security Secretary. The chiefs of the four federal law enforcement agencies (Policia Federal (federal police), Gendarmeria Nacional (border police), Policia de Seguridad Aeroportuaria (airport police) and the Prefectura Naval Argentina (coast guard)) are invited to attend when necessary. Five chiefs of provincial police (on a rotational basis), provincial governors, members of the congressional security committees, other specialists, advisors and guests may also be invited if the need arises.

In emergencies, Crisis Committees can be convened under the HSC to coordinate police forces or where local law enforcement is overwhelmed and the involvement of military forces is required. The Ministry of Security convenes the Committee, which can include the Defence Minister and the Chair of the Joint Chiefs of Staff where military support is required. In these circumstances, the

---

[10] Homeland Security Law, op. cit., Article 14.

Figure 2.1 Structure of the Argentine Homeland Security Council.[11]

President chairs the HSC as commander in chief. Military involvement is allowed in two circumstances:

- In support of police forces (mainly through logistics because under the defence law and its regulation they are not allowed to perform policing activities);[12]
- When and where a state of emergency is declared,[13] and strictly to re-establish security when local law enforcement forces are unable to do so. In this case, the President becomes the operational commander of all police and military forces.[14]

---

[11] Source: author.
[12] Homeland Security Law, op. cit., Article 27.
[13] Constitución Nacional [National Constitution], Article 75(29).
[14] The last declaration of a state of emergency occurred during the social crisis and economic meltdown at the end of 2001. Through Presidential Decree 1678/2001, President De la Rua declared a state of emergency for thirty days across all Argentine territory. This measure was thought to be unnecessary, was unpopular and, therefore, widely rejected by the population. President De la Rua resigned one day later.

While the law describes to whom the Council is accountable, there are no formal mechanisms for ensuring accountability. Most of the decisions are taken through consensus, but those who do not abide by the agreements rarely face the consequences. In this sense, it appears to be too susceptible to political pressure from the Executive to enforce its agreements.

Another weakness exists in terms of the level of resourcing. The Council's secretariat is significantly understaffed with a permanent body of fewer than fifteen officials. However, the small staff does mean the Council can access a broad range of expertise as necessary. This is enshrined in the law, which clearly states that the Minister may call any relevant individual whose presence is required, like academics or former public officials.

Thus, while the HSC has been relatively successful in achieving its domestic objectives and had strong support from the Executive, especially during the last five years, it has not become a full National Security Council. It has never acted as a national think tank responsible for developing a long-term national security assessment or its corresponding strategy. This competence remains with the National Defence Council, crippling the HSC's capacity to design comprehensive long-term security strategies.

COVID-19 and the HSC

At the start of the pandemic, the HSC was the only body called to intervene. Argentina reacted quickly, with President Fernandez declaring a total and mandatory quarantine for Argentina on 20 March 2020 – the first country to do so.[15] The HSC was very active during the initial phase of the pandemic, first meeting in April to coordinate provincial efforts not only from law enforcement of the lockdown, but also of the Provinces with the health system. Working in support of the HSC, the Ministry of Security quickly introduced a unified command system to coordinate law enforcement and border assistance actions to mitigate the impact of COVID19. The HSC coordinated additional measures between the Ministry of Security and the twenty-three provincial police forces to cover border controls and return Argentineans from abroad.

---

[15] Priscila Palacio (21 July 2020). 'COVID-19 and the Economic Crisis in Argentina'. *E-International Relations*, at www.e-ir.info/2020/07/21/covid-19-and-the-economic-crisis-in-argentina/, accessed 30 August 2021.

Having quickly introduced some of the toughest controls on movement in the world, Argentina seemed to be doing well. Widespread acceptance of the restrictions and compliance by the public at the start was effective; one month after the national lockdown started, use of public transport had decreased by 80 per cent.[16] However, over time the HSC's influence diminished significantly. In Argentina's federal system, it proved unable to cohere activity with the Provinces over movement between provinces or how provincial borders were managed. With increasing popular discontent with the harsh lockdown arrangements, each province started to devise its own territorial control strategy.[17] This series of autonomous decisions by the provinces showed the HSC's limited influence amid a crisis in which clear leadership was missing. Its role got more political, and it became focused on issues that were not as urgent but less contentious, such as the reform of the national drug law. By June 2020, the National Ministry of Security was still struggling to reinstate the HSC's meetings.[18] The last meeting, held in October 2020, was run virtually with the main agenda item being the anniversary of the national Drug Act. The meeting was supposed to start a debate on the modification of that law, which showed how far the Council had relinquished any operational coordination in the national security response to COVID-19. Currently, the only venue at which the different departments and agencies come together is the Cabinet, but different political factions in Cabinet make adopting a single approach difficult. With no single body in charge of coordinating the COVID-19 response, management of the crisis occurs as a series of bilateral discussions with communication emanating from the Chief of Cabinet.

The HSC's performance during the COVID-19 crisis confirms that it lacks proper authority and is only as strong as the National Minister of Security. As in the past, without clear leadership the Council loses its ability to manage operational aspects of a crisis and reverts to being a mere deliberative body without practical authority for delivery.

---

[16] Santiago Filipuzzi, 'Cuarentena: como cambio la movilidad de los argentinos según Google', *La Nación,* at www.lanacion.com.ar/tecnologia/cuarentena-como-cambio-movilidad-argentinos-segun-google-nid2350415, accessed 30 August 2021.

[17] 'Chaco: cierran las ingresos a la provincia y endurecen las medidas', *El Ancasti, at* www.elancasti.com.ar/nacionales/2020/6/15/chaco-cierran-las-ingresos-la-provincia-endurecen-las-medidas-436620.html, accessed 30 August 2021.

[18] 'COVID-19: qué planes tienen los ministros de Alberto Fernández en medio de la pandemia', *Observatorio Metropolitano,* www.observatorioamba.org/noticias-y-agenda/noticia/la-agenda-paralela-al-covid-19-que-planes-tienen-los-ministros-de-alberto-fernandez-en-medio-de-la-pandemia, accessed 30 August 2021.

Conclusion

The difficulty in developing integrated long-term strategies against drug trafficking has shown how badly Argentina needs a fully functional National Security Council. Three issues explain Argentina's failure to develop a security and defence council that fulfils the functions of an integrated National Security Council.

Firstly, the inability to forge a broad conception of 'security'. In Argentina, there is a very clear and understandable philosophical, legal and institutional tension between security and defence. However, separating domestic security from defence has seriously limited the possibility of having a single agency to concentrate and coordinate the various state agencies involved in managing national security. As Martin Van Creveld stated almost thirty years ago, 'the Trinitarian way of conflict is disappearing, and national borders will become meaningless as rival parties pursue each other freely across them.'[19] Similarly, the Argentine Ministry of Defense's last strategic assessment in 2018, describes an international context characterized by great power struggles, the use of hybrid warfare and the impact of non-state actors.[20] This demands an integrated view of defence and security matters, as the threats require the integration and involvement of military and civilian assets, including law enforcement.

Second, the HSC has been highly dependent on the Executive, which is an advantage in terms of political support (when the Executive is supportive) but cripples the Council's autonomy. The Council had minimal use between 2011 and 2015 when the administration was hostile to it, but was extensively used between 2015 and 2019 during President Macri's administration. Under President Macri, the number of meetings of the HSC tripled, with more than twenty agreements signed between the federal government and local authorities.[21] It successfully managed requests for resources, provided advice to local law enforcement agencies and defined the direction for security reform, for example by introducing legislation forming new joint provincial commands. During this period, the HSC not only worked as a forum for gathering federal and provincial authorities but also exercised its decision-making powers.[22] In 2021 the

---

[19] Martin Van Creveld (1991). *The Transformation of War* (New York: The Free Press), 282.

[20] Directiva de Política de Defensa Nacional [National Defense Policy Directive] 2018.

[21] Federico Saettone (20 February 2020). '¿Un Consejo Federal de Seguridad Interior?', *Infoabe*, at: www.infobae.com/opinion/2020/02/20/un-consejo-federal-de-seguridad-interior/, accessed 30 August 2021.

[22] These agreements included the strategic document 'Argentina sin Narcotrafico' [Argentina without drug-trafficking], which established the basis for a new national drugs strategy that led to a 71 per cent increase in cocaine seizures and 24 per cent increase in cannabis seizures.

Homeland Security Council partially resumed activity, holding a coordination meeting in April to coordinate enforcement of the decree on COVID-19 movement restrictions,[23] and a meeting in August to coordinate several citizen security issues.[24]

Third, the traumatic history of military rule created fears among some parties that the creation of a comprehensive National Security Council might empower the military again. Since the return of democracy in 1983, however, the military has not only showed its willingness to operate under democratic control, but also demonstrated its capacity to engage in activities other than war, such as natural disasters assistance and peace operations. This challenge to creating a fully functioning National Security Council is less forceful today.

President Fernandez stated early in his Presidency that he will create a National Security Council, although this commitment has not been repeated recently. If he does, he will be addressing one of the main organizational problems that currently restrain the coordination of national security policies. This Council should learn from the performance of the HSC during the COVID-19 pandemic, and needs to resemble the one that existed during the 1960s. It should answer to the President and be responsible for drafting the national security strategic assessment and strategy. It should articulate policies working with other agencies while retaining a fair degree of autonomy, allowing the participation of experts and allowing expert groups to work independently and not only under the executive's request. The Council will need a strengthened secretariat, which could be provided by the Secretariat of Strategic Matters that was created in 2015. Repurposing this agency, with additional resources, would create an ideal coordination capability for this new, integrated National Security Council.

Chequeado, a well-known Argentine non-profit organization devoted to checking Politian's statements has reminded the government that President Fernandez's pledge on creating a National Security Council remains undelivered.[25] It seems that developing such a Council may remain a 'bridge too far' for Argentina.

[23] 'El Consejo de Seguridad Interior abordó las restricciones en el marco de la Emergencia Sanitaria', *Ministerio de Gobierno y Justicia, at :* www.entrerios.gov.ar/mingob/index.php?codigo=&cod=2151 &codtiponoticia=1&noticia=ver_noticia&modulo=noticia, accessed 4 September 2021.

[24] 'Consejo de Seguridad Interior: el Ministerio continúa su trabajo federal y firma Convenios con las provincias', *Ministerio de Seguridad,* at: www.argentina.gob.ar/noticias/consejo-de-seguridad-interior-el-ministerio-continua-su-trabajo-federal-y-firma-convenios, accessed 4 September 2021.

[25] Manuel Tarricone (9 December 2020). 'Alberto Fernández: 'Crear un Consejo de Seguridad para que el problema de seguridad deje de ser el problema de un gobierno', *Chequeado,* at: https://chequeado. com/promesas-chequeadas/alberto-fernandez-crear-un-consejo-de-seguridad-para-que-el-problema-de-seguridad-deje-de-ser-el-problema-de-un-gobierno/, accessed 30 August 2021.

3

National security in Canada

Hugh Segal and Ann M. Fitz-Gerald

Introduction

The structures and operational reach of key national security instruments at Canada's federal level derive from events since 1970 that re-shaped Cold War frameworks towards internal threats. While some instruments originated in the First World War's War Measures Act 1914, instruments for threat analysis, operational advice to the federal cabinet, lawful surveillance and interdiction date from 1970.

Before the September 11 terrorist attacks on the United States, Canada's national security focus had been largely shaped by Pearsonian peacekeeping deployments, an ongoing commitment to, and presence within, NATO, and a strong bilateral focus on the defence and security relationship with the United States. Canada's post 9/11 national security posture saw the gradual diminishing of peacekeeping roles, a sustained commitment to NATO and greater consideration of internal threats and the development of robust legal frameworks which attempt to balance security and civil liberty. The system remains, however, strategically less-than-fully developed.

This chapter will give an overview of the development of Canada's national security structures and the functions comprising the current system, highlighting both advantages and challenges.

Structural and formative foundations of the contemporary Canadian security establishment

Canada's discussion on how to define national security has been ongoing since the 1970s. In 1979, the McDonald Commission proposed a simple definition: the need to preserve Canadian territory from attack and to preserve and maintain the democratic process of government.[1] Canada's most recent policy contribution to national security, published in 2004, described the concept as concerning threats that had the potential to undermine the security of the state, which were closely linked to both personal and international security and which required a national response.[2] A 2017 document for the National Security and Intelligence Committee of Parliamentarians took a still broader perspective, defining national security as 'protecting the safety and security of Canada's territory, government, economy and people, and the promotion and protection of Canadian interests'.[3] The latest definition reflects the more integrated, whole-of-government approach that Canada has taken in addressing issues concerning security, as well as its support for the broader human security agenda that Canada promotes both nationally and through its multilateral partners. These definitions notwithstanding, reflecting on historical links to national security is helpful in promoting a better understanding of the evolution of Canada's national security structures.

The Front de liberation du Quebec's abduction of a British Trade Officer in Montreal in October 1970,[4] and murder of the Honourable Pierre Laporte, the provincial Minister of Labour during the same crisis, saw the proclamation of an 'apprehended insurrection' under the War Measures Act. Federal troops were deployed to Montreal, Quebec City and Ottawa, civil liberties (freedom of assembly, of the press, expression, habeas corpus) were suspended, and hundreds of people were incarcerated following house-to-house sweeps by local police. Most of those detained, in some cases for weeks, were never charged.

Public disquiet and subsequent allegations of sporadic wrong-doing by the Royal Canadian Mounted Police (RCMP) in Quebec, involving arson and illegal entrapment, resulted in a Royal Commission of Inquiry (the McDonald Commission).[5] The Commission recommended removing the RCMP's security and intelligence role, and a separate Canadian Security and Intelligence Service

---

[1]   Minister of Supply and Services Canada (1979). *Commission of Inquiry Concerning Certain Activities of the Royal Canadian Mounted Police, Security and Information,* First Report, 15.
[2]   Government of Canada (2004), *Securing an Open Society: Canada's National Security Policy,* vii.
[3]   Privy Council Office (2017). *'What is National Security?' Document provided to the National Security and Intelligence Committee of Parliamentarians,* 3.
[4]   Jenish D'Arcy (2020). *The Making of the October Crisis* (London: Penguin/Random House).
[5]   Minister of Supply and Services Canada (1979–1981). *Commission of Inquiry Into Certain Activities of the Royal Canadian Mounted Police.* First Report, *Security and Information,* 1979; Second Report, *Freedom and Security under the Law,* 1981; Third Report, *Certain RCMP Activities and the Question of Governmental Knowledge,* 1981.

(CSIS) was formed; enforcement activities remained with the RCMP and provincial and municipal police forces. This separation, formally underwritten by the Canadian Security Intelligence Service Act 1984, is at the centre of Canada's national security infrastructure.

Both CSIS, and the Communications Security Establishment (CSE)[6] focused on external threats such as Islamist extremism (Al Qaeda, ISIS, Hamas, Hezbollah), homegrown related risks or cyber-attacks on key infrastructure by Chinese, Russian, Iranian and North Korean-based agencies. They work closely with the other 'Five-Eyes' partners: the UK, US, Australia, and New Zealand. However, the roots of much of the Canadian national security establishment reflect the dynamics and politics of internal security challenges.

The impact of internal security challenges

Prime Minister Pierre Trudeau, who invoked the War Measures Act in 1970, introduced the Charter of Rights and Freedoms[7] during the 1981–1983 constitutional reform negotiations. This followed the defeat of the proposed 'Sovereignty Association'[8] in a Quebec-wide referendum in October 1980. The proposal for Quebec sovereignty had been advanced by the Parti Quebecois Government in 1976, elected in part because of the controversy over the use of the War Measures Act in 1970.

The Charter, and the repatriation of the British North America Act from Westminster in 1982 and 1983, established a new structural reality that sought to balance civil liberties and security. Much of the police and armed forces' action in Quebec during the 1970 crisis would have not been legal under the Charter. It has also been used to water down hastily passed anti-terrorist legislation following the 9/11 terrorist attacks in New York and Washington, and 7/7 attacks in London in 2005, which culminated in a Senate Special Committee on Anti-Terrorism review between 2006 and 2010.[9]

Modifications to the operation of CSIS, and the national security structure, had already been necessitated by the 1985 bombing of Air India flight 182 from

---

6 Government of Canada, Communications Security Establishment, at www.cse-cst.gc.ca/en/inside-interieur/, accessed 30 August 2021.
7 Department of Justice (2018). *The Canadian Charter of Rights and Freedoms (revised 2018-09-13)*.
8 University of Alberta (2019). Centre for Constitutional Studies, Sovereignty-Association, at https://ualawccstest.srv.ualberta.ca/2019/07/sovereignty-association/, accessed 30 August 2021.
9 Kent Roach (2007). 'Better Late than Never? The Canadian Parliamentary Review of the Anti-Terrorism Act', *Choices* vol. 13(5).

Toronto to London[10] – Canada's largest terrorist event which resulted in the deaths of all 329 passengers. As the bomb was put on the aircraft as checked baggage in Canada, extensive inquiries into the failure of Canadian security and police forces to prevent the tragedy exposed clear operational and instrumental failures of coordination between the CSIS and RCMP. A critical failing concerned the analysis and intelligence work undertaken by CSIS, on which it had no enforcement authority, being forwarded to the RCMP and local and provincial police establishments who lacked urgency in converting it into action.

Canadian security culture often reflects the level of interest and engagement on security demonstrated by the Prime Minister. The Air India event, advice from security agencies and recommendations from several inquiries into the tragedy, led the Harper Government (2006–2015) to introduce legislation addressing issues of 'lawful access' for police and security organizations to telephone, digital and electronic data for crime and terrorism prevention. Prime Minister Harper's robust engagement with the Afghanistan mission and the security issues that emerged, his enthusiastic support for Israel and his discomfort with what some typified as excessive judicial activism,[11] all contributed to an increased focus on the efficacy, coordination and linkages between security agencies. This blended with enhanced defence budgets for the Afghanistan mission and growing cyber operational and defence needs. Striking an appropriate balance between security and liberty continued to tax the government. New 'lawful access' proposals were opposed by some, largely because legislative oversight provisions were missing.

A newly elected Liberal government in 2015 refreshed the framework of national security operations conferring statutory authority where it had not clearly existed before. Bill C59 introduced a combined statutory framework that provided 'lawful access' with a prescribed approval process requiring ministerial and, in some circumstances, judicial sign-off. It also strengthened parliamentary oversight via the 'National Intelligence and Security Committee of Parliamentarians',[12] reflecting the UK model. It also created new authorizations for 'active measures' by agencies like CSIS and CSEC. The mix of measures and

---

[10] Government of Canada, *Remembering Air India Flight 182*, at www.publicsafety.gc.ca/cnt/ntnl-scrt/cntr-trrrsm/r-nd-flght-182/index-en.aspx, accessed 30 August 2021.

[11] Jeremy Keehn (23 October 2014). 'Stephen Harper and the Question of Canadian Security', *New Yorker*.

[12] National Security and Intelligence Committee of Parliamentarians (18 December 2020), *2020 Annual Report* at www.nsicop-cpsnr.ca/press-releases/pr-cp-2020-12-18/pr-cp-2020-12-18-en.html, accessed 30 August 2021.

oversight was recommended in part by the Special Senate Committee on Anti-Terrorism.[13]

The period between 2003 and 2015 could therefore be characterized as a transformation from an external, Cold War, focus towards internal considerations such as terrorism; a transformation that proved challenging while simultaneously dealing with attempts at infiltration and interference by traditional autocratic adversaries.

National security agencies, executive power and parliamentary oversight

Today, the key national security agencies/security-focused departments in Canada's security establishment include: the Department of National Defence, CSIS, Financial Transaction Analysis Centre, Public Safety Canada and the Cabinet Committee that oversees the broad scope and direction of these agencies. The 2003 creation of Public Safety Canada, dubbed as a 'homeland security' equivalent brought a mandate to ensure coordination across federal departments and agencies responsible for national security and the safety of Canadians from risks such as natural disasters, terrorism and crime. The institution served as the overarching authority and line manager for the RCMP, CSIS and the Canadian Border Security Agency. The agencies have specific scopes of operations and, in some but not all cases, budgetary allocations are passed by parliament in the usual way.

Above these agencies sit Cabinet Committees, supported by various Deputy Minister (DM) committees. Whereas Canada has no single National Security Council, the collective role of the Cabinet Committees, and the DM committees that support them, substitute. Chief among them is the Cabinet Committee on Global Affairs and Public Security (CCGAPS), on which the ministers of public safety, transport, industry science and technology, defence, foreign affairs, immigration, justice, and international development sit. Others can be invited as necessary. The Centre for Cyber Security within the CSE is represented by the Defence Minister.

The Prime Minister is an ex officio member of every cabinet committee. In the Privy Council Office (PCO), three senior officials advise the Prime Minister

---

[13] Thomas Walkom (23 June 2017). 'Justin Trudeau's Security Bill: a lot like Stephen Harper's', *Toronto Star*.

on national security: the National Security and Intelligence Advisor (NSIA) to the Prime Minister; the Assistant Secretary to the Cabinet for Security and Intelligence; and the Assistant Secretary to the Cabinet for Intelligence Assessment. The latter presides over an Intelligence Assessment Group which has been developed to produce more concise, evidence and issue-based policy briefs that have helped facilitate a tighter relationship between the Prime Minister's Office and the NSIA.[14] Each of the assistant secretaries is supported by a team which, in the case of the Intelligence Assessment Group, numbers approximately thirty. The NSIA's team is also the prime liaison function with the US NSC and National Security Adviser and analogous operations in other friendly and Five-Eyes partner countries.

The CCGAPS meets regularly, to approve legislation on security matters, consider cabinet submissions from any of the constituent departments or at the call of the Chairperson. When cabinet committees meet, each Minister is traditionally accompanied by their DM or relevant agency head. Anything urgent or unexpected not given to an existing or newly created committee is managed by the Incident Response Group, an ad hoc grouping of ministers, who gather as required in response to natural disasters, pandemics or other crises which require urgent cross-ministry cooperation and action. The COVID-19 pandemic highlights how a matter sufficiently urgent and important may warrant the creation of a new Cabinet Committee. The newly developed 'Cabinet Committee on COVID-19' met regularly, providing whole-of-government leadership, coordination and preparedness for a response to the health and economic impacts of the virus.

Whereas the Cabinet Committee structure and the Incident Response Group were, prior to 2018, performed by a Security and Intelligence Committee, the reformed structure gives Cabinet the ability to consider medium- to long-term national security challenges, giving immediate focus to unexpected serious events. In some respects, this has provided a more responsive high-level structure akin to the UK's emergency management committee – COBR.

DM Committees play a critical role in informing the work of the Cabinet Committees. There are four DM Committees for national security: DM Policy Committee on National Security Issues (DMNS); Foreign Affairs and Defence Committee (FAD); DM Operational Coordination Committee (DMOC); and DM Intelligence Assessment Committee (DMIC) – see Figure 3.1.

---

[14] Author interviews with former PCO senior officials.

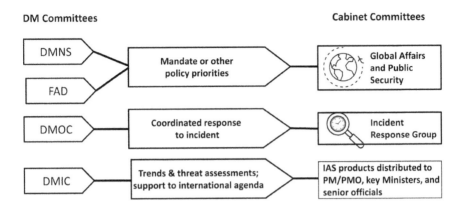

DM Committees   Cabinet Committees

Sensitive political and/or political issues could be discussed at **Operations**

Figure 3.1 Relationship of Cabinet and DM Committees.[15]

Whereas the DMIC oversees the peer-review of outputs from the Intelligence Assessment Group in the PCO, the DMOC plays a critical role in crisis response and in supporting the Incident Response Group within the CCGAPS. The DMOC convenes weekly, enabling relationship and trust-building for officials to convene rapidly and agilely in times of crisis to support the Incident Response Group and its strategic communications effort.[16] While the plethora of committees creates a community of security awareness within the upper reaches of the Cabinet and bureaucracy around national security challenges, it is not clear that it is as efficient or agile as a National Security Council structure might allow. In a majority government (2015–2019), the Prime Minister's freedom to act is essentially unchallenged. Within the vagaries of minority parliaments (a more frequent Canadian context) a measure of across-the-aisle consultation is often required.

Challenges

The tension between civil liberties and the need for security has been a constant theme in Canadian national security. The scope of the security threat is described broadly as:

- espionage or sabotage that is against Canada or detrimental to the interests of Canada or any activities in support of such espionage or sabotage;

---

[15] Source: Daniel Jean, Canada School of Public Service.
[16] Author interviews with former PCO officials.

- foreign-influenced activities within or related to Canada that are detrimental to the interests of Canada and are clandestine or deceptive or involve a threat to any person;
- activities within or related to Canada, toward or in support of the threat or use of acts of serious violence against persons or property for the purpose of achieving a political, religious or ideological objective within Canada or in a foreign state;
- activities directed toward undermining by covert unlawful acts, or directed toward or ultimately to lead to the destruction or overthrow by violence of the constitutionally established system of the Government of Canada, but does not include lawful advocacy, protest or dissent, unless carried on in conjunction with the activities referred to in paragraphs (a) to (d) above.[17]

These broad definitions do not limit scope in any meaningful way, particularly with the presence of an Incident Response Group. However, the process is largely secretive with public reports and relatively vanilla anti-terrorism strategies being published or updated annually or as required. Scrutiny has improved, with parliamentary and judicial oversight, and new complaint procedures that have added a new dimension to how security agencies and the entire system are held accountable.

Public scrutiny is less robust. The 2019 federal election lacked significant debate on issues concerning foreign affairs or national security, and the absence of a national security strategy or concept paper discourage engagement. While an annual Intelligence Priorities Process is undertaken, the lack of defined strategic security direction risks making these annual labour-intensive exercises too all-encompassing and not tightly focused on, or supportive of, declared priorities. However, non-government centres, such as the Citizen Lab at the University of Toronto's Munk School, play a constructive role, especially in cybersecurity analysis, which aids the public awareness of issues immensely. This public awareness is supported by a wider socialization of relevant national security threats and challenges via parliamentary oversight and media engagement. Canada's Department of National Defence also funds networks[18] that link cross-Canada knowledge hubs and align directly with the policy challenges articulated in Canada's 2017 Defence Policy.[19] The policy is relatively

---

[17] Canadian Security Intelligence Act 1985, Article 2.
[18] See DND's MINDS Collaborative Networks at https://www.canada.ca/en/department-national-defence/programs/minds/collaborative-networks.html accessed 30 August 2021.
[19] Government of Canada (2017). *Strong, Secure, Engaged: Canada's Defence Policy.*

forward-thinking and reflects wider security issues, such as pandemic preparedness, cyber, artificial intelligence, Arctic security and continental defence, in which wider cross-government security agencies also have an interest. But as Defence is a line-ministry function that should support wider national goals and objectives in coordination with other line ministries, strategic and coherent security direction from the government is still absent. The absence of clear national security goals and priorities does not risk security-related departments operating independently as much as it risks undermining efficient organization and coordination of resources.

Generally speaking, national security planning work and in-depth analysis in advance of prospective threats has been variable. The Canadian system does not engage with the coherence or intellectual rigour of others, e.g. US National Security Council. For example, while a cybersecurity agency has been stood up for some time, Canada's inability to make a timely, prophylactic decision, either way, on Huawei's desire to build Canadian 5G networks, alone among its allies, speaks to the extent to which lack of focus, or a policy of measured dithering at the top, delays vital deliberation.

There are strengths in the system. Constructive inter-agency cooperation led to the arrest of the 'Toronto 18' – a mix of adults and older teens believed to be inspired by extreme and violent Islamist doctrine were alleged to be planning attacks in federal and financial hub locations in the Toronto region. The successful integration of electronic intelligence, focused surveillance and pro-active engagement of local police meant the suspects were arrested before harm was done. What is less clear from experience to date is the acuity and adaptability of the intelligence, national security and police infrastructure in the face of increasing right-wing extremism. Recent events in the United States and elsewhere underline the importance of an analytical, surveillance and prophylactic focus in this area, which can be incited by hostile states; CSIS heads have expressed concerns about the activities of Russian and Chinese agents.[20] In these cases, the national security challenge is more about undue influence over policy or intimidation than violence. The addition of neo-Nazi groups to the official list of terrorist groups in February 2021 might not have happened without the attacks on the US Congress on 6 January 2021. On balance, the Canadian

---

[20] See David Vigneault (9 February 2021). 'National Security, Economic Prosperity and Canada'. *CIGI Speaker Series*, at www.canada.ca/en/security-intelligence-service/news/2021/02/remarks-by-director-david-vigneault-to-the-centre-for-international-governance-innovation.html, accessed 30 August 2021.

system of security agencies appears to be engaged with both a coherent real-time and reactive focus with sufficient resources. But apprehensive acuity, and the resultant will on enhanced intelligence, is less sharp, intense or developed, largely because Canadian governments usually move to the tempo of the political leadership's engagement with the issue.

Conclusion

The development of Canada's current national security structures and traditions has been shaped by reactions to events starting with internal tensions and instability in the 1970s and 1980s. The impact of increased terrorist activity domestically and internationally between 1985 and 2015 resulted in reforms to make Canada's national security structures and processes more agile and responsive. One could argue that this greater level of agility builds on the country's efforts between 2006 and 2015 to evolve its legislative framework to accommodate better levels of intelligence gathering and sharing while upholding its Charter of Rights and Freedoms. The strength of the national security structure in Canada is the power of its coordination mechanisms to 'convene'; more specifically, to react in an agile way to Cabinet Committee information requirements and to respond to and coordinate communications on sudden emergencies or anticipate imminent threats. In this context, the role of the Incident Response Group is important.

However, despite improvements and adaptations at the functional level, Canada's national security structure will continue to be weakened by the lack of political will to support a more strategic discussion and declared direction on national security. The COVID-19 pandemic has reminded Canadians how incidents on the other side of the world can threaten safety at the community level across Canada's provinces and territories. National security may gain new strategic ground and prominence as Canadians begin to feel 'threatened' once again.

4

Colombia's National Security Council and the fluid architecture for presidential counselling

Oscar Palma

The institutional architecture

Conceptions of security and defence in Colombia have been conditioned by the internal conflict against armed insurgent groups and shaped Colombia's institutions. The current institutions date from 1965, one year after the appearance of the two main insurgent groups: the Revolutionary Armed Forces of Colombia (FARC) and the National Liberation Army (ELN). In response, the Superior National Defence Council (SNDC) was formed with high State officials to coordinate and legitimize government action in the face of social turmoil and increasing unpopularity.

For many years, security and defence agendas were separate. Defence issues, which since the 1950s included the police, were handled by the Defence Ministry, while security, understood as internal public order, was handled by the Government Ministry and a separate Security Council. The Security Council focused on public order and exchanging information among national (not regional) government organizations.[1] In 1992 the Councils merged to create a unified National Security and Defence Council (NSDC), later renamed the National Security Council.

As this chapter shows, the Colombian institutional architecture is not rigid. It has changed according to three factors: the context; how the government understood 'security'; and the influence of the National Security (and Defence) Advisor (NSA).

---

[1] República de Colombia, *Ley 52 de 1990*. [Law 52/1990]. Article 22.

Context

From the 1950s to the 1970s, economic inequality (especially land distribution), state abandonment, and social marginalization in remote regions motivated the emergence of rebel groups. The political system was highly centralized, tightly managed by political elites, but it marginalized many: peasants, indigenous communities, communists and the poor. The tough social and economic conditions met the revolutionary spirit of the 1959 Cuban Revolution, providing a platform for rebel groups.

Popular uprisings forced the President to declare a state of emergency, in the hope that special measures, including the creation of the SNDC, would restore public order.[2] Chaired by the President it involved the Ministers of Defence, Government,[3] Foreign Relations, Economy, Justice, Communications, and Infrastructure, the Joint Commander and the Second Commander of the Military Forces. Its functions were to: coordinate military and civil activities; evaluate strategic intelligence; formulate recommendations on national defence; and monitor the implementation of the President's Defence actions.[4]

The conflict continued for decades, as violent actors intensified their operations. A burgeoning narcotics economy through the 1970s to the 1990s, saw the emergence of drug cartels and well-funded rebel groups. Reactionary deaths squads, also known as paramilitary groups, involving wealthy citizens, especially landowners and stockbreeders, formed to fight the rebels. They used and benefited from the cocaine economy, and cooperation existed, unofficially, between many military units, regional political and economic leaders and the paramilitaries. Further institutions, such as the Security Council, were created to address the rising violence.

The creation of the NSDC in 1992 brought this architecture together, with the NSA acting as the NSDC secretary. Besides the Security and Defence Councils, the NSDC incorporated specialized commissions, such as the one created in 1989 to confront right-wing paramilitary groups.

---

[2] Presidencia de la República de Colombia, *Decreto 3398 de 1965*. [Decree 3398/1965].

[3] The Government Ministry was responsible for dealing with internal 'political' affairs: political parties, Congress, human rights, indigenous and Afro-Colombian affairs – the police fall under the Ministry of Defence. It was renamed the Ministry of Interior in 1995.

[4] *Decree 3398/1965*, op. cit., which became a Law of the Republic through República de Colombia, *Ley 48 de 1968* [Law 48/1968].

The NSDC was charged with:

- advising the President and recommending security and defence policies;
- coordinating security and defence policies with other state agencies;
- analysing national security and defence conditions;
- assessing national security objectives and recommending courses of action;
- evaluating national strategic intelligence policies and formulating recommendations;
- monitoring implementation of security and defence policies;
- promoting the exchange of information among state institutions for public order;
- proposing specific security and defence plans to address public order and external security; and
- formulating recommendations for the coordination, military assistance and operational control of military forces and security agencies.[5]

The understanding of 'security'

The government's understanding and interpretation of security issues, and the roles of the security actors impacted substantially on the institutional architecture. For decades, the struggle against armed groups was seen as the responsibility of the Military Forces, and politicians abrogated leadership to them. The evolution in membership from the 1965 to 1992 Councils reflects this; the NSDC was dominated by the Military and the Police who took a narrow view of security and acted accordingly.

In 2002, the Democratic Security Policy broadened the understanding of security.[6] It now encompassed economic, social and development matters, as well as the traditional fight against armed groups. The struggle began to be understood as a State responsibility in which all institutions had a role in a 'whole-of-government' approach. This brought into play non-military and non-police responses, such as development of economic activity, and disrupting the coca economy and armed groups through better coordination of state institutions in conflict-affected regions. The Policy recognized that the lack of institutional coordination was a major flaw, so it sought to coordinate and unify the action of

---

[5] Presidencia de la República de Colombia, *Decreto 2134 de 1992* [Decree 2134/1992]. Article 5.
[6] República de Colombia. *Política de Seguridad Democrática (PSD)* [Democratic Security Policy]. Ministerio de Defensa Nacional (2002).

government agencies, especially integrating that of the Military Forces with the other State institutions through the NSDC.[7]

However, the Council's new role was not itself decisive. Coordination was often achieved through implementation agencies like the '*Centro de Coordinación de Acción Integral*' (which became the 'Consolidation Bureau'). This Agency oversaw different Ministry and Presidential programmes at local level aimed at building institutions and implementing development projects in conflict-affected regions. There were also local security councils, down to municipalities, headed by the President who made decisions concerning local security.[8] The Policy worked: a strong state offensive, including action at a very local level, weakened the criminal economy and hit armed groups severely. FARC and ELN were left considering a negotiated solution to the conflict.

Organized crime, robbery, gangs, theft, micro-trafficking, have been more relevant to Latin American security that conventional defence problems. The securitization of these public security issues motivated changes to the Council's structure in 2010 to reflect this wider notion of security. Renamed as the National Security Council (NSC), the Ministers of Justice, Government, Foreign Affairs and Economy returned as permanent members, improving coordination between civilians and the Military, and a new Presidential Advisor on Public Security was appointed.[9] The Presidential Advisor on Public Security[10] would define a strategy against crime in the cities,[11] while the NSA focused on wider security, e.g. armed groups, guerrillas, major criminal gangs and external threats.[12] At the same time, the Operative National Security Committee was created to support and oversee implementation of the Council's decisions.[13] Both security advisors were members, with the rest of the Committee composed of the deputies of Council members.

The decision to negotiate and implement a peace process with FARC in 2012 implied a deep transformation of the security council architecture. Military

---

[7]   PSD, op. cit.

[8]   President Alvaro Uribe was seen by critics as a micro-manager, travelling to crises to lead local security councils and making decisions to resolve local security problems.

[9]   Presidencia de la República de Colombia, *Decreto 4748 de 2010* [Decree 4748/2010]. Article 3.

[10] Presidencia de la República de Colombia. *Decreto 3445 de 2010* [Decree 3445/2010]. Article 18.

[11] República de Colombia. *Política Integral de Seguridad y Defensa para la Prosperidad* [Comprehensive Security and Defence Policy for Prosperity]. Ministerio de Defensa Nacional (2010).

[12] Explanation by President Juan Manuel Santos. Revista Semana, *Gobierno crea Consejo de Seguridad Nacional y Consejería de Convivencia Ciudadana*, at: www.semana.com/nacion/articulo/gobierno-crea-consejo-seguridad-nacional-alta-consejeria-convivencia-ciudadana/122147-3, accessed 30 August 2021.

[13] *Decree 4748/2010*, op. cit., Article 5.

operations reduced in favour of cease-fires and dialogue with the rebels. In 2014, the position of 'Advising Minister for Post-conflict, Human Rights and Security' was created to oversee all issues related to conflict, peace and security. He replaced the NSA as the technical secretary of the NSC and a 'Director of Security' was appointed beneath him, but with less power.[14]

While not yet formally defined, national security is given a wide interpretation, and the environment has become a key dimension of Colombian national security. Colombia has the second highest biodiversity worldwide, and one of the highest amounts of drinking water, so natural resources are now perceived as strategic assets. This expanded definition of national security resulted in an expansion in the permanent membership of the Council to include the Environment Minister and Director of National Planning who are responsible for these areas.

The NSA's importance

The system relies on the personality of the President and NSA, and their power within government. During Juan Manuel Santos's Presidency (2010–2018), the first NSA, Sergio Jaramillo, was close to the President and powerful. When he was appointed chief negotiator and High Peace Commissioner, the prominence of the office moved with him.

Under Ivan Duque (2018–present) the narratives and priorities changed. As a member of the party that opposed the Peace Process, Duque rejected the discourse on 'peace', and focused on regaining security and achieving stability in the context of a growing threat from armed groups, including FARC's dissidents. The Council architecture changed again, eliminating post-conflict positions, and reinstating the figure of the NSA.[15] He appointed Rafael Guarín, a security and defence expert close to Duque who re-established the NSA's central position within decision-making circles.[16] Guarín's career and expertise contrasted with Minister of Defence Guillermo Botero's lack of experience,[17] and he has become

---

[14] Presidencia de la República de Colombia, *Decreto 1649 de 2014* [Decree 1649/2014]; Presidencia de la República de Colombia, *Decreto 724 de 2016* [Decree 724/2016].

[15] Presidencia de la República de Colombia, *Decreto 1784 de 2019*. [Decree 1784/2019]. Article 4.

[16] The Government appointed a Presidential Advisor for Stabilization and Consolidation who continued the post-conflict agenda, although the narratives changed. Discourses including concepts like 'peace', 'post-conflict' or 'internal conflict' were replaced by 'stabilization', 'consolidation' and 'internal threats'.

[17] Botero was a businessman and head of the National Federation of Traders (FENALCO). He had no previous experience in the security and defence sector.

the dominant figure in the security agenda: for the first time, the National Security Policy has been signed by both the NSDA and Minister of Defence.[18]

Duque's Security and Defence policy intends to reinvigorate the NSC, guided by the concept of multidimensional security that continues the multi-sector and multi-agency approach for which Council coordination is essential.[19] The Council has been very active, meeting seven times in the first eighteen months to define key security issues, and approve the National Intelligence Plan (one of its traditional duties).[20] The most recent reform to the Council reflects this notion of multidimensional security. It has added the Ministers for Information Technologies, Environment and Health (an obvious consequence of the pandemic), and the Director of National Planning as new members.[21] Recent Council acts include categorizing armed groups according to their level of threat,[22] defining territorial zones of state intervention (ZEIIs)[23] and, for the first time, adopting a list of global terrorist organizations.[24] The Council can also authorize further peace negotiations with armed groups and, is now required to develop a National Security Strategy, which has never been officially adopted in Colombia before.[25]

Supporting the NSA is a very small permanent staff, no more than ten, dealing with key elements of the security agenda, including producing a National Security Strategy for the first time in Colombia's history.[26] The staff handles the 'Zonas Futuro' programme for the development of conflict affected areas,[27] leads

---

[18] República de *Colombia, Política de Seguridad y Defensa para la Legalidad, el Emprendimiento y la Equidad* [Security and Defence Policy for Legality, Entrepreneurship and Equity]. Ministerio de Defensa Nacional (2019). The Presidential Advisor on Public Security was disestablished by President Santos in the reshuffles linked to the Peace Process.

[19] Legality, Entrepreneurship and Equity Policy, op. cit..

[20] Author interview with Rocío Pachón, former Deputy Director for Security and Defense at the National Planning Department.

[21] Presidencia de la República de Colombia. *Decreto 741 de 2021* [Decree 741/2021]. Article 2.

[22] Legality, Entrepreneurship and Equity Policy, op. cit.; República de Colombia, *Ley 1941 de 2018* [Decree 1941/2018].

[23] Legality, Entrepreneurship and Equity Policy, op. cit.; El Espectador (29 January 2020). '¿Zonas Futuro en Jaque? Corte Constitucional define demanda que busca tumbarlas'. At: www.elespectador.com/noticias/judicial/zonas-futuro-en-jaque-corte-constitucional-define-demanda-que-busca-tumbarlas-articulo-901994, accessed 30 August 2020.

[24] Colprensa (20 January 2020). 'Colombia adopta listado de organizaciones terroristas que ya no incluye a las FARC'. *El País* at: www.elpais.com.co/colombia/colombia-adopta-listado-de-organizaciones-terroristas-que-ya-no-incluye-a-la-farc.html, accessed 30 August 2021.

[25] Decree 741/2021, op.cit., Article 3, No.10.

[26] Legality, Entrepreneurship and Equity Policy. op. cit.

[27] The Havana agreements resulting from the peace process with FARC, prioritized several municipalities for development. 'Zonas Futuro' is a focused programme for state institutions to develop specific areas in those municipalities. See: https://id.presidencia.gov.co/Paginas/prensa/2020/proposito-Zonas-Futuro-mejorar-seguridad-territorios-generar-desarrollo-cambiar-economias-ilicitas-Comisionado-Paz-200129.aspx , accessed 30 August 2021.

public security programmes, and it is starting to lead in cybersecurity.[28] It also wants to create a permanent committee structure since both the National Security Council and supporting Operative National Security Committee only meet when they are convened by the NSA.[29]

Responding to COVID-19

Although Colombia's widened understanding of security includes human security, for which health is a core part, the COVID-19 pandemic did not trigger a significant response by the NSC. Lacking any public health institutions, which would have been essential to decision-making during the pandemic, and with Council members who do not have experience in dealing with public health issues, the NSC was not a major actor in Colombia's response. Instead, the NSC remained focused on dealing with rebel groups and bespoke mechanisms were developed for COVID-19.

Throughout, the President has been advised on how to address the spread of COVID-19 by health officials, epidemiologists and the Ministry of Health. Institutions like the military and the police have had a role, for example, in the control of the population during the lockdown and combating criminal groups that sought to exploit the quarantine by exerting their control over territory. However, the strategies and plans used by the armed forces and police did not involve the NSC as the route to collaboration with other institutions.

The military launched *Operación San Roque* (named after the Catholic patron saint of those affected by contagious diseases) as their approach to action through the crisis. It had four lines of action: assisting the civilian authorities in humanitarian assistance; continuing and developing operations for border control; keeping troops on the first level of combat readiness; and preserving the health and integrity of the men and women of the Military Forces.[30] It involved 30,000 soldiers being deployed to border areas to prevent massive illicit immigration and providing support to the population during the challenges of lengthy lockdowns. Clearly this required interagency coordination, including with the Border Police, the General Prosecutor's Office, the National Migration

---

[28] Rocío Pachón interview, op. cit.
[29] Rocío Pachón interview, op. cit.
[30] Fuerza Aérea Colombiana (2 May 2020). *'Operación San Roque': Plan de Contención Institucional Frente al COVID-19*, at: www.fac.mil.co/%E2%80%9Coperaci%C3%B3n-san-roque%E2%80%9D-plan-de-contenci%C3%B3n-institucional-frente-al-covid-19, accessed 30 August 2021.

Agency, consulates, local governments, and even the security forces of neighbouring countries.[31] However, the coordination was done at the operational level and in local settings, not nationally, meaning that NSC decision-making was not required. Similarly, while the National Police is a single hierarchical organization, in operational terms it depends on the command of local authorities (mayors and governors), so many of the decisions related to deploying the National Police during the pandemic were made by local rather than national authorities.

Reflecting the separate management mechanisms set up for dealing with the pandemic, the NSDA's agenda continued to be focused on the development of *Zonas Futuro*, and the response to urban threats from rebel groups. According to the government, these groups infiltrated social protests throughout September 2020, and threatened public order in several cities.

Conclusion

The institutional architecture advising the President of Colombia in security and defence has been fluid and highly dependent on the context. Rather than being rigid and solidly institutionalized, it has evolved according to the way in which the state has conceived security, which for much of the time has been driven by the struggle against armed groups. The relevance of the National Security Council has also varied over time; its structure and the themes it has overseen depending on the political and security context and a broadening understanding of what is meant by 'security'.

A general perception of the Council is that it has been inadequate.[32] For long periods, the Council existed in name only, not being convened despite circumstances in which coordination would have been beneficial. Even when it has met, it has not impacted on the decisions of policy makers, and rather than delivering real interagency coordination, the Council has played a more passive role, informing other state institutions about the security and defence agenda rather than acting as an executive authority that sets the agenda. The Supporting

---

[31] Presidencia de la República de Colombia (4 April 2020). *En Operación San Roque, más de 30 mil hombres de la Fuerza Pública están protegiendo las fronteras*, at https://id.presidencia.gov.co/Paginas/prensa/2020/En-Operacion-San-Roque-mas-de-30-mil-hombres-de-la-Fuerza-Publica-estan-protegiendo-las-fronteras-200415.aspx, accessed 30 August 2021.

[32] Original research included informal conversations with researchers at the Universidad del Rosario (Julio Londoño; Sebastian Beltrán, and Francesca Ramos), and a member of the Security Council who wished to remain anonymous.

Committee has met on fewer occasions than the Council itself, and there is no written record of Council meetings from past governments. A key problem remains the lack of an understanding by many agencies about their role in the security agenda: many still believe that the problems are for the traditional security sector actors alone. This will be a significant limitation as the understanding of security expands and demands better mechanisms for responding to environmental, cyber and public health risks. It still needs to be seen if the pandemic will motivate further changes in the composition of the NSC to bring these experts into the structure.

Looking at the current dynamic of the NSA's Office and activity of the Council, it is possible that these institutions could serve a purpose, but their success is currently too highly dependent on the will of the President. The Council continues to be a non-permanent institution without a bureaucracy of its own, and its members meet sporadically. If the President empowers the NSA and the Council, the arrangements can be effective, but work still needs to be done to embed the structures and authority formally within the bureaucracy. The fact that in July 2021, for the first time, the Council has been directed to enact a National Security Strategy could be a positive sign, but it is too early to judge. It remains to be seen if the Strategy will be developed successfully, and how the members of the Council will interpret its scope. Furthermore, it is unknown if the Council will be able to effectively assess the strategy's implementation, and whether this will grant it a greater role in security and defence governance. Despite this, Colombia has successfully, if slowly, embraced whole-of-government coordination in the past when bringing insurgents such as FARC to the negotiating table, so there are grounds for optimism if the lessons can be learned and applied.

5

Centralized decision-making in France: The non-permanent Defence and National Security Council

Patrick Chevallereau

Introduction

After the Second World War, France, as a permanent member of the United Nations Security Council, became a significant international actor in the management of global defence and security issues. Drawing on lessons from the trauma of the 1940 military defeat and occupation, Charles de Gaulle, the founding president of the Fifth Republic, established a centralized decision-making system strongly anchored at the level of the Head of the State. The centralization of decision-making is a core national concept and applies to all kinds of crisis situations covering times of peace and war. It is not just for crisis management, however; it is also responsible for dealing with long-term security issues and resilience. Unlike in many nations though, the French pyramidal system does not rely on any permanent 'National Council'.

Defence and National Security Council

At the heart of the French system of decision-making on defence and security issues is the *Conseil de Défense et de Sécurité Nationale* (CDSN) – the Defence and National Security Council. It takes a very broad view of defence and security that represents an evolution from the narrowly focused *Conseil de la défense nationale* defined in the original Constitution of the Fifth Republic in 1958 by Charles de Gaulle.

Under Article 15 of the French Constitution, the CDSN is chaired by the President in his role as Commander in Chief ('*Chef des Armées*'). Technically a non-permanent institution, the CDSN is activated at the instigation of the President only when necessary. Its role illustrates and reinforces the centralized approach to decision-making that places authority in the hands of the Executive branch, which is a fundamental principle of the Fifth Republic.

While the CDSN is the ultimate decision-making body, the French government is guided by a much broader national defence concept. This guiding concept defines how the country organizes its national defence and security. Security is seen broadly, going beyond the traditional military domain. It is concerned with direct or indirect threats and risks that could threaten the existence of the nation, whether originating at home or abroad, and to which France, its territory, population and security interests could be exposed. Consequently, a wide spectrum of the state's means and resources (Armed Forces, National Security Forces and Sécurité Civile), can be harnessed, as well as the decentralized territorial entities and Operators of Vital Importance's assets (OIV).[1] The approach is most concretely defined in the 2004 'Code de la défense' which exists as a Standing Law. Article L111-3 defines three formats for the CDSN:

- The Defence and National Security Council establishes the general political guidance on defence issues, resilience and crisis management.
- The Restricted Defence and National Security Council is a sub-format of the CDSN, focused on decision-making specifically related to the military dimension of defence and security issues and crises.
- The Intelligence National Council is a specialized format of the CDSN, focused on intelligence issues.

Importantly, the CDSN establishes the guidelines and priorities for deterrence,[2] military procurement, operations abroad, large-scale crisis planning, intelligence, economic and energy security, home security planning and the fight against terrorism ('Code de la défense', Article R*1122-1). Its role, therefore, covers both short- and long-term issues.

The CDSN has a variable geometry format, composed of both permanent and occasional members. Aside from the President of the French Republic, the Prime Minister (Head of the government), the Foreign Affairs Minister, the

---

[1] While no complete public list of the related organizations exists, it is known to include areas like Water Supply, Industry, Health etc.
[2] To be understood as 'Nuclear deterrence'.

Interior Minister, the Defence Minister and the Finance Minister are permanent members. Occasional members are invited to participate depending on the specific agenda, e.g. the Justice Minister, the Health Minister etc.

Over time, the CDSN has evolved to include preparation for all the threats and risks faced by the country and its citizens. Its scope reflects the comprehensive 'defence-security continuum' that is at the core of the most recent national strategic reviews: the 2013 *Livre Blanc*[3] and its continuation, the 2017 Defence and National Security Strategic Review[4] and the January 2021 Strategic Update.[5] These documents address the blurred delineation between the notions of defence and security. The State's fight against terrorism typifies this approach. It encompasses police-led anti-terrorism action at home and military-led counter-terrorism operations abroad, such as in the Sahel and in the Middle East, with the military, which includes the Gendarmerie, operating in both the homeland and overseas.

Other documents also reflect the centralized but integrated nature of the French system. The 2009 'Blue book, a National Strategy for the Sea and Oceans' is inter-ministerial by nature and articulates France's ambition as a maritime power, including its economic and environmental dimensions.[6] The President tasked development of this strategy to the Prime Minister, whose Secretary General for the Sea then drafted the strategy and coordinated the responses for Prime Ministerial approval.

Crisis-management can also be delivered through a CIC (Inter-ministerial Crisis Cell) without requiring a CDSN meeting.[7] Generally, the Prime Minister's inter-ministerial direction is delegated either to the Minister of Interior for crises occurring on French territory,[8] or the Foreign Affairs minister if the events happen abroad. Using the governmental plans established under the auspices of the General Secretariat for Defence and National Security (SGDSN), the crisis cells cover three domains: situation management, anticipation (oversight on the short-term future – scenarios, exit strategy. . .), and public information (the interaction with the public – e.g. press conference, communiqués . . .). The short chain of command relies on the inter-ministerial role of '*Prefects*', who are the permanent depositaries of the State's authority in

---

[3] République Française (2013). *Livre blanc sur la défense et la sécurité nationale* [French White Paper. Defence and National Security].
[4] République Française (2017). *Revue stratégique de défense et de sécurité nationale*.
[5] Ministère des Armées (2021). *Actualisation stratégique*.
[6] République Française (2009). *Livre bleu: une stratégie nationale pour la mer et les océans*.
[7] For example, the COVID-19 crisis is being managed by a CIC rather than the CDSN.
[8] The term 'French territory' includes the French Overseas Territories.

each French *départements* (region).[9] The *Prefects* are in charge of the conduct and coordination of the operations on the ground.

This principle also applies to the concept of State Action at Sea, which is closely linked to France's needs for surveillance and intervention in the second-largest maritime domain worldwide (Exclusive Economic Zone – EEZ). Again, the government does not necessarily need to rely on the CDSN in order to act – especially in case of major maritime accidents or policing illegal actions at sea. The inter-ministerial chain of Command is short, passing directly from the Prime minister-level to the Secretary-General for the Sea (*SG Mer*) to the Maritime Prefects whose responsibilities cover the maritime façades and their adjacent maritime domain (the territorial waters and the EEZ).

Supporting the CDSN

The Council is supported by the SGDSN, which reports to the Prime Minister. It is a permanent inter-ministerial body of almost 1,000 officials – civil servants and military – that assists the design and implementation of security and defence policies. Apart from preparing for CDSN meetings, it also provides advice and support to the political decision-making process. Its areas of expertise include strategic defence and security matters including military programmes, nuclear deterrence, domestic security, economic and energy security, counterterrorism and crisis response plans. The SGDSN has three main missions:

- monitoring security threats, resilience planning (pandemic, civil nuclear accident, response to a terrorist attack, cyberattack etc.) and coordinating public crisis management;
- advising government, and drafting bills and decrees relating to matters of security and defence;
- operational tasks ranging from security clearance and classified document management to the protection of government communications (via the

---

9   *Départements* are the administrative territorial entities on the French mainland and in overseas territories. There are *Prefects* in the French '*départements d'Outre-mer*' (La Réunion, Mayotte, Martinique, Guadeloupe, Guyane, Saint-Pierre et Miquelon). They have the same authority as *prefects* on the French Mainland. In the two French territories of French Polynesia and Nouvelle Calédonie (which have a different status than the *départements*), the French Republic is represented by the Commissioner of the Republic (*commissaire de la République*) who have the same responsibilities as a Prefect in the event of a crisis. They coordinate action with the local government.

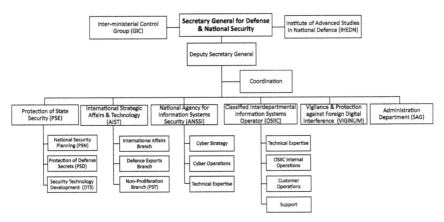

Figure 5.1 SGDSN Organization.[10]

Centre de transmissions gouvernemental and cybersecurity. A national agency within SGDSN ('*Agence Nationale de la sécurité des systèmes d'information*' – ANSSI) is specifically in charge of the latter.

Adapting to changing threats and emerging risks

The 14 July 2016 terrorist attack in Nice was a turning point for the CDSN, whose meetings are now held much more frequently; in practice, the CDSN now meets on a weekly basis.[11] These meetings take place before the whole government meeting (*Conseil des ministres*), which is also chaired by the President. Additional meetings are convened as necessary. Since the beginning of the COVID-19 crisis, its magnitude and scope meant the CDSN met regularly to respond to the health and other elements of the crisis, such as economics, industry etc. This involved new occasional members in the CDSN as the pandemic impacted parts of government that had not traditionally been engaged in security or major crisis response. That they have been integrated effectively is a sign of the strength and adaptability of the centralized system.

In recent years, some of the most visible outcomes of the CDSN meetings have been the rapid decisions to deploy French military forces in power and force projection operations (e.g. Libya 2011, Mali 2013, Central African Republic

---

[10] Source. SGDSN Website at www.sgdsn.gouv.fr/, accessed 30 August 2021.
[11] Prior to 2016, the CDSN typically met two to three times each year.

2013 and Strikes against Syrian President Assad's regime in April 2018). Just as political decision making is quick, so too is the action in Defence, enabled by a short chain of command, from the political-strategic guidance to the execution level. The Chief of Defence ('*Chef d'Etat-Major des Armées*' – CEMA) is the pivotal authority within this chain of command, that is political-military by nature. By necessity close to the President as well as to the President's senior military advisor,[12] the CEMA is in charge of the conduct of all military operations. To fulfil his mission, he has the French Strategic Headquarters ('*Centre de Planification et de Conduite des Opérations*' – CPCO) from which military operations are planned and conducted. It is noteworthy that although the CEMA is not a permanent member of the CDSN, he routinely attends them; he is at the core of the political-military articulation of the French organization.

A typical illustration of how reactive this chain of command can be is the complex but successful deployment of a joint expeditionary force to Mali in January 2013. Just a few hours after the decision was taken by the President at an urgent CDSN meeting, French expeditionary forces were able to project land and air power to prevent heavily armed and motorized Jihadist forces from overwhelming the capital city, Bamako. Without this capacity to turn decisions into action rapidly, there would have been catastrophic strategic impact across the entire Sahel region.

A unique approach

The concentration of powers in the hands of a few authorities has always been a key principle of how the French government organizes its crisis-management response. And it ensures the ability to respond rapidly to emerging crises, which is a strength of the French system.

Article 15 of the French Constitution gives the President the sole authority to engage military forces in operations abroad, with the Legislative branch playing a relatively marginal role compared to the Executive. The French Parliament must be informed by the government within three days of the beginning of any military operation. At this point, a parliamentary debate can be held as was the case in 2015 about the extension of the French Air Force operations against ISIS to include action in Syrian territory. But the Parliament has no power to veto the President's

---

[12] The President's Senior military advisor is a General officer (the '*Chef de l'Etat-Major Particulier du Président*' (CEMP)) who heads a small team of senior officers located at the Elysée Palace.

decision. However, there is a legal provision that if a military operation lasts more than four months, then the government is obliged to submit the extension for Parliament's authorization. Parliament has a strong tradition of bipartisan support in security matters, and these extensions have always been granted.

This division of roles between the Executive and Legislative has never been seriously challenged by the mainstream parties despite historical opposition by a small wing of anti-interventionists. However, it is fair to question whether this sixty-year-old constitutionally-based system is still suited to today's world, where society is more open than ever before, with more intense demand for democratic processes. It is also fair to observe that it offers less scrutiny from the other branches of the French political system than the decision-making organizations in comparable democracies. In this context, we may wonder and watch for a greater public or parliamentary push for involvement in or transparency over the French government's defence and national security actions. But for now, the indicators point in the other direction with speed and effectiveness seemingly being more important to most people than transparency.

Unlike the United Kingdom, France's strategic peer and most important military partner in Europe, no 'Chilcot report'[13] has demanded greater transparency or an increased role for the French Parliament so far. While the growing frequency and magnitude of terrorist attacks on French territory in recent years means the population is demanding more protection and security. The COVID-19 crisis may, however, shape public views about the relative value of speed of action through a centralized model and greater decentralization in delivering targeted outcomes.

The COVID-19 crisis

Although the 2013 Strategic review ('Livre Blanc') captures the threat of a major pandemic, the outbreak of COVID-19 and, above all, the magnitude of its consequences, constitutes what we can call a strategic surprise similar to events like the 9/11 attack on the World Trade Centre or the 2008 financial crisis. The French crisis management permanent organization – because of its pyramidal system and inter-ministerial nature – reacted quickly and provided a sound basis for the State's response at first. Responding to the crisis, the Health Ministry

---

[13] The British public inquiry into the nation's role in the 2003 Iraq War, at www.gov.uk/government/publications/the-report-of-the-iraq-inquiry, accessed 30 August 2021.

and its regional bodies ('*Agences Regionales de Santé*') activated multiple local 'white plans' and 'reinforced white plans' aimed at establishing priorities and re-orientating resources at hospitals. Through a lead and supporting ministry approach, many ministries provided means and resources (medicalized fast trains, Navy amphibious ship between the island of Corsica and the continent, medically equipped aircraft etc.). Beyond the purely national, even though public health remains primarily a national responsibility, the European Union can complement national policies and encourage cooperation between Member States. Accordingly, a European response, although largely improvised, was implemented. Among other things, this provided for patients to be treated in neighbouring countries' medical facilities and the coordination of bulk purchasing of protective equipment.[14]

However, the crisis quickly revealed a unique character due to both its unexpected duration and the severity of its impact on the economy and the society. Therefore, the existing crisis management system and procedures had to be adapted to deal with these unchartered circumstances, with the activation of a CIC under the coordinating authority of the Ministry of Interior leading, supported by a cell focusing on the Health aspects located at the Health Ministry (CORRUSS: Operational Centre for Management and Response to Health and Social Crisis). The CORRUSS was already included in standing procedures for pandemics, but its systems had to be adapted in light of the breadth and complexity of the COVID-19 response to allow to the various components needed to work together effectively. Iterations on how to deal with this long-lasting crisis are still going on at the time of writing.

At this stage, two main lessons can be drawn from a French perspective:

1. However integrated and credible the crisis management organization and its plans are, ultimately the level of resilience in society is a key factor. And while it is difficult to anticipate the level of resilience needed, trust in the process as much as the outcome is crucial.

2. While the centralized nature of the State organization enabled a rapid and solid initial response that facilitated synergies across government action, the French system seems less comfortable in providing an efficient decentralized answer. As the intensity of the pandemic varies a lot with sometimes

---

[14] The legal basis for EU action in public health is established in Articles 4, 6 and 168, Treaty on the Functioning of the European Union. The EU COVID-19 response is described in more detail at: *The Common EU Response to COVID-19*, at https://europa.eu/european-union/coronavirus-response_en, accessed 30 August 2021.

significant geographical differences, local entities like regions or municipalities are important partners for central government and could be better brought into the process, both for crisis management and for the long-term management of the problem.

Conclusion

The French decision-making system is highly centralized and capable of rapid response, which makes it well suited to a world where security crises of all kinds are developing faster and faster, are multifaceted, with strong multinational dimensions and often more complex than ever before. In this environment, the role of the CDSN and the concentration of the decisional power in the President's hands seem consistent with France's objective to remain an active contributor to international security. It also fits with its tradition of not being shy in using its hard power when required.

The model is culturally attuned to the Constitution, with power vested in a strong Executive that is subject to limited oversight by the Legislative. This makes it adaptable and decisive, even if it seems to offer less transparency than comparable foreign organizations. It also requires a strong and professional Secretariat to ensure the burdens on the Executive are manageable with their other responsibilities. Their central role allows the experience gained in crisis management to inform national plans and strategies in an iterative manner, although capturing and integrating the lessons learned could be improved.

No system is perfect, however. Being highly centralized and heavily rooted in state culture, the official policy circles are filled by a staff structure that could benefit from being more open to outsiders especially for long-term planning deliberations. The think tank world in Paris – less developed than in places like Washington, London or Berlin – generally gets quite limited access to decision-makers but could benefit them by bringing fresh perspectives. Similarly, no decision-making process is neutral. While the standing inter-ministerial structures are solid, the different political weight of some ministries – Interior, Defence, Finances – can skew the debate or shift the direction of the outcomes towards their own strengths. This is just a reality, whether for good or not. Finally, as COVID-19 shows, even a highly centralized system needs to be able to accommodate decentralized actors and action. However, despite the absence of a permanent security council, the French system has numerous strengths, including the ability to adapt to new situations and evolve.

6

A National Security Council: Georgia's historic challenge to get it right

Natia Seskuria

Georgia has had a challenging path to creating a comprehensive National Security Council (NSC). Since regaining independence in 1991, and having inherited corrupt institutions and tough economic and social conditions, the priority was to democratize. This required building strong institutions and a robust national security architecture. Russia's continuing desire to control its neighbourhood means Georgia constantly faces security threats. Thus, territorial protection and restoring territorial integrity despite limited resources have always been the primary security challenges, especially since the 2008 August War with Russia that resulted in 20 per cent of Georgia's territories being occupied.

For historic as much as current reasons, Georgian security thinking is dominated by the Russian threat. The presence of a foreign enemy has resulted in a classic security and defence focus. In recent years, Russian aggression towards Georgia has become multifaceted, employing more sophisticated tools to destabilize the country and subordinate Tbilisi to Moscow's will. Today, Georgia faces myriad challenges from Russia, internal and external, varying from military aggression to cyberattacks and disinformation. Facing such complex national security challenges has broadened the understanding of national security and requires a whole-of-government approach that demands effective national security coordinating mechanisms. The NSC, therefore, plays a key role in strategic decision-making in response to Georgia's most pressing issues.

A rocky road

When it formed on 24 January 1996, the NSC had substantial executive powers under the 1995 Constitution.[1] It was subordinated to President Eduard Shevardnadze as a Presidential advisory body for decision-making on strategic, defence and foreign policy matters, development of the Georgian Armed Forces, and elaboration of the National Security Concept. The NSC comprised the President as Chair, the State Minister, Ministers of Foreign Affairs, Defence, State Security, Internal Affairs, and the Secretary of the Council, who also served as National Security Adviser (NSA).[2] The permanent members and other invited members, e.g. the Chairman of the Parliament and Chairmen from the supreme representative bodies of the Autonomous Republics of Adjara and Abkhazia, were directly appointed by the President.

From its outset until February 2002, Shevardnadze's closest political ally, Nugzar Sajaia, was the Council's Secretary. His personal relationship with the President made him a highly influential figure, but the NSC's authority was too dependent on his personal links and influence over the political processes and decision-making at the highest level.[3] The lack of institutional traditions, and a highly centralized and corrupt political system meant the NSC was used largely to exercise control over the law enforcement agencies. It lacked strategic foresight or the ability to exercise oversight with regards to external and internal security threats.

The 2003 Rose Revolution brought systematic changes to the country with President Mikheil Saakashvili's Western-oriented Government, but the NSC's functions did not alter dramatically. Chaired by President Saakashvili, the permanent members were the Prime Minister, Chairman of Parliament, Ministers of Foreign Affairs, Defence and Internal Affairs, Chairman of Parliament's Defence and Security Committee, Chairman of the Foreign Relations Committee, Secretary of the Council (who remained NSA to the President) and the Chief of the General Staff of the Georgian Armed Forces.[4] Despite democratic changes and Western support in institution building, the NSC still lacked long-term planning or future threat preparation capabilities,

---

[1]   საქართველოს კონსტიტუცია (1995). [Constitution of Georgia], Article 99.
[2]   საქართველოს კანონი 'ეროვნული უშიშროების საბჭოს შესახებ' [Law of Georgia 'On the National Security Council'] 1996.
[3]   Author's interview with anonymous senior NSC official, November 2020.
[4]   საქართველოს კანონი 'ეროვნული უშიშროების საბჭოს შესახებ' [Law of Georgia 'On the National Security Council'] 2004.

and the much-needed authority and ability to coordinate the relevant state agencies. Dependence on informal coordination arrangements significantly undermined the NSC's role and credibility. Furthermore, it remained highly reliant on the authority of key individuals with decision-making restricted to the President and his inner circle. The concentration of power in the hands of a few reduced the NSC's ability to impact on the decision-making process. The NSC remained in the shadows without much power while its lack of clear authority hindered the ability to build trust across government structures.

A tale of two councils: Lack of coordination and duplication of functions

The 2008 August War exposed the shortcomings in Georgia's national security architecture, the lack of inter-agency cooperation and the NSC's difficulty functioning as the highest political decision-making body on national security.[5] Its role in crisis management was insignificant. The War served as a wake-up call to address the gaps. The NSC staff took charge of updating and elaborating strategic documents, such as the National Security Concept and Threat Assessment, to reflect the changing security environment and developed a much-needed, if nascent, capacity for foresight and planning.

In 2012, the new 'Georgian Dream' government altered the NSC's role again, reflecting its vision. The 2013 constitutional amendments transitioned Georgia from a presidential to a mixed parliamentary democracy. Executive power moved into the hands of the government; although the President remained commander-in-chief of the armed forces, they lost leverage over Georgia's national security policy decision-making. Reflecting this, in January 2014 the State Security and Crisis Management Council (SSCMC) was established to advise the Prime Minister on security matters. Chaired by the Prime Minister, it included the Foreign Minister, Ministers of Defence, Finance and Internal Affairs, Head of the State Security Service, and the Secretary of the Council who also served as a NSA to the Prime Minister – the Secretary of the NSC remained the President's NSA.[6] The SSCMC and staff were responsible for national security policy and planning on strategic matters related to state security,

---

[5]   Author's interview with anonymous senior NSC official, October 2020.
[6]   საქართველოს კანონი 'ეროვნული უსაფრთხოების პოლიტიკის დაგეგმვისა და კოორდინაციის წესის შესახებ' [Law of Georgia *'On Planning and Coordination of the National Security Policy'*] 2015.

elaboration of strategic documents and managing crisis situations at the highest political level, through the Operational Center for Crisis Management. Staffed by professional civil servants with experience in the security sector, the SSCMC took ownership of the national threat assessment document. Yet, the Council had a vast range of responsibilities that exceeded its capacity and undermined its effectiveness. It created confusion as formally both NSC and SSCMC were responsible for planning and coordinating national security policy and, despite clear overlap, coordination between them remained poor, weakening the credibility and authority of both. Furthermore, the two Councils were hostage to the tense personal relationships between then President and Prime Minister,[7] which provoked an unhealthy rivalry that Georgia, as a country facing critical threats and challenges, could ill-afford.

Georgia's quest for a suitable model

Despite significant pressure from Moscow, Georgia has retained a pro-Western foreign policy and reform-oriented agenda that seeks to integrate the country into European and Euro-Atlantic structures. Such aspirations have led the Kremlin to orchestrate activities aimed at weakening Georgian democracy. Russia's active pursuit of 'Borderization'[8] aims at gradual expansion of the zones of illegal occupation by pushing the so-called 'administrative border lines' further into Georgian territory allowing a creeping occupation of Georgia.[9] Russia has also actively pursued militarization of the occupied regions of Abkhazia and (so-called) 'South Ossetia'. Russia is also trying to destabilize the security environment by spreading disinformation and using the cyber domain.

Georgia has a comprehensive view of national security that covers state and non-state actors, energy, public health, the environment and links its security to the Black Sea and Euro-Atlantic regions.[10] This requires a whole-of-government

---

[7] Liz Fuller (21 March 2017). 'Conflict Between Georgian Parliament, President Intensifies'. *Radio Free Europe* at www.rferl.org/a/caucasus-report-president-parliament-conflict-intensifies/28382686.html, accessed 30 August 2021.

[8] US Embassy, Georgia (21 August 2019). *The Department of State's Spokesperson Morgan Ortagus at the Department's Press Briefing on August 21 commented about 'borderization' in Georgia*, at https://ge.usembassy.gov/the-department-of-states-statement-on-borderization-in-georgia-august-21/, accessed 30 August 2021.

[9] Natia Seskuria (2019). *Russia's 'Silent' Occupation and Georgia's Territorial Integrity*. RUSI Commentary.

[10] საქართველოს კანონი 'ეროვნული უსაფრთხოების პოლიტიკის დაგეგმვისა და კოორდინაციის წესის შესახებ' [Law of Georgia 'On Planning and Coordination of the National Security Policy'] 2015.

approach and a capable NSC that can respond effectively to existing threats and increase the country's resilience to future security challenges. The twin Councils (NSC and SSCMC) were unhelpful, and in 2017 the SSCMC was abolished. A new Constitutional framework in 2018 also abolished the NSC in its old form, which created an institutional vacuum in the security sector that was filled in 2019 by the establishment of a new NSC.[11] The constitutional amendments also provided the President with a wartime consulting body, the National Defence Council, but only during periods of martial law. It comprises: the President as Chair; the Prime Minister; Chairman of Parliament; Minister of Defence; and Chief of Georgian Defence Forces.[12]

The new NSC is the principal security body, acting as a coordinating and advisory/consulting body directly subordinated to the Prime Minister.[13] The initial aim was to reduce bureaucratic burdens by optimizing the size of departments and staff numbers while making the Council and its staff effective and flexible. This included developing an improved capability for foresight and responsibility for national security policy planning and coordination at a strategic level. In the development phase, extensive communication with strategic partners, such as the United States and the United Kingdom, took place to determine good practices. Recommendations were taken into consideration, but were adapted to fit Georgia's needs and reflect the importance of hard security given the Russian threat, regional challenges and non-traditional internal and external security threats.

The NSC has eight permanent members: the Prime Minister as Chair; Ministers of Defence, Internal Affairs, Foreign Affairs and Finance; Head of the State Security Service; Head of the Georgian Intelligence Service (for the first time); and the Chief of Georgian Defence Forces.[14] Where necessary, NSC meetings can be attended by non-permanent members. The President of Georgia can also nominate a trusted individual from their office to attend the meetings.

In contrast to past experience, the Secretary of the NSC is not the NSA; the secretary role is given to one of the Council members by the Prime Minister. They are responsible for coordinating the overall functioning of the Council and

---

[11] საქართველოს კანონი 'ეროვნული უსაფრთხოების საბჭოს აპარატის დებულების დამტკიცების თაობაზე' [Law of Georgia 'On the Approval of the Statute of the Office of the National Security Council'] 2019.

[12] საქართველოს კონსტიტუციური კანონი „საქართველოს კონსტიტუციაში ცვლილების შეტანის შესახებ' საქართველოს კონსტიტუციურ კანონში ცვლილების შეტანის თაობაზე' [*Constitutional Law of Georgia 'On the Amendments to the Constitution of Georgia*] 2018.

[13] Civil.ge (2018). *New Security Council to Operate under Prime Minister*, at https://civil.ge/archives/272173, accessed 30 August 2021.

[14] Approval of the Statute of the Office of the National Security Council (2019), op. cit.

organizing NSC meetings, including setting the agenda. While this ensures the NSC has the highest political support, limiting the choice to Council members may compromise the long-term stability of the NSC given frequent cabinet reshuffles; in its two years of existence, two Prime Ministers have left office and it has had three secretaries. Moreover, the permanent member serving as Secretary to the NSC is also a political figure with responsibility for an interested agency, potentially making it difficult to remain neutral.

The Office of the NSC is headed by a politically neutral civil servant, who acts as the honest broker and manages the activities of the NSC staff on a daily basis.[15] The Office is responsible for planning and coordinating national security policy, providing analysis to the Prime Minister and preparing relevant recommendations for decision-making, as well as providing national-level crisis management by the Prime Minister at a political level. It is also responsible for the elaboration of strategic and national-level documents and inter-agency coordination. Its forty-six staff members include administrative and management staff, advisers and experts covering all aspects of national security: societal, economic, political, ecological and energy, civil and information security, as well as domestic and foreign policy threats, defence and crisis management. The structure reflects strategic priorities, with teams responsible for developing a new national security concept, a threat assessment, and analytical work on regional and thematic issues including non-traditional threats such as cyber. On a practical level, its aim is to function like a think tank, providing analytical support to the NSC on national security matters. It is made up of practitioners with a broad experience of the civil service, but its small size means it has been trying to balance the think-tank element with its policy-making function.

The lack of a functional coordinating national security body and an institutional vacuum in the security sector prevented the renewal of key documents, such as the Threat Assessment and National Security Concept (last updated in 2011). Georgia's complex threats and challenges make a systemic approach to fixing such shortcomings vital. Although COVID-19 delayed things, the NSC Office is working to deliver these essential strategic national security documents. These will be crucial for establishing credibility in the relatively newly established NSC and its Office.

The NSC's Office is also active in managing crises at an operational level. In August 2019, tensions erupted over the construction of a Georgian police

---

[15] Approval of the Statute of the Office of the National Security Council (2019), op. cit.

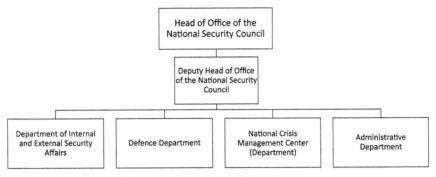

Figure 6.1 Structure of the Office of the NSC.[16]

checkpoint in Chorchana, within the Tbilisi-controlled Khashuri municipality, close to the Russian-occupied village of Tsnelisi, where Russia is actively pursuing 'borderization'.[17] The de facto leadership of the Russian-occupied Tskhinvali region gave the Georgian Government an ultimatum to dismantle the checkpoint, threatening an escalation of tensions. Following extensive negotiations between the sides and with the direct engagement of the Head of the NSC Office, the crisis was averted.[18] The Chorchana incident served as an operational example of multi-layered crisis management, with intergovernmental coordination provided through the NSC's Office. Moreover, the Chorchana case has been the first successful attempt at drawing a red line when it came to Russian 'borderization', boosting the newly established NSC's credibility, despite scepticism given the past performance of national security coordinating bodies in Georgia. Similarly, the escalation of the conflict between Armenia and Azerbaijan in September 2020 placed Georgia in a difficult situation. The NSC suspended the transit of military cargo through its territory to both countries and established Georgia as a neutral broker able to contribute to the peaceful resolution of the conflict and hosting a dialogue in Tbilisi, earning domestic and international praise.[19]

[16] Source: Author from National Security Council (2020). *Departments*, at https://nsc.gov.ge/en/ OFFICE-OF-THE-COUNCIL/Departments, accessed 30 August 2021.
[17] Civil.ge (30 August 2019). 'Security Officials Meet Over Disputed Police Checkpoint', at https://civil. ge/archives/318359, accessed 30 August 2021.
[18] First Channel (30 August 2019). 'Kakha Kemoklidze – Police checkpoint at Chorchana village will remain at its current place', at https://1tv.ge/en/news/kakha-kemoklidze-police-checkpoint-at-chorchana-village-will-remain-at-its-current-place/, accessed 30 August 2021.
[19] Government of Georgia (2020). *Statement by the National Security Council of Georgia, at* http://gov. ge/index.php?lang_id=ENG&sec_id=288&info_id=77419, accessed 30 August 2021.

COVID-19: A test for the new NSC

The COVID-19 pandemic was a completely new kind of challenge for which the NSC's classic defence and security focus was not optimized. Such a large-scale and unprecedented challenge represented a real test for the NSC and its Office. From early on, it was clear that COVID-19 needed a broad, whole-of-government approach with effective planning and coordination between a wide range of relevant agencies. Throughout, the NSC and its office were directly involved in planning, crisis response and coordination of the inter-agency process.

From January 2020, when few anticipated that the coronavirus would spread across the world with such intensity, the NSC was actively involved in inter-agency coordination at the highest political level to develop a national response that included relevant agencies at local and regional levels. When the situation in Europe became alarming, the emergency measures and proposal for a declaration of a state of emergency were discussed by the NSC on 16 and 19 March. At the same time, the NSC's Office moved to an emergency mode of operation. It activated the National Situation Room that serves as the Operational Headquarter during states of emergency working under the Interagency Coordination Council, which was established in January 2020 specifically to combat COVID-19.[20] The Situation Room, established in 2016 with the aid of the British government and based on the British model, plays a critical role in managing the health crisis, bringing the representatives of all relevant agencies together to provide timely and effective implementation of necessary measures.

A prompt crisis response and inter-agency coordination allowed Georgia to manage its first wave of COVID-19 with one of the lowest death rates in the world.[21] Yet, the outcomes of the second and the third waves, still underway at the time of writing, have differed with more cases and higher death rates. This was due to complex reasons, some beyond the NSC's competence, such as ensuring the timely supply of vaccines. The level of societal resilience is also an important factor, and COVID-19 has clearly shown deficiencies with this regard, but will be addressed in a new national security concept.

Like many countries, the novelty of such an unprecedented challenge forced Georgia's government to make prompt decisions; some turned out to be

---

[20] Government of Georgia (2020). *Measures Implemented by the Government of Georgia Against COVID-19 Report*, at https://stopcov.ge/Content/files/COVID_RESPONSE_REPORT__ENG. pdf, accessed 30 August 2021.
[21] Natia Seskuria (2020). *An Unusual Suspect: Georgia as a Success Case in Addressing the Coronavirus Challenge*. RUSI Commentary.

successful while others were less so and were eventually dropped. The pandemic demonstrated the enduring importance of improved coordination between agencies during times of crisis, for which the NSC was essential. While the world is still tackling the pandemic, it is too early to assess the success and failures of respective countries definitively, yet, Georgia's NSC has shown it can adapt to emerging challenges and mobilize its resources in a timely manner.

Conclusion

The changing security environment in the South Caucasus and the Black Sea region and Russia's aggressive foreign policy towards Georgia have shown how badly Georgia needs a fully functional and effective NSC. It needs to be able to develop long-term strategic foresight regarding complex threats and challenges to Georgia's national security and support cross-government crisis management. An integrated and whole-of-government view on defence and security matters is crucial. The NSC has a vital role in enabling the Prime Minister to have a synthesized and in-depth understanding of the security context and make appropriate strategic decisions.

Georgia's turbulent history, with past NSC's becoming too dependent on individual personalities or executive power, has clearly demonstrated that national security bodies depending on personalities for their ability to coordinate others are doomed to failure. Georgia is trying to move beyond that, but despite a promising start, the new NSC has yet to prove that it can remain effective and functional in its current form in the face of political reshuffling. It has to play a critical role in ensuring stability and security in Georgia over the long term. It needs to: without a functioning NSC, Georgia will be unable to effectively protect its state interests. The longevity and stability of the NSC will be a crucial factor in terms of Georgia's ability to cope with its complex threats and challenges in the future.

7

Ghana's National Security Council: Negotiating institutional and political decision-making processes

Kwesi Aning and Naila Salihu

Introduction

Even after independence in 1957, Ghana's use and application of the word 'security' reflects its colonial experience, being perceived as an elite tool to control the masses. As a term, its elasticity has enabled those who provided or controlled the security apparatus to apply it in ways that were personalised, unaccountable and, to a large extent, coercively used to control citizens. The nebulous nature of 'security' and its application gave it an aura of secrecy, fear and a sense of violence in its application. In the immediate post-independence period, however, endeavours were undertaken by the newly established government led by the Convention Peoples Party (CPP) and its Prime Minister, Kwame Nkrumah, to establish a National Security Council (NSC) culture.

This chapter considers how different governments sought to create NSCs with an institutional ethos and proven channels of community cultures, hierarchical structures, command and control measures. However, development has been fraught with stop gap measures, reversals and NSCs that until 2020 functioned without a national security strategy. This may change following the 2020 National Security Strategy (NSS) and supporting Security and Intelligence Agencies Act.[1] While the NSS was met with cautious optimism, there was a healthy dose of scepticism about its ability to bring about a sense of transparency and reduce the abuse of the term 'national security' in infringing citizens' rights. Finally, it touches on the response to COVID-19, and argues that dealing with

---

[1] Security and Intelligence Agencies Act 2020 (Act. 1030).

the health and non-health aspects through media and public engagement improved collaboration with local sources of authority, power and knowledge to community level. This became critical to building strategic alliances and passing on important messages that could help remove the colonial stigma associated with 'national security', despite other parts of the COVID-19 response that may have damaged public trust.

Tentative steps

In the immediate period between Ghana achieving self-rule in 1951 and independence (1957), the policy discussions covering national security apparatus were characterized as 'complex dialogue[s]'.[2] They were held at cabinet level and sought to come to grips with Ghana's security challenges. Multiple agencies competed to lead discussions around issues relating to a structured security decision-making process centred around Prime Minister Nkrumah. In the search for a structured approach to security and its coordination, five main services were established: this started with the establishment in 1960 of a Bureau of National Security (BNS) to 'coordinate and direct more effectively the security and intelligence services of the country':[3] Military Intelligence was created in 1961 under M. M. Hassan; a Special Intelligence Unit, established in early 1963 and directed by Ambrose Yankey; the Presidential Detail Department, which was principally responsible for the Prime Minister's personal safety, headed by Mr Eric Otoo, and finally; the Foreign Service Research Bureau, under Benjamin 'Ben' Forjoe. Subsequently, the Security Service Act 1963 (Act.202) brought these services under the Prime Minister's direct control. They operated independently of the regular armed and police forces, which resulted in a growing chasm between Nkrumah and the Ghana Armed Forces. These tentative steps, however, started the learning process for the establishment of Ghana's NSC that sought to reduce the toxic loyalties among different institutions and personalities.

Three critical dynamics have shaped Ghana's national security developmental processes. First, the overarching role of executive control in shaping the functioning and reporting of the performance of the council. Second, political party infiltration into the structures that subjected professional and technical

---

[2] John Valentine Clune (2014). *The Abongo abroad: military internationalism, travel, training, and peace in Ghana and the United States, 1960–1992* (PhD dissertation University of Kansas), 129.
[3] Government of Ghana (1960). *Bureau of National Security*, Chief Secretary's Office, SECRET, 08/10/1960. File RG2/4/26 Public Records and Archives Administration Department, Accra.

analyses to the whims and caprices of party loyalists who were inserted into the services. Third, how national security was predominantly driven by internal imperatives of weaving competing ethnicities into a diverse but unified nation. This Nkrumah-ist perspective of national security has underpinned Ghana's endeavours to establish a functional, credible and responsive national security framework, though horizontal management functions are still not fully embedded within the bureaucracy.

Towards a structured approach to national security

President Nkrumah was overthrown in 1966, partly due to the divisive, competing and repressive nature of national security institutions. In the thirty years to 1996, all governments (National Liberation Council (1966–1969); Progress Party (1969–1972; National Redemption Council (1972–1978); Supreme Military Council I; Supreme Military Council II (1978–1979); Armed Forces Revolutionary Council (June–September 1979); Peoples' National Party (1979–1981); and Provisional National Defence Council (1981–1992)) operated NSCs to avoid this. However, all lacked two things: there was no legislation defining the NSC's functions and no NSS to guide its work.

In 1996, four years after the Fourth Republican Constitution (1992), Jerry Rawlings' National Democratic Congress (NDC) government enacted a Security and Intelligence Agencies Act to fill the gap.[4] This recognized the factionalism, competition and in-fighting that had hobbled the effectiveness of earlier NSCs, and compromised the credibility and effectiveness of its work under the PNDC (1981–1992) when different revolutionary organs performed competing functions. The Act inaugurated a NSC, defined its membership, meeting procedures and functions, and established subsidiary regional, metropolitan, municipal and district security councils.[5]

Chaired by the President, the NSC comprises: the Vice-President, Ministers of Foreign Affairs, Defence, Interior and Finance. The Chief of Defence Staff, and two other members of the Armed Forces are also members, as are the Inspector-General of Police, two other members of the Police Service (one of whom is the Police Commissioner for Criminal Investigations), the Director-General of the

---

[4]   Security and Intelligence Agencies Act, 1996 (Act. 526). This was subsequently repealed by Act. 1030 (op. cit.), but many provisions are identical.
[5]   The NSC is established under Art. 83 of the Constitution but defined in detail in Act 1030. The Metropolitan and Municipal levels were added by the Local Government Act 2016 (Act. 936).

Prisons Service and the Directors of External Intelligence, Internal Intelligence and Military Intelligence, and the Commissioner of Customs, Excise and Preventive Service. The President can appoint three other persons to the NSC, and any other ministers as required.[6]

The NSC's functions include: considering and taking appropriate measures to safeguard Ghana's internal and external security; collection of information relating to Ghana's security and the integration of the domestic, foreign and security policies to enable the security services and other departments and agencies of government to cooperate more effectively in matters relating to national security; assessing and appraising military risks to Ghana; and, taking appropriate measures regarding the consideration of policies on matters of common interest to the departments and agencies of the government concerned with national security.[7] The Act also empowers different Security Councils (Regional (REGSEC); Municipal (MUSEC) and District (DISEC)) as committees of the NSC[8] to provide early warning to government of the existence or likelihood of security threats at the regional or district level.[9] See Figure 7.1.

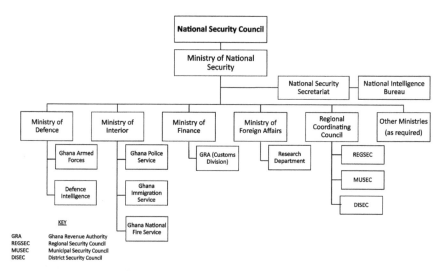

Figure 7.1 Institutional Representational Structure of Ghana's National Security Council.[10]

---

[6]   Act. 1030, ss. 1(2), 1(3) and 2(2).
[7]   Act. 1030, s. 4.
[8]   Act. 1030, s. 5(2).
[9]   Act. 1030, ss. 7(b) and 9(b).
[10] Source: Authors, from Act. 1030.

Act. 526 brought the performance and oversight of the security and intelligence services under the NSC's authority, which Act. 1030 continues. This subjected them to (very limited) Parliamentary and Judicial oversight, similar to the initial efforts of 1963. It also authorized the President to appoint a Minister for National Security, who must present an annual report to parliament on the operations of the intelligence agencies. It was envisaged that such processes would ensure 'political neutrality' of the intelligence agencies,[11] and address and end the stylized provision of security in which violence had become a norm.[12]

Between rhetoric and praxis: from 1996 to today

Almost twenty years after Act. 526, and with a new government in 2017, the President used his powers to appoint a Minister for National Security.[13] While not the first Minster for National Security since 1996, this was qualitatively different. It involved updating the law under Act. 1030, which repealed Act. 526. Act. 1030 made provision for a new Ministerial Security Coordinating Committee[14] and reflected a determination to link the performance of the NSC to the presence of an NSS. The NSS specifies the threats, the nature of the structure and reporting and coordination guidelines to bring clarity and, above all, reverse the historical misuse of the term 'national security' as an all-encompassing term for misbehaviour.

The NSS was finally completed in 2020 under the bombastic sub-heading *'A Secure and Prosperous Ghana, with Regional, Continental and Global Reach and Influence'*. According to the President:

> Once operationalized, the Strategy will optimise the effectiveness of the security and intelligence sector, by evolving the current systems and structures. It will prioritise the use of our resources, and *promote effective decision-making*, through an *institutional system* that will ensure *integrated and efficient*

[11] Kwesi Aning. 'Resurrecting the Police Council in Ghana' in Alan Bryden and Fairlie Chappuis eds. (2015). *Learning from West African Experiences in Security Sector Governance* (London: Ubiquity).

[12] Kwesi Aning, Emma Birikorang and Ernest Lartey (2013). 'Developing a democratic intelligence culture in Ghana', in Kristian Gustafson and Philip Davies (2013). *Intelligence Elsewhere: spies, and espionage outside the Anglosphere* (Washington, DC: Georgetown University Press).

[13] Jeffrey Owusu Mensah. (4 January 2017). 'Akufo-Addo names Kan Dapaah as Nat'l Security Min; Appoints Nat'l Security Adviser & Coordinator', *PrimeNews.com*.

[14] President of Ghana (7 June 2021), at https://presidency.gov.gh/index.php/briefing-room/news-style-2/1927-president-akufo-addo-commissions-national-security-ministry-building-launches-national-security-strategy, accessed 30 August 2021. The Committee has not yet been created so the impact is unknown.

coordination in all spectrums of national security. It will also provide a *new institutional structure,* which will be equipped to tackle strategic security and crisis management issues requiring rapid, coordinated and comprehensive responses.[15]

Critical issues – interim assessment

Despite the recent developments, concerns remain. First, relates to how the NSC works, both its nature – whether it is an implementing or coordinating agency – and the continued lack of transparency over any Standard Operating Procedures (SOPs). Second, is the influence of political parties within the bureaucracy. Finally, there are questions over the NSC's supporting systems.

How the NSC works

According to an official, the current structure of the national security architecture:

> can only continue to produce insecurity because factional elements have been clothed with national security powers to maximize security for the government. As a result, they do not operate under any known laws of the land and, therefore, are not held accountable. [Individually] all the agencies … have their SOPs [standard operating procedures] to guide their operations. Security institutions must, therefore, remain there and be called upon to perform their duties when needed by national security.[16]

Under Act. 1030, coordination, cooperation, integration and supervision among the different agencies remain the main functions of Ghana's NSC. It is clear that, irrespective of the operational situation, the NSC does not implement policy or action. It simply ensures that other agencies in the National Security arena (including independent experts and think tanks) are coordinated to assess threats to Ghana as identified in the NSS. Any actual operational activity or physical implementation is for independent institutional agencies under the NSC. This is because they have their legal mandates (captured within their respective legislative Instruments and their SOPs) that guide their operations and against which they are held accountable.

Herein lies the critical coordinating lacunae that confronts the NSC. There are no provisions in any of the establishment Acts of the NSC, neither Act. 526

---

[15] Republic of Ghana (2020). *National Security Strategy*, v. Italics ours.
[16] Author interview with anonymous Senior National Intelligence Bureau official, Accra – 28 July 2021.

nor its replacement, Act. 1030, authorizing the NSC to act as an implementing agency. The deliberate political misinterpretation of the NSC's powers and functions under these Acts and its performance in operational roles have become the subject of public condemnation. The challenges and dilemmas of negotiating between political exigencies and developing an institutional culture that follows established procedures was seen in May 2021. In taking disciplinary action against officers who had acted improperly in assaulting a journalist, the Ministry and NSC noted that 'its investigative committee established that the arrest and subsequent assault . . . violated the Ministry's operating standards' and as a result the individuals were to report to their parent organizations for the necessary disciplinary measures.[17] Clearly, both the Ministry and the NSC lacked the authority to act, suggesting they remain coordinating institutions with fewer controls than the other ministries who 'own' their people.

Party influence

Another challenge concerns the dichotomy between technocratic and personality/party elements within the NSC's structures. Sixty years after independence, the role and influence of party elements within the general security apparatus and the NSC's structure remain an ongoing cause of friction. A former Deputy Minister of the Interior, James Agalga, argued that, '[w]e need to purge the security agencies of all the people who were unqualified but somehow managed to infiltrate the ranks of the agencies.'[18]

Support to the NSC

The Minister for National Security asserted that Ghana's national security would be based on 'a whole-of-Government and a Whole-of-Society approach'.[19] This expansive approach requires resourcing and given the NSC's ambitions and the optimism raised by the NSS for enhanced efficiency, the NSC Secretariat should become the fulcrum around which any success will revolve. The Secretariat needs to provide and have the technical capacities to analyse and offer options.

---

[17] Marian Ansah. (13 May 2021). 'We're probing assault on Citi News journalist – National Security Ministry', *Citinewsroom.com.* Subsequently, the Ministry of National Security withdrew four officers over this assault on the journalist. Adwoa Adubia (22 May 2021). 'National Security withdraws four officers over assault on Citi-FM journalist', *Thesunghana.com.*

[18] James Agalga (9 June 2021). 'Review Criteria for recruitment into State security agencies – James Agalga', *IndexNews.*

[19] Letter from Ministry for National Security, 20 May 2021, 2.

However, the numbers, budget, size and actual roles performed by the Secretariat are still shrouded in secrecy, perpetuating concerns about transparency.[20]

A National Security Coordinator, currently retired Major General Francis Adu Amanfo,[21] heads the NSC Secretariat, making this one of the most powerful security positions in Ghana. Appointments are the prerogative of the President, and a question relates to the calibre and type of individuals appointed. The nebulous nature of the structure, however, poses two challenges. One relates to the tense relationship between the Coordinator and the Minister for National Security,[22] with Act. 1030 not clear on their boundaries. The Minister's role, described in s. 24, is crucial, but while the National Security Coordinator 'coordinates, on a daily basis, the operational activities of the intelligence agencies'[23] the Minister oversees the intelligence agencies, provides policy direction and orients, guides and directs them. Section 24(b), could create the impression of politicizing the intelligence agencies because Ministers often prioritize intelligence collection and collection methods. Furthermore, repeated use of 'efficient and effective' in the Coordinator's and Minister's functions is also problematic, since the meaning has not been defined, e.g. ss. 23(1) and 24(c). The second challenge concerns the command and control mechanisms between the National Security Coordinator and his regional counterparts. Because a number of regional coordinators are party appointments, their willingness to follow the chain of command is often weak, challenging the National Security Coordinator's authority and position.[24]

While the new NSS offers cautious hope for improved effectiveness, confusion about the limits on its functional powers (coordinating and vested in the Minister for National Security rather than executive authority) limits its ability to deliver. Despite Act. 1030, merely changing the NSC's role in law still leaves it vulnerable in performance terms, as exhibited through departmental factionalism and competition for influence and power that leads to excesses.[25] Such challenges reflect both a maturing process and the ability, or otherwise, of the NSC's bureaucracy to handle horizontal forms of security governance.

---

[20] News (10 December 2015). 'Recruitment scam hits Ghana's National Security', *Nsempii.com*.
[21] Sammi Wiafe (9 February 2021). 'Akufo-Addo appoints new National Security Coordinator'. *Citinewsroom.com*.
[22] Senah (7 February 2018) 'Gov't To Demote National Security Coordinator', at https://senahsite.wordpress.com/2018/02/07/govt-to-demote-national-security-coordinator/, accessed 30 August 2021.
[23] Act 1030, s. 21(b).
[24] 3News.com (19 May 2021). 'National Security Minister, Coordinator must sit up', at www.ghanaweb.com/GhanaHomePage/NewsArchive/National-Security-Minister-Coordinator-must-sit-up-COP-Bright-Oduro-1265752, accessed 30 August 2021.
[25] Letter from Ministry for National Security, 20 May 2021, 2.

Responding to COVID-19

The first two cases of COVID-19 in Ghana were identified on 12 March 2020. By 19 April, more than 1,000 confirmed cases of COVID-19 and nine deaths had been reported.[26] The government adopted and promoted World Health Organization (WHO) recommendations, which included avoiding or limiting physical contact, regular handwashing with soap under running water, rubbing of hands with alcohol-based sanitizer, and reducing large gatherings among the general populace.[27] A highly securitized approach was adopted in the management of COVID-19 through extraordinary security measures including enacting an emergency law;[28] a twenty-one day partial lockdown in some urban areas; banning public gatherings; closure of air, sea and land borders; and closure of schools and religious institutions.[29]

To enforce the above-mentioned measures, institutional mechanisms made up of public health and sectoral experts were initiated to guide the pandemic response, using the REGSECs. An Inter-Ministerial and Presidential taskforce on COVID-19, separate to the NSC, was constituted with the President at the head and chairing most of the meetings, with membership similar to the NSC.[30] Inter-Ministerial committees meet daily to assess the interventions and advise the Presidential Taskforce for effective coordination.[31] This highlighted the national security imperatives attached to the emergency response. The outcomes, however, have been mixed as the public, including officials, violated the protocols.

Due to the manner in which the COVID-19 pandemic response was securitized, several security institutions became integral to and played diverse support roles in the implementation of public health and security policies. *Operation COVID Safety* – the national security task force established to enforce the COVID-19 safety protocols and lockdown – was launched in March 2020

---

[26] Ghana Health Service (12 March 2020). *Ghana Health Service COVID-19 Situation update*, at https://ghanahealthservice.org/covid19/, accessed 30 August 2021.

[27] World Health Organization. (30 April 2020). *Coronavirus disease (COVID-19) advice for public*, at www.who.int/emergencies/diseases/novel-coronavirus-2019/advice-for-public, accessed 30 August 2021.

[28] Imposition of Restrictions Act (2020), Act. 1012.

[29] Emma Birikorang and Naila Salihu (Forthcoming). *The Securitization of Health and the Security Sector; Ghana and Covid-19.*

[30] The principal ministries include Ministries of Health, Interior, Defence, National Security. Other state agencies include Health Service, Information Services Department, Armed Forces, Police Service, Immigration Service, Noguchi Memorial Institute for Medical Research among others.

[31] Ministry of Health (22 May 2020). *Ghana to enhance the 3Ts in its Covid-19 fight*, at www.facebook. com/101563631288390/posts/ghana-to-enhance-the-3ts-in-its-covid-19-fightthe-minister-for-health-hon-kwaku-/244018220376263/, accessed 30 August 2021.

with a combined team of police, armed forces and other security agencies.[32] The involvement of security forces, especially the military, in such civic duties occasionally had unintended consequences. There have been concerns about human rights violations, arbitrariness and excessive use of force by security personnel. These developments undermined public trust and cast doubts about the professionalism of the security sector.

Conclusion

For most of Ghana's political history since independence, the processes towards establishing a NSC have been fraught with stop-gap measures and reversals. The immediate post-colonial era association of national security with internal control, politicization of the security system and a lack of transparency have all impacted negatively, and continue to do so sixty years later. Moreover, the NSCs have had to function without a comprehensive strategy; there are, however, some signs for optimism. In 2020 a new Security Law was passed (Act. 1030) to strengthen institutional arrangements for national security, and a NSS was adopted, which provides an opportunity for bringing coherence to national security decision-making and operationalization in the country.

While encouraging, it is too soon to assess the full impact of the changes and important questions remain over what has really changed with regards to the clarity of roles of the institutions under this strategy and whether the strategy sets the tone for the development of a defence policy. What is clear is that a fundamental shift in institutional cultures is essential to bring about the professionalism, effectiveness and efficiency in Ghana's national security architecture that the nation needs.

---

[32] Kwesi Aning (29 July 2020). 'COVID-19 and its impact on violent extremism in Ghana and West Africa'. *COVID-19 In-Depth Analysis*. ACCORD.

8

India's National Security Council: Addressing a strategic gap

Aaditya Dave

Introduction

India's geostrategic location and large population, combined with a state capacity that has struggled to keep up with the country's economic and technological boom, have created traditional and non-traditional security challenges for New Delhi. Unresolved territorial disputes with Pakistan and China have seen multiple conflicts along land borders that remain potential flashpoints, particularly as India becomes a more assertive regional power. These antagonistic relationships are coupled with, and sometimes fuel, threats from terrorism and insurgencies in Jammu and Kashmir and central and northeast India. The intensifying great power competition between China and the US, meanwhile, creates strategic challenges and opportunities as India attempts to manage its ties with the former while expanding its security relationship with the latter and becoming a more influential presence in the Indo-Pacific.

Non-traditional security threats, including climate change and resource scarcity, cyber threats and disinformation, as well as social fragmentation and political polarization, pose significant domestic concerns, particularly as New Delhi faces an uphill battle to deliver economic growth capable of sustaining India's growing population and alleviating poverty.

This chapter considers how India's National Security Council (NSC) and supporting structures tackle the country's security challenges. It outlines the NSC's evolution before describing its mandate, briefly noting its role in responding to COVID-19. It then assesses how the NSC and associated bodies have impacted national security decision-making processes.

Evolution of India's NSC

Upon independence in 1947, India inherited a three-tiered national security decision-making system that comprised a committee led by the Prime Minister, supported by a Defence Minister's Committee and Chiefs of Staff Committee. There was no NSC, but the structure enabled basic coordination in classical security decision-making. However, PVR Rao, Defence Secretary between 1962 and 1966,[1] observed that before the 1962 Sino-Indian War, national security decisions were 'considered ad hoc by the Prime Minister, Defense Minister, Chief of the Army Staff and some senior Army officers', while the formal bodies within the chain of command were either ineffective or 'appraised of decisions mostly post facto'.[2]

India's defeat in the 1962 War cruelly exposed the civilian leadership's lack of expertise, spurring changes to the decision-making process. However, while defence expenditure and the military's operational independence increased, the military's ability to shape defence policy did not change substantially.[3]

In August 1990, noting the 'changing equilibria of power' at the end of the Cold War, the VP Singh government constituted a NSC to take 'a holistic view of national security issues in the light of the external, economic, political and military situations and their linkages with our domestic concerns and objectives'.[4] Chaired by the Prime Minister, it included ministers of defence, finance, home affairs and external affairs, with other ministers, state chief ministers, and experts invited as required. Supporting the NSC were a Strategic Core Group comprising bureaucrats and service chiefs, a Secretariat and National Security Advisory Board (NSAB) drawn from chief ministers, members of parliament, academics, and other experts.[5] However, the VP Singh government was short-lived, and the NSC met only once before a change in leadership in November 1990.

Prime Minister PV Narasimha Rao (1991–1996), was sceptical about the NSC and NSAB, seeing them as inconsistent with India's parliamentary system,

---

[1] Equivalent to the UK's Permanent Secretary of the Ministry of Defence.
[2] PVR Rao (1970). *Defence without Drift* (Bombay: Popular Prakashan), cited in D. Shyam Babu (2003). 'India's National Security Council: Stuck in the Cradle?', *Security Dialogue*, vol. 34(2), 215–230.
[3] Frank O'Donnell and Harsh Pant, 'The Evolution in India's National Security Apparatus: Persisting Structural Deficiencies', in Harsh Pant ed. (2016), *The Routledge Handbook of Indian Defence Policy: Themes, Structures and Doctrines* (London: Routledge), 327; Shyam Babu, op. cit.
[4] Gazette of India (22 September 1990), 652, https://egazette.nic.in/WriteReadData/1990/O-0541-1990-0038-23207.pdf, accessed 30 August 2021.
[5] Ibid.

and overlapping with similar functions under the jurisdiction of individual cabinet ministers.[6] Moreover, the Cabinet Committee on Security (CCS), comprising the Prime Minister and the ministers of defence, home affairs, finance, and external affairs, remained the apex decision-making body for national security, including policy, appointments and expenditure, with an almost identical membership.[7]

Following the 1998 nuclear tests by India and Pakistan, the Atal Bihari Vajpayee government re-established the NSC, emphasizing the need for 'integrated thinking and coordinated application of the political, military, diplomatic, scientific and technological resources of the State to protect and promote national security goals and objectives'.[8] The structure largely mirrored the short-lived 1990 NSC, the most significant difference being the creation of a National Security Adviser (NSA). The NSA would be part of the NSC along with the Deputy Chairman of the Planning Commission (now the Vice Chairman of the NITI Aayog) and Deputy NSAs (appointed in 2018). State chief ministers were excluded.[9]

The Strategic Policy Group (SPG) replaced the Strategic Core Group to facilitate bureaucratic coordination and integration of ministry inputs, and undertake a long-term strategic defence review. The SPG is an Officials group, chaired by the NSA, that includes the cabinet secretary (until 2018, the SPG chair), Chief of Defence Staff (CDS), chiefs of the three branches of the military, the governor of the Reserve Bank, director of the Intelligence Bureau (India's domestic intelligence agency), and secretaries from several key government departments.

A new NSAB, formed in December 1998, was tasked with conducting long-term analysis and providing non-binding advice to the NSC. Unlike the 1990 NSAB, it entirely comprised experts from outside government, and, in the aftermath of India and Pakistan's 1999 Kargil War, was responsible for producing a draft nuclear doctrine.[10] The Modi government discontinued the

[6] Anit Mukherjee (2011). 'Facing Future Challenges: Defence Reform in India'. *RUSI Journal*, vol. 156(5), 30–37; Jaswant Singh (1999). *Defending India* (Basingstoke: Macmillan), 271–274.
[7] Cabinet Secretariat, 'Composition of the Cabinet Committees (as on 09.10.2020)', at https://cabsec. gov.in/writereaddata/cabinetcommittees/english/1_Upload_2448.pdf, accessed 30 August 2021.
[8] Gazette of India (16 April 1999), 4, https://egazette.nic.in/WriteReadData/1999/E_94_2013_050. pdf, accessed 30 August 2021.
[9] Gazette (16 April 1999), op. cit.; Neeta Sharma (5 October 2018), 'With 3 Deputies Under Him, NSA Ajit Doval Has Become a Major Power Centre', *NDTV*.
[10] Ministry of External Affairs (17 August 1999). *Draft Report of National Security Advisory Board on Indian Nuclear Doctrine*.

NSAB in 2015, with reports suggesting that the prime minister was not 'enthused by former bureaucrats, military and intelligence officials, scholars doing studies which are analytic in nature'.[11] However, he reinstated it in 2016 with members drawn from the same pool of experts.[12] Its written reports to the NSC are classified so the degree to which it provides fresh challenge is unclear.

The 1999 Order creating the NSC also created an NSC Secretariat (NSCS) to support the NSC, NSAB, SPG and ad hoc taskforces falling under them.[13] The Indian National Congress-led government in 2004 restructured the NSCS into four divisions: a Joint Intelligence Committee (JIC), previously a separate body now merged with the NSCS, to verify intelligence inputs and prepare assessments; a Policy Division to prepare policy options; a Project Division monitoring other countries' nuclear doctrine; and a Defence Division, focusing on defence modernization and the credibility of India's nuclear deterrence.[14] A further reorganization of the NSCS in 2018 brought in multi-disciplinary experts from within and outside government and created four verticals: Strategic Affairs, dealing with strategic and security interests in the neighbourhood and key regions; Technology and Intelligence, working on integrating new technologies for intelligence, civil and military applications and plugging technology gaps; Internal Affairs, focusing on next-generation threats, security issues in Jammu and Kashmir and Northeast India as well as counter-terrorism and counter-insurgency; and Military, examining military developments in India's neighbourhood and defence requirements in India's strategic environment. The first three are headed by Deputy NSAs while the Military Vertical is led by a Military Adviser.[15]

---

[11] Jayanth Jacob (11 June 2015). 'Modi govt may discontinue security advisory board started by Atal govt', *Hindustan Times*.

[12] Staff (10 October 2016). 'National Security Advisory Board Reconstituted, But With Fewer Members', *The Wire*; Snehesh Alex Philip (31 December 2018). 'National security advisory panel set to induct 3 more members', *The Print*.

[13] Gazette (16 April 1999), op. cit., 7.

[14] SD Pradhan. 'National Security System—Evolution', in Satish Kumar ed. (2010). *India's National Security: Annual Review 2010* (New Dehli: Pentagon Press), 442–445.

[15] PS Raghavan (2019). 'The Evolution of India's National Security Architecture', *Journal of Defence Studies*, vol. 13(3), 33–52.

Figure 8.1 India's National Security Structure.[16]

Despite the bureaucracy surrounding the NSC, India lacks a published national security doctrine or strategy that comprehensively assesses India's security challenges and outlines policy responses.[17] Its absence has frequently been criticized given India's numerous security threats and frequent security crises, with the need for such a document repeatedly highlighted.[18]

---

[16] Source: Author.

[17] India's primary opposition party, the Indian National Congress, produced a draft national security strategy prior to the 2019 general elections – see https://manifesto.inc.in/en/national_security_strategy_gen_hooda.html, accessed 30 August 2021. The current Modi government has not suggested a similar document, but by opening the debate at the political level, it raises the possibility of a national security strategy being adopted in future.

[18] B.S. Raghavan (18 March 2011). 'National Security Doctrine for India', *The Hindu Business Line*; BD Jayal, VP Malik, Anit Mukherjee and Arun Prakash (2012). 'A Call for Change: Higher Defence Management in India', *IDSA Monograph Series No.6*; Arjun Subramaniam (28 August 2018). 'It's time for India to formulate a national security doctrine', *The Print*; Arun Prakash (18 February 2019). 'India urgently needs a national security doctrine, clear red lines', *Indian Express*; Shyam Saran, 'Need for a Comprehensive National Security Strategy', in Centre for Policy Research (4 June 2019). *Policy Challenges 2019-2024: The Key Policy Questions for the New Government and Possible Pathways*; Rudra Chaudhuri (12 April 2021). 'India Needs an Honest National Security Document for the Next Decade, Just Like Britain Made', *The Print*.

Role and responsibilities

The NSC's scope goes beyond India's traditional security focus, with the 1999 notification highlighting that 'national security needs to be viewed not only in military terms, but also in terms of internal security, economic security, technological strength and foreign policy'.[19] Its mandate covers:

- external security;
- security threats involving atomic energy, space and high-technology;
- economic security threats covering energy, foreign trade, food, finance and ecology;
- internal security, including counter-insurgency, counter-terrorism and counter-intelligence;
- patterns of alienation, especially those with a social, communal or regional dimension;
- security threats posed by trans-border crimes, e.g. smuggling and trafficking; and
- coordinating intelligence collection and tasking.

The NSA's brief is similarly broad. They head the National Technical Research Organisation, India's technical intelligence agency, and coordinate intelligence from across agencies for the prime minister. Additionally, they chair the Executive Council of India's Nuclear Command Authority, which supports decision-making by the Nuclear Command Authority and executes directives from the Political Council, the only body that can authorize the use of nuclear weapons.[20] Since 2003, the NSA has also been India's Special Representative for talks with China on the disputed Sino–Indian boundary.[21]

Under Prime Minister Modi, NSA Ajit Doval's powers expanded further, making him a central figure in security-related decision-making. In addition to chairing the SPG (from 2018), he was the first NSA given cabinet rank, placing him on a par with key ministers in the CCS.[22] Doval was also made chair of a

---

[19] Gazette (16 April 1999), op. cit., 5.

[20] Prime Minister's Office (4 January 2003). 'Cabinet Committee on Security Reviews Progress in Operationalizing India's Nuclear Doctrine'.

[21] MEA (21 December 2019). '22nd Meeting of the Special Representatives of India and China' at https://mea.gov.in/press-releases.htm?dtl/32234/22nd_Meeting_of_the_Special_Representatives_of_India_and_China, accessed 30 August 2021.

[22] Elizabeth Roche (4 June 2019). 'Ajit Doval to stay as NSA, gets cabinet rank with 5-year term', *Livemint*.

new Defence Planning Committee (DPC), tasked with preparing a national security strategy, an international defence engagement strategy, a roadmap for building a defence manufacturing ecosystem, a strategy to boost defence exports, and priority capability development plans.[23] This broad portfolio makes Doval more influential than previous NSAs, even if it impacts the capacity to focus on any part of the portfolio.[24] To support him, the NSCS was formalized in 2019,[25] enabling them to access relevant cabinet proposals and participate in inter-ministerial discussions without having to go through the Cabinet Secretary.[26]

The reconstituted NSAB has taken on a slightly broader role, with its chairman noting that NSAB members would 'try to spread wider public understanding of India's national security challenges, perspectives and policies', including through seminars and lectures by members and acting as a bridge between think tanks, academia and the national security establishment.[27] This suggests that, in addition to advising the NSC (and subsequently the CCS), the NSAB may also receive top-down direction on certain topics.

Responding to COVID-19

Despite its broad mandate, the NSC did not play a significant role in India's COVID-19 response, and the Prime Minister's informal COVID-19 task force did not include the NSA.[28] The only notable instance of the NSA intervening during the first COVID wave was to defuse communal tension at a New Delhi mosque that became a hotspot during the initial days of the virus's spread.[29] This lack of involvement is perhaps unsurprising as neither the NSC's mandate nor the restructured NSCS verticals include health security, and the border crisis with China that flared up in May 2020 demanded most of the NSC's attention. During the (devastating) second wave, however, the NSA was actively involved

[23] Shishir Gupta (19 April 2018). 'India to create super-committee for defence planning', *Hindustan Times*.
[24] Vijaita Singh (11 July 2020). 'Ajit Doval: The spy who came in from the cold', *The Hindu*.
[25] Gazette of India (6 August 2019), 2, https://egazette.nic.in/WriteReadData/2019/210353.pdf, accessed 30 August 2021.
[26] Pranab Dhal Samanta (3 October 2019). 'NSA gets teeth, Secretariat put in government business rules', *Economic Times*.
[27] Dipanjan Roy Chaudhury (14 January 2019). 'National security advisory board's aim is to spread "security understanding"', *Economic Times*.
[28] Uday Mahurkar, (9 April 2020). 'Inside PM Modi's COVID-19 task force', *India Today*.
[29] Manjeet Negi (1 April 2020). 'Markaz leadership agreed to vacate Nizamuddin mosque after NSA Ajit Doval intervention', *India Today*.

in diplomatic outreach and attempts to secure assistance from abroad.[30] Rather than a wider role for the NSC, however, this is possibly a reflection of current NSA Ajit Doval's personal prominence in the government's decision-making processes.

The NSC's performance

When re-established in 1999, India's NSC filled an important gap in national security decision-making, enabling strategic thinking and long-term policy planning as well as coordinating and implementing security policies.[31] This was particularly important given India and Pakistan's nuclear tests, which significantly changed the region's security dynamics. It also allowed India to demonstrate the institutional framework necessary to evaluate security threats and develop nuclear doctrine.[32]

Nevertheless, the NSC failed to address a key criticism of India's national security decision-making: that military officials were relegated below multiple layers of civilian bureaucracy.[33] This was particularly acute before the appointment of a CDS in 2020 to foster integration and 'jointness' among the Services. The CDS is the principal military advisor to the political leadership. As a result, there are now effectively two key security advisors to the political leadership. Potential overlap exists between the NSA and CDS in bodies like the DPC, which the NSA chairs but deals with areas within CDS' charter, and the SPG, which the CDS and the Service chiefs sit on but which supports the NSC and is chaired by the NSA. How the CDS role develops will be important to avoid complicating the security picture.

Although the same ministers sit on the NSC and CCS, the two meetings serve different functions. The NSC is a deliberative platform that considers security issues, creates threat assessments, evaluates policy options and coordinates action across different security agencies and government departments. The CCS is ultimately responsible for security and determines

---

[30] The White House (25 April 2021). 'Statement by NSC Spokesperson Emily Horne on National Security Advisor Jake Sullivan's Call with National Security Advisor Ajit Doval of India'; Geeta Mohan (28 April 2021). 'Turkey extends support To India in Covid crisis, President's spokesperson speaks to Ajit Doval', *India Today*.

[31] Shyam Babu, op. cit.

[32] PR Chari (2000). 'India's Nuclear Doctrine: Confused Ambitions', *Nonproliferation Review*, vol. 7(3), 123–135.

[33] O'Donnell and Pant, op. cit.; Raghavan, op. cit.

action on issues raised by specific ministries based on advice from the NSC, such as troop deployments or equipment procurement.[34] There are considerable links between the CCS and NSC. All notes for CCS approval are sent to the NSCS, which comments and sends them to the relevant ministry. The ministry may modify the note before sending for CCS consideration alongside the NSCS's comments. Furthermore, the NSA attends all CCS meetings to represent the NSC structures when the CCS considers proposals sent by the ministries.[35]

When India has faced major security threats, e.g. the 2008 Mumbai attack or the Sino–Indian border crisis in 2020, concerns have been raised about the NSCS's intelligence coordination function. Observers have criticised failures of intelligence assessments and dissemination both in 2008, when the JIC was a separate division of the NSCS, and in 2020 after it was absorbed into the structure.[36]

Another issue is the centralization of power under the NSA, which has been a persistent feature of the system. The first NSA, Brajesh Mishra, also served as Prime Minister Atal Bihari Vajpayee's principal secretary, dividing his efforts between two full-time roles. The third NSA, MK Narayanan, also acted as gatekeeper to the prime minister, allegedly 'micromanaging the intelligence agencies'.[37] The current NSA's large number of additional responsibilities may also prevent him from focusing on specific issues effectively. Numerous changes by the Modi government have reinforced the importance of the personality serving as NSA, but this creates a sense of uncertainty and impermanence around their decisions and a lack of accountability. The 2019 formalization of the NSCS and NSA's purpose may change this, but the impact remains to be seen.

Finally, while the NSAB was intended to be the NSC's think-tank, producing long-term analysis, its previous iterations became bloated and frequent reshuffles made it difficult for the body to function effectively.[38] Moreover, the NSAB's lack of access to classified information made the value of its advice to policymakers unclear. The revived NSAB partially addresses these issues; it is smaller, with

---

[34] Pradhan, op. cit.

[35] Ibid.

[36] (2008) 'Terror in Mumbai', *Strategic Comments*, vol. 14(10), 1–2; FP Staff (17 July 2020). 'Galwan Valley clash: Defence experts question dismantling of JIC, say it "weakened" system of assessing intel', *Firstpost*.

[37] Vikram Sood, 'The Indian Intelligence System: Meeting the Challenges of a New World', in Harsh Pant, op. cit., 341.

[38] Janaki Bahadur Kremmer (1 February 1999). 'In the Tower of Babel: The NSC's Advisory Board is a Battleground of Diametrically Divergent Views and Inflated Egos', *Outlook*, 45–46, cited in Shyam Babu, op. cit.; Tara Kartha (17 October 2018). 'The Rejig of India's National Security Architecture Has Been a Long Time Coming', *The Wire*.

experts from a range of sectors, including academia and the private sector, but again it is too soon to determine the impact of the changes.

Conclusion

As the key coordinating and supporting agency for national security decisions made by the CCS, the NSC has considerable responsibility. However, there is scepticism about its effectiveness given the overlapping composition with the CCS and the opacity in its functioning. The effectiveness of the NSAB too is unclear given its purely civilian make-up. A persistent weakness, though, is the absence of a national security strategy to cohere NSC activity. Should one be developed, that will provide an opportunity for more effective coordination of national security, with the NSCS a logical focal point for collating perspectives from different government departments and civilian expertise received via the NSAB.

The NSA plays a critical role in the national security decision-making process. While all Indian NSAs have been close to the prime ministers they served, the Modi government's decisions to elevate the NSA to cabinet rank and appoint them as chair of the SPG and DPC reflect the fundamentally political nature of the appointment. Constitutional recognition of the NSA was only granted in 2019, and while this underpins and frames its formal authority, in practice it does not constrain the role, which remains highly flexible based on the prime minister's demands and the NSA's personality. These dependencies raise concerns about the level of centralization and top-down control in the system, and the NSA's capacity.

The Modi government has made significant changes to India's national security and defence mechanisms, installing a CDS and initiating reforms in both defence procurement and planning. Largely welcomed by the strategic community, the introduction of a CDS is a step towards addressing the longstanding criticism of military exclusion from national security decision-making. Whether these decisions enable more effective policy-making or create unintended bottlenecks will be crucial to India's future security.

9

Iraq's National Security Council: From Repression to Inclusive Security

Manuel Almeida and Aram Habeeb

Introduction

Created in 2004 as part of the US-led 'nation-building' project, Iraq's National Security Council (NSC) is, in its current form, a relatively new institution. The attempt to implement an imported model in a very distinct institutional, normative, and security environment left a gap between the NSC's formal role as envisioned by the Coalition Provisional Authority (CPA), and the body's operationalization. The de-Ba'athification laws that dismantled Iraq's entire security apparatus and greatly strengthen the insurgency compounded the NSC's challenges.

The obstacles to creating an effective NSC must be understood against the Ba'ath Party's legacy. For decades, the army and other security institutions were primarily instruments of internal control and repression.[1] The NSC under Saddam Hussein coordinated the various armed forces, intelligence and security institutions, including paramilitary and police. Chaired by Saddam, the NSC's weekly meetings were usually presided over by his second son Qusai, a testament to the personalized nature of the regime.[2]

Military defeat in the 1991 Gulf War, the imposition of UN-led economic sanctions, military pressure from US administrations and US support to the umbrella opposition group the Iraqi National Council, contributed to the regime's

---

[1] Between 1963, when the Ba'ath Party overthrew General Abd al-Karim Qasim, and 1980, when the Iraq–Iran war began, the Iraqi army had no external engagements. Kanan Makiya (1998) *Republic of Fear: The Politics of Modern Iraq* (London: University of California), ix–xxxi and 21.

[2] GlobalSecurity.Org. *National Security Council*, at: www.globalsecurity.org/intell/world/iraq/nsc.htm, accessed 30 August 2021.

heightened sense of threat and vulnerability.[3] This sense – magnified by Ayatollah Khomeini's intention to export the Iranian revolution and tap into Iraq's repressed Shiʿa majority – was accompanied by a Baʿathist perception that Iraqi society was growing increasingly restless, despite the brutality of the state's security institutions. The regime turned increasingly towards the active promotion of sectarianism and tribalism as instruments of control and legitimation. Thousands of Shiʿas and hundreds of thousands of Kurds were systematically killed.[4] The NSC, as the coordinating body of the various security and military institutions, was integral to the repression.[5] The legacy of authoritarianism, tension between state and human security, state weakness, external interference in Iraqi affairs, sectarian institutions, and endemic corruption remain significant challenges to re-building inclusive national security.

The Ministerial Committee for National Security

The post-2003 US-led efforts to build Iraq's security sector and institutions faced significant political, security and cultural challenges. The George W. Bush Administration was determined to transform Iraq into a functioning liberal democracy quickly. Their vision included reconstructing Iraq's security institutions to oversee what was expected to become a thriving civil society.[6] A central aspect of the vision was an understanding of Iraqi society as one irremediably divided along ethnic and religious lines between three main – homogeneous and antagonistic – communities of Shiʿas, Sunnis and Kurds.[7] One

---

[3] F. Gregory Gause III (2010) *The International Relations of the Persian Gulf* (New York: Cambridge University Press), 122–124.

[4] Although the principle of *muhasasa taʾifia* (sectarian apportionment) came to dominate Iraq's political scene and institutions in the post-2003 period, the sectarianisation of Iraqi politics began decades earlier. British colonial policy empowered the Sunni Arab elite to the detriment of other confessional groups, which fostered sub-national identities and proved an obstacle to the creation of an Iraqi national identity. The *muhasasa taʾifia* system was mostly developed in the early 1990s by a group of exiled Iraqi politicians. In October 1992, an opposition conference in Salah al-Din defined the proportional allocation of state jobs to Iraq's three main confessional groups (the 'Salah al-Din principles'). Ranj Alaaldin (2018). *Sectarianism, Governance and Iraq's Future*, Brookings Doha Center Analysis Paper No. 24. Also, Toby Dodge (18 September 2018). *Tracing the Rise of Sectarianism in Iraq after 2003*, LSE Middle East Centre Blog, at: https://blogs.lse.ac.uk/mec/2018/09/13/tracing-the-rise-of-sectarianism-in-iraq-after-2003/, accessed 30 August 2021.

[5] An Iraqi intellectual described, 'People are terrified of what they see. If the regime falls, you can imagine the chaos that will result, with the poor attacking the less poor. Nearly everyone has arms, and the country is slipping into chaos. Sometimes I think the regime encourages the idea of a breakdown. It's like saying, 'See what could happen… if they were no longer around?'. Makiya, op. cit., xxxi.

[6] Charles Tripp (2007). *A History of Iraq* (New York: Cambridge University Press), 277.

[7] Toby Dodge (2005). 'Iraqi Transitions: from regime change to state collapse', *Third World Quarterly*, vol. 26(4–5), 705–721.

expert noted that this vision was explicit across 'Central Intelligence Agency reports, National Security Council briefing papers, [and] documents drawn up by both the State Department and Defense Department.'[8]

In May 2003, the caretaker authority Office of Reconstruction and Humanitarian Assistance was abolished. Paul Bremer, an official with no Middle East experience, was appointed the Administrator of the newly created CPA. Bremer's first two orders had long-lasting consequences for efforts to stabilize Iraq and re-build its security institutions.[9] CPA Order No. 1 abolished the Ba'ath party, removed party members from positions of authority, and prohibited many members from holding positions in state institutions.[10] Order No. 2 dissolved the ministries of Defence, Information and Military Affairs and all other national security institutions, including the NSC, Iraqi Intelligence Service, all branches of the Iraqi Army, Republican Guard, Directorate of Military Intelligence, and all militias and paramilitary organizations associated with the Party.[11] Approximately 300,000 Ba'athists lost their jobs and livelihoods, breeding deep resentment against coalition forces especially in the Ba'athist strongholds of Mosul and Fallujah.[12]

Shortly before sovereignty was formally handed to the Iraqi Interim Government, CPA Order No. 68 established the Ministerial Committee for National Security (MCNS) to 'facilitate and coordinate national security policy among the ministries and agencies of the Iraqi government tasked with national security issues'. Chaired by Bremer, it operated under his 'authority, direction and control', 'pending full transfer of governance authority to the Iraqi Interim Government'.[13] Its permanent advisory members were the senior military advisor, the Director General of the Iraqi National Intelligence Service (INIS), and national security advisor (NSA). The NSA was the primary advisor to the Administrator and the MCNS on national security, and managed the National Security Advisory Staff. However, the establishment of theoretically representative institutions contrasted with the breakdown of law and order, the rise of the insurgency, widespread sectarian violence, and endemic corruption.

[8] Dodge (2018), op. cit.
[9] Tripp, op. cit., 278–283.
[10] Coalition Provisional Authority Order No. 1: *De-Ba'athification of Iraqi Society*, 16 May 2003.
[11] Coalition Provisional Authority Order No. 2: *Dissolution of Entities*, 23 May 2003.
[12] Andreas Krieg (2017). *Socio-Political Order and Security in the Arab World: From Regime Security to Public Security* (London: Palgrave Macmillan), 219.
[13] Coalition Provisional Authority Order No. 68: *Ministerial Committee for National Security*, 4 April 2004.

Al-Maliki's NSC

Between 28 June 2004 – the CPA's formal handover of sovereignty to Prime Minister Ayad 'Allawi – and May 2006, when Nuri al-Maliki became prime minister, Iraq's two cabinets were, in practice, caretaker governments with limited power. The governments of 'Allawi and his successor, Ibrahim al-Ja'fari, lacked the necessary institutional capabilities and, as the violence increased in level and complexity, were greatly dependent on the United States, politically and militarily. During 'Allawi's premiership, security-related decisions, e.g. the creation of a new intelligence agency, re-instating dismissed Ba'athists while continuing the de-Ba'athification process, and the creation of various military and paramilitary units, muddied an already complicated situation.

The appointment of a Sunni Arab, Ghazi al-Yawar, sheikh of the Shammar tribe, as interim Iraqi President, reflected the institutionalization of sectarian and ethnic representation in the political system. 'Allawi's defence minister lasted less than a year, and al-Ja'fari's equally short stint as prime minister marked a power shift from Sunni to Shi'a, with a cabinet dominated by Shi'a ministers who outnumbered Kurds, Sunni and Christians combined.[14] Growing suspicion and hostility from a significant proportion of Iraqis towards the new government and rising levels of sectarian violence went hand in hand with the growing influence of Iran. This fluid and complex political and security environment prevented an effective post-Saddam NSC from taking root.[15]

In 2006, Nouri al-Maliki, from the Islamic Dawa Party, took office. He re-appointed fellow party member Mowaffak al-Rubaie as NSA – previously a NSA under the CPA but dismissed by 'Alawi. The NSC included the ministers of interior, defence, national security, foreign affairs, finance and justice, as well as the senior military advisor and the director general of the INIS. At the beginning of al-Maliki's premiership, the NSC seemed to embody the vision of its creators in both scope and relevance. As former Minister of State for National Security, Shirwan al-Waili, noted, 'the NSC represented a mini government that dealt with major internal and regional security issues and discussed the structure of various ministries'.[16]

However, al-Maliki's sectarianism, and the cronyism and patronage entrenched in key security institutions undermined the NSC's ability to address

---

[14] Tripp, op. cit., 292–300.
[15] From al-Maliki's premiership onwards, the unofficial term NSC has been used instead of its official (MCNS) name, although no law formally reflects this.
[16] Author Interview, 9 June 2020, Iraq.

Iraq's security and reconstruction challenges. Al-Qaeda in Mesopotamia exploited this, inflaming sectarian tensions by targeting Shi'a civilians and religious sites, while using Sunni resentment to invite responses in kind. The period of sectarian violence, known as the 'Iraqi Civil War' (2006–2009), saw thousands killed. Opportunities to build more inclusive policies and embrace Sunni constituencies were missed. Notably, between 2005 and 2006, al-Maliki's government did not capitalize on the decision by Sunni tribes from Anbar – with US support – to turn against al-Qaeda, wasting an opportunity for community reconciliation.[17] The Shi'a-dominated government was at best a reluctant participant in the process: 'US commanders in Iraq, backed by the US Ambassador, succeeded in getting Prime Minister Nouri al-Maliki to incorporate former insurgents into the security forces and other official bodies. But the reversal of this policy following the departure of US forces suggests that he was not committed to the project.'[18] The Iraqi Army began arresting the leaders of the 'Sons of Iraq', as the Awakening Councils were also known. The government's strategy to demobilize the Sunni rank-and-file, already excluded from Iraq's Security Forces (ISF) and government structures, then evolved into extrajudicial killings, imprisonment and expulsion from Iraq. Protests from Sunni communities, notably in Anbar, were met with lethal force.[19]

This sectarian approach to security was translated into the composition of the NSC. As Dr Mahmud Azzo, a political science lecturer at Mosul University notes, 'al-Maliki worked on adopting a Shi'a political vision regarding Iraq's national security, by which he excluded representatives from the Kurdistan Region from the council's membership'.[20]

In late 2010, al-Maliki was confirmed for a second term, during which the monopolization of power undermined the NSC.[21] Ministers of defence, interior, and state national security, were not appointed. Al-Maliki established the Office of Commander-in-Chief of the Armed Forces (OCAF) with the roles and responsibilities of the defence and interior ministers and the army's Chief of Staff.[22]

---

[17] Bernard Stancati (2010). 'Tribal Dynamics and the Iraq Surge', *Strategic Studies Quarterly*, vol. 4(2), 88–112.

[18] Greg Shapland (February 2018). *Elite Bargains and Political Deals Project: Iraq's Sunni Insurgency (2003–2013) Case Study*, Stabilisation Unit.

[19] Shapland, op. cit.

[20] Author interview, 2 June 2020, Iraq.

[21] Al-Maliki's second term followed a nine-month election impasse. Qassem Soleimani, the head of Iran's Revolutionary Guards and commander of the Quds Force, orchestrated various backstage deals with Shi'ite and Kurdish leaders that paved the way for al-Maliki's appointment. See Dexter Filkins (20 September 2013). 'The Shadow Commander', *The New Yorker*.

[22] Al-Maliki only appointed a defence minister in 2011 and remained Minister of Interior throughout his second term.

Falih al-Fayyadh, a senior member of the National Reform Movement, was appointed as the NSA, overseeing key security and intelligence agencies such as the Iraqi National Security Services (INSS) and the INIS. The appointment in 2011 of another member of al-Maliki's Islamic Dawa Party, Adnan al-Asadi, as deputy interior minister and acting interior minister allowed the party to dominate the NSC. These steps all contributed to a weak and ineffective NSC.

Security conditions deteriorated and the threat from violent extremist groups grew. Compounding this, in 2011 the US completed its troop withdrawal. By August 2014, the Islamic State of Iraq and the Levant (ISIL) had control of over a third of the country with Iraq's army unable to respond. Amid a global outcry and internal pressure, al-Maliki stepped down.

Al-Abadi's NSC: Responding to ISIL

The new prime minister, Haider al-Abadi, included all the ministers that formally should be members of the NSC and saw the roles of defence and interior ministers re-gain relevance, appointing Khaled al-Obaidi and Mohammed al-Ghabban respectively. The minister of state for national security and OCAF posts were abolished. Ridha al-Haidar, an Iraqi MP and head of the Security and Defence Committee, however, viewed the NSC's increased membership as a management challenge given the greater complexity of its decision-making process.[23]

On 21 October 2015, the NSC approved Iraq's new National Security Strategy (NSS), which was developed by the NSA with international advice and assistance through the United Nations Development Programme (UNDP). The NSS was approved by the Council of Ministers in March 2016. The NSS, still effective at the time of writing, places human security at the core (in theory) and describes the security landscape as follows:

> the legacy of the former regime, the rapid transition from dictatorship towards democracy, and changes in the strategic environment are all characterised by violent political conflict, corruption, the outbreak of sectarian violence, terrorism and crime, and all serve collectively to weaken the social structure, which accelerates insecurity and instability.[24]

---

[23] Author interview, October 2020.
[24] Republic of Iraq, National Security Council (1 March 2016). *The National Security Strategy*, 2.

The issues to be addressed and managed are then grouped into risk areas: political, economic, diplomatic (namely foreign interference) and security.

Security in this period was dominated by the response to ISIL, which included the formation of predominantly Shi'a Popular Mobilization Units (PMUs). The rise of the PMUs followed a *fatwa* (religious edict) issued in mid-June 2014 by Grand Ayatollah al-Sistani, Iraq's top Shi'a cleric, as a call to arms against ISIL. The PMUs, many Iranian-backed, became a double-edged sword; key actors in the war against ISIL but representing a serious threat to the state's monopoly on the use of armed force. The PMUs' indiscriminate violence and expansion into Sunni areas bred further Sunni resentment against the government in Baghdad.

NSA al-Fayyadh was appointed Head of the PMU Commission soon after its creation but was temporarily removed from both positions in 2018 by al-Abadi who claimed al-Fayyadh's political affiliation with Hadi al-Amiri's pro-Iranian Fatah bloc affected his neutrality as NSA. Al-Fayyadh returned to his dual posts in late 2018 during Adil Abdul Mahdi's administration.

Under Abadi, the NSC's role coordinating the military and civilian spheres of government improved, positively impacting the security and humanitarian dimensions of the government's operations. There was also early progress in military coordination between the various security bodies; the ISF, PMUs, and Kurdish Peshmerga forces. However, tensions arose between ISF/PMUs and Kurdish forces in October 2017 after the former took over areas within the disputed territories that the Peshmerga had taken control of during the fight against ISIL. The disputed areas became a locus of competition between the various security forces, which the NSC struggled to manage.

Al-Khadimi's NSC and COVID-19

Adil Abdul Mahdi became prime minister in October 2018 but faced massive anti-government demonstrations in October 2019. Despite multiple NSC meetings calling for the protection of civilians at peaceful protests, security forces and militias responded with excessive force, killing dozens of unarmed protesters. Abdul Mahdi resigned within a year of his appointment, but not before ordering the PMUs to integrate fully into the state security forces, in line with efforts to rein in these militias.[25]

---

[25] Ali Younes (1 September 2019). 'Adel Abdul-Mahdi, an Iraqi prime minister "doomed to fail"', *Aljazeera*: Ali Mamouri (8 July 2019). 'Shiite militias react angrily to decree integrating them into Iraqi forces', *Al-Monitor*.

In May 2020, Mustafa al-Kadhimi, the former intelligence chief and long-standing member of the Iraqi opposition during the pre-2003 Ba'athist regime, became prime minister. He was the third PM-designate nominated by the president following Abdul Mahdi's resignation. Al-Kadhimi's appointment was supported by key Shi'a, Sunni and Kurdish blocs, as well US and Iran.[26] He introduced significant changes, including replacing heads of key governmental bodies and security positions. Al-Fayyadh, the NSA and head of the INSS, was removed in July 2020 and replaced by Major-General Qassim al-Araji and former interior minister Abdul Ghani al-Asadi respectively. Al-Fayyadh remained chair of the PMUs but al-Kadhimi's move was widely seen as a step towards excluding PMU figures from top security positions and institutions, and an attempt to win public support.

The NSA, al-Araji, is supported by the small Office of the National Security Advisor, and uses al-Nahrain Center for Strategic Studies for research. He can also call on staff in the Ministries and the Council of Ministers. Al-Kadhimi also chose US-trained General Othman al-Ghanimi, a former military chief of staff and a powerful tribal chief from southern Iraq, as Minister of Interior. These and other measures reflected al-Kadhimi's willingness to reform Iraq's security sector, implement centralized command and control structures and sideline factionalism to professionalize the security forces.[27] There are positive signs, but it is too early to claim success.

COVID-19 exacerbated Iraq's already significant security and governance challenges. Under al-Khadimi the NSC directly addressed the health crisis, whereas with Abdul Mahdi the NSC appeared more concerned about the socio-economic impact of the pandemic and ISIL's attempts to exploit the security forces' focus on implementing lockdowns. The health response was led by the Supreme Committee for National Health and Safety to Combat Coronavirus, formed in March 2020 as a crisis cell headed by the health minister. However, articulating the response to the pandemic fell within the NSC's formal objective of strengthening the state's capacity to respond to and manage crisis and disasters.[28] While the NSC does not include the health minister, who has not participated in its meetings, the PM chairs both the NSC and Supreme

---

[26] Washington Institute for Near East Policy (7 May 2020). 'New Iraqi government confirmed: Mustafa al-Kadhimi named prime minister'.

[27] Michael Knights (19 May 2020). 'Kadhimi as Commander-in-Chief: First Steps in Iraqi Security Sector Reform', *PolicyWatch 3317, Washington Institute for Near East Policy*.

[28] Government of Iraq (30 March 2020). 'Abdul Mahdi chairs first meeting of the supreme committee for national health and safety'.

Committee, ensuring leadership and coordination of the decisions and pandemic response measures. For example, on 27 June 2020, al-Kadhimi's NSC directed the Ministry of Health to issue protocols for hospitals and called on the Ministries of Health and Higher Education to allow medical students voluntarily to support hospital medical staff.

During 2021, the NSC met on several occasions to discuss COVID-19 curfews and lockdowns, but also ISIL's attacks, the Iranian-backed PMUs parade in Baghdad in May and US airstrikes against PMU positions on the Iraq–Syria border in June as retaliation for persistent rocket fire against US bases in Iraq. Under al-Kadhimi, the NSC has, therefore, widened its role in national security, a development that should provide useful lessons for its approach to other, broader, security challenges.

Conclusion

The history of Iraq's NSC illustrates the challenges of implementing an inclusive concept of national security in a context where human security has systematically been a casualty of sectarianism, factional infighting and despotic rule. In addition, perennial state weakness has been an open invitation to foreign interference.

The NSC's ability to coordinate an effective government response to Iraq's myriad security challenges is likely to depend less on the technical capacity of the body's membership and support staff and more on a broader set of factors. These include the government's commitment to, and political capital for, Security Sector Reform (SSR), reigning in parallel security structures such as the PMUs, countering factionalism, and tackling endemic corruption. However, the various governance and development issues, such as the urgency of economic diversification, poor water management, or the closure of internally displaced person (IDP) camps, speak to the importance of the NSC adopting and coordinating a whole-of-government human security approach. At the technical level, effective coordination across relevant ministries and between Baghdad and the provinces, as well as external assistance for capacity building, will be required to ensure a more inclusive, accountable and sustainable security provision.

10

Israel's National Security Staff comes of age[1]

Charles (Chuck) Freilich

Introduction

In 1999, some fifty years after Prime Minister Ben-Gurion first considered the idea, Israel's National Security Council was finally established. Much like the American NSC, on which it was modelled, Israel's NSC (renamed the Israel National Security Staff – NSS) was the outcome both of domestic politics and strategic developments.

Announcing the NSS's establishment just two weeks before the 1999 elections was a political ploy by Premier Netanyahu, then completing his first term in office. In a country preoccupied with national security affairs, Netanyahu clearly hoped – forlornly as it transpired – that the announcement would improve his electoral prospects by generating the impression of a reform-minded leadership adopting a critical new decision-making innovation.

Strategically, in the decades following the 1973 Yom Kippur War, an intolerable gap had emerged between Israel's increasingly complex external environment, and the existing national security machinery's ability to cope with the demands it generated. Most of the threats Israel had long faced remained, and new, even more dangerous ones were added. Cracks also began appearing in the previously monolithic wall of Arab hostility, presenting unprecedented opportunities for diplomatic engagement that required an entirely new set of considerations. Israel's relations with a variety of countries, including the United States, Russia, some Arab states and even distant ones like China and North Korea, were also changing rapidly. Although a tiny nation, the spectrum of national security concerns Israel faced were worthy of a major power.

---

[1] Except where explicitly stated, this chapter draws on interviews conducted with senior officials of the NSS, current or recent, and the author's own experience having served on the NSS in its early years. It also draws on the following works by the author: Charles Freilich (2012). *Zion's Dilemmas: How Israel Makes National Security Policy* (New York: Cornell), and (2013) 'National Security Decision-Making in Israel: Improving the Process', *Middle East Journal*, vol. 67(2), 257–267.

Responding to the threat

Israeli national security thinking had long been predicated on a fundamental perception, shared by decision-makers of all stripes, that Arab hostility was so extreme as to pose an existential threat of genocide, not just the danger of politicide faced by other states. Moreover, Israel's external environment was characterized by nearly constant and sweeping change. The combined effect of Arab hostility and Middle Eastern volatility was a belief that Israel's ability to materially shape its external environment was highly circumscribed and decision-making in the early decades consisted primarily of responses to Arab actions.

Israel also responded by developing outsized defence capabilities and a decision-making style focused on ad hoc solutions to immediate threats. In these circumstances, the absence of an entity charged with policy planning at the prime ministerial and cabinet level, an otherwise glaring gap in Israel's national security structure, becomes somewhat less surprising, if no less significant.

Early years

With Netanyahu's defeat in the 1999 elections, the NSS languished in bureaucratic obscurity under his successors Barak and Sharon, neither of whom believed it offered significant value and considered it an unnecessary bureaucratic competitor to the Israel Defense Forces (IDF). Israel's trauma over the ill-fought 2006 Lebanon war, in which Hezbollah, a non-state adversary, succeeded in fighting the IDF to a standstill and causing significant damage to the home front, ushered in a period of introspection. A National Commission of Inquiry severely criticized Israel's wartime decision-making process (DMP) and paved the way for the 'NSS Law' in 2008. With the NSS' existence enshrined in statute, the question became what kind of role it would play, rather than whether it should exist. Recognizing that Israel, unlike the US, already had a National Security *Council* – the Cabinet – the law changed the name to the more appropriate National Security *Staff*.

Surprisingly, perhaps, for a country so preoccupied with national security affairs, Israel has never formulated a formal national security strategy, nor adopted an accepted definition of the term national security. Given Israel's strategic environment, however, the NSS was always going to focus on the 'hard' (foreign and defence) dimensions of national security policy, rather than 'softer' domestic issues, which were dealt with by other agencies, or in some cases orphaned. This focus was clear from the outset in the ambivalent attitude towards the NSS's Domestic Affairs Division. Initially, the Division dealt with issues such as Jewish–Arab relations, alternative models of military service and societal resilience and considered the challenges to Israeli democracy. The Division was disbanded when it was deemed more appropriate in a democracy for a civilian agency to deal with issues of this nature, rather than a military-dominated national security establishment, but was subsequently reconstituted.

The NSS's primary focus has thus been on Israel's external challenges, such as the proliferation of weapons of mass destruction, especially Iran's nuclear programme, Iranian regional expansionism, Hezbollah, the Palestinians and Hamas, relations with the US, Russia, the primary Arab countries, Europe and various strategic partners such as India. Much of the emphasis has been on military and diplomatic threats, but also opportunities, such as the NSS's important role in negotiations leading to the peace agreements with the UAE and Bahrain in 2020.

Following the NSS Law, Prime Minister Olmert instituted an extraordinarily highly structured and rigorous DMP. Meetings of the Ministerial Committee on Defense (MCoD) were scheduled one year in advance, with the NSS chairing a demanding inter-agency process in preparation for these and other meetings. As might have been expected, this trauma-induced and untenably structured process began dissipating rather quickly, but some of the procedures took root.

The NSS started coming into its own following Netanyahu's re-election in 2009 and uninterrupted tenure until 2021. In practice, Netanyahu was premier for more than half of the NSS's life, and almost the entire period since the NSS Law was passed. It thus largely came to be his creation and its influence grew steadily, gaining a central role in the Israeli DMP. This influential role has continued under Prime Minister Bennett.

NSS today

The NSS has a professional staff of some seventy-five people today, not including support personnel. The structure has changed considerably over the years, reflecting new strategic exigencies and the priorities of different Premiers and NSAs. In addition to the original four divisions (Defence, Foreign Affairs, Domestic Affairs and Counter-Terrorism, as well as a legal and economic advisor), the NSS has added: a Middle East, Special Relations and Africa Policy Division; an Intelligence, Integration and Ministerial Committees Division, responsible for preparing Cabinet meetings, MCoD and other senior forums;

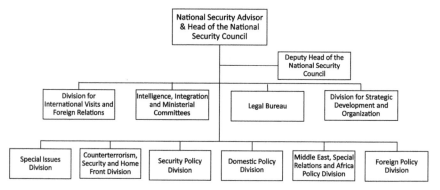

Figure 10.1 NSS organization.[2]

a Special Issues Division dealing with particularly sensitive issues such as Iran; and an International Visits and Foreign Relations Division, responsible primarily for organizational aspects of the Premier's trips abroad.

Policy formulation. In Israel, as elsewhere, an advisory body that is not engaged in day-to-day affairs risks bureaucratic irrelevance, as was the case in the NSS's early years. Consequently, it has become deeply engaged in day-to-day servicing of the premier's affairs, but has thereby undermined the unique role intended for it as the primary body in Israel's national security establishment charged with in-depth, national level strategic planning. With other agencies consumed by current affairs, the NSS should have provided sorely needed balance and reduced Israel's proclivity for improvisational and sequential decision-making. In practice, the NSS conducts few fundamental policy reviews. One important exception, after a number of faulty starts, is the institutionalization of the annual national net assessment mandated by the NSS law.

The NSS provides a systematic process today for substantive preparation of the Premier prior to meetings with foreign dignitaries in Israel and on trips abroad, replacing the more haphazard preparations of the past. Preparation of meetings with other senior Israeli officials, however, including ministers, remains spotty and unstructured. Crucially, the NSA, or one of the other senior officials from the NSS, participates in virtually all of the Premier's meetings on diplomatic and most defence issues, although those of a clearly military nature remain the bailiwick of the Premier's Military Secretary, his liaison to the IDF.

Meetings of the cabinet and MCoD are better prepared than in the past, with an orderly process in place, though not the extraordinarily structured one of the late Olmert era. The NSS sets the agenda, holds preparatory inter-agency meetings, prepares background papers and especially the critical 'decision proposals' (*hatzaot machlitim*), which are usually the basis for cabinet discussion and decision. The NSS typically briefs the Premier prior to meetings of the cabinet and MCoD, as well as interested ministers. The NSS also maintains a list of the primary issues requiring cabinet attention, updated on a quarterly basis, prepares '100-day plans' for incoming cabinets, which happened three times during the politically volatile 2019–2020 years, and maintains a regularly updated list of Israel's objectives and interests on the different military fronts.

In most cabinet meetings today, the NSS presents policy options and often recommendations. The absence of systematic presentation of options was long considered a critical failing of the Israeli DMP and this change is an important improvement. The nature of the process for developing options, however, remains deficient. Time pressures and ministerial rivalries mean that agency representatives in the preparatory meetings cannot always present options that have been formally approved by their agencies. This problem appears to be greater for those meetings chaired at divisional-head level than those chaired by the NSA.

An even greater problem is posed by the ongoing division of authority between the NSA and the Military Secretary, an IDF General, whose importance rivals that of the NSA. Attempts by at least one previous NSA to subordinate the Military Secretary to the NSS encountered strong opposition from the IDF and succeeding NSAs chose, probably wisely, to abandon the fight. The Military Secretary remains the gatekeeper of all national security information flowing to the Premier. He is the first and last person to brief the Premier on events throughout the day, accompanies him at all times, and is the only official present in every national security meeting the Premier holds. Although the Military Secretary lacks a supporting staff, and in that sense is at an organizational disadvantage compared to the NSA, he has the entire IDF at his disposal and is responsible for preparing meetings dealing with matters of a clearly military nature. Consequently, the NSA has not achieved, and is unlikely to achieve, complete control over the preparation and management of the Premier's national security affairs. Under Netanyahu, the position of Advisor to the Premier for Diplomatic Affairs, previously another leading rival for influence, was merged with that of the head of the NSS Foreign Affairs Division, but has reemerged as an independent player under Bennett. It is not yet clear whether this is a permanent change.

For most of his tenure as Premier, although not in the latter years, Netanyahu convened an informal grouping of senior ministers, originally seven, later eight and ultimately nine, which proved to be an effective, discrete and expeditious sub-cabinet forum for considering issues of particular importance and sensitivity. Lacking statutory authority, these groups could not make formal decisions, but their recommendations usually carried decisive weight with the MCoD, or cabinet plenum. Despite the importance of these groups, their meetings were not typically prepared by the NSS.

Policy integration. Policy integration and the inter-agency process remain areas in which further progress is required. To the extent that the NSS's cabinet presentations and policy papers reflect an integrative process, it remains overwhelmingly intra-NSS. Numerous inter-agency meetings are convened and the NSS takes the agencies' positions into account. A hierarchical process, however, starting with low-level meetings, followed by more senior ones and finally a 'Principals' forum, as in the US, does not exist. Moreover, NSS cabinet presentations and policy papers do not usually reflect an iterative process involving the different agencies. Most policy papers are not circulated for comment and the NSS does not typically serve as an 'honest broker' when differences arise, usually leaving it to cabinet ministers to iron out differences. Integration appears to be limited primarily to the process of drawing on agency inputs and then formulating an NSS paper.

Formulation of clearly defined policy objectives, the basis for any truly systematic DMP and a critical failing of the Israeli process in the past, also remains partial. Coalition maintenance remains the Premier's foremost objective, rather than decision-making clarity. As a result, objectives tend to be ad hoc, issue-specific and tactical in nature, rather than broad strategic ones. To the extent that formulation of fundamental strategic objectives and options does take place, it is mostly in the context of the annual net assessment and a few in-depth policy papers that the NSS does prepare, not in the ongoing flow of policy papers and cabinet presentations.

One important area in which considerable progress has been achieved is in the statutory mandate to deepen the NSS's role regarding the defence budget and major procurement projects. Opposition from the IDF and Ministry of Defense to the NSS dealing with these matters, along with personnel limitations, long hampered its ability to effectively address these areas, but it has developed impressive capabilities in recent years, nevertheless.

Post-decision functions. A formal process for follow-up on cabinet decisions has been put in place, but has not become fully institutionalized, due to bureaucratic resistance and because of decision-makers' reluctance to have their achievements assessed by subordinate officials. Further complicating the picture, cabinet and MCoD decisions are often intentionally worded in a manner designed to make an assessment of their success difficult, a practice that is politically expedient, especially in Israel's coalition system, while the rapid pace of developments in Israel's external environment often outpaces decisions. In many cases, cabinet decisions are largely declaratory, without any actual intention that they are implemented.

Operational responsibility. Although the NSS is neither designed nor structured to be an operational agency, in some areas it has gained considerable operational responsibility. It has gained particular importance in the conduct of negotiations with foreign governments and management of a variety of 'strategic dialogues' and other senior forums. This role has caused tensions with other agencies, especially the Foreign and Defense Ministries, which either chaired these forums in the past, or expected to do so.

The NSS's National Situation Room is responsible for preparing a one-stop, integrative, national briefing paper for the premier and MCoD, designed to replace the deluge of daily briefings and raw data produced by the various agencies. It is also responsible for the management of a highly secure wartime decision-making facility for the national leadership, reportedly safe even from nuclear attack.[3]

NSA. The NSA himself has become an important trouble-shooter and special envoy for the Premier, meeting with foreign leaders on issues of particular national security importance or sensitivity. On rare occasions, the NSA has also served as an envoy to domestic political figures on particularly charged issues having national security dimensions.

The NSA's twin role, as the head of the NSS (part of the national security establishment), and as a political appointee and senior advisor to the Premier, has been a long-standing source of tension. In the former capacity, the NSA is expected to make recommendations based on purely professional considerations, serving, in effect, as an impartial national security 'magistrate'. In the latter, the NSA is expected to take account of the Premier's political considerations to offer politically aware advice, while at the same time maintaining professional integrity. Most NSAs have wrestled with this dilemma.

For Yossi Cohen, formerly a senior official in the Mossad, the position of NSA was a steppingstone to his appointment as director of Mossad. Netanyahu apparently intended to name Cohen's successor, Meir Ben-Shabbat, a former senior official in the Shin Bet, to head that Agency. His appointment was stymied both by internal opposition and Netanyahu's electoral defeat. To the extent that

---

[3]   Ofer Petersburg (27 August 2007). 'National Command Bunker being Built'. *YNet News*.

the role of the NSA becomes a steppingstone to the most senior positions in the national security establishment, it will be quite a change from even a few years earlier, when premiers, including Netanyahu, had to scrabble around to find almost anyone willing to take what appeared to be an uninfluential and career-ending position.

The NSS and COVID-19

From the outset, the NSS was deeply involved in coordinating the inter-agency process responsible for formulating Israel's response to the COVID crisis and even its implementation in the early months. By April 2020 the NSS had developed a comprehensive plan for addressing the crisis in consultation with the relevant ministries, public sector institutions, think tanks, academics and a special NSS COVID task force. Its limitations as an operational body rapidly became apparent, however, and responsibility for implementation was transferred to an inter-agency task force headed by the IDF and Mossad, and subsequently – and prematurely – disbanded.[4]

What had initially appeared to be a highly successful response, rapidly deteriorated into one of the least successful ones in the developed world. Partisan politics, including rivalries between Prime Minister Netanyahu and other leaders, exacerbated by bureaucratic politics, especially between the Health and Finance Ministries,[5] largely account for the change. In a desperate attempt to contain the spread of the virus, a special 'Coronavirus Czar' was appointed, although the NSS remained an important source of advice to the Premier and continued to provide the support mechanism for the 'Corona Cabinet'. In the end, a dramatic vaccination programme, for which Netanyahu deserved much of the credit and in which Israel was a world leader, saved the day.[6]

---

4 See: Staff (31 March 2020). 'Official: Lockdown may ease after Passover, but life to be entirely different', *Times of Israel*; Noa Landau (13 April 2020). 'Hi-tech and Preschools First, Malls and Sports Last: Israel's Coronavirus Exit Strategy', *Haaretz*; Amos Harel (28 May 2020). 'Israel's COVID-19 Experts: the Lockdown saved the country, but Steps are Needed to Avert Another', *Haaretz*.

5 See: Ido Efrati (10 June 2020). 'Israel Fails to Break Chain of Coronavirus Infections – and the Numbers are Rising', Haaretz; Staff (13 April 2020). '2-month phased rollback of lockdown pushed by National Security Council-report', *Times of Israel*; Ido Efrati (29 September 2020). 'Israel Coronavirus Mortality Rate Surpasses U.S. for First Time Since Pandemic Began', Haaretz.

6 See: AP (1 July 2021). 'Israel Scrambles to Curb Jump in COVID Infections', *The Independent*; Healthmanagement.org, Why is Israel's Vaccination Programme so successful, at https://healthmanagement.org/c/hospital/news/why-is-israels-vaccination-programme-so-successful, accessed 30 August 2021.

Conclusion

The NSS has faced broad criticism from within the national security establishment and beyond, for its ostensible failure to fulfil the roles assigned to it and its lack of influence. While some of the criticism has certainly been warranted, it also reflected a degree of bureaucratic rivalry and, no less importantly, a lack of understanding of what an NSC type body is actually designed to do. When viewed from this perspective, and once it had been assigned a role of importance by the Premier, the NSS rapidly became a major player. Prime Minister Netanyahu took to stressing publicly that various issues of importance had been considered by the NSS and that policies adopted reflected its recommendations. In so doing, the NSS became the public face of policy and provided an important degree of policy legitimization.

With the election of Naftali Bennet in mid-2021, a relative neophyte in national security affairs, a new era for the NSS has begun. At the time of writing, it is still far too early to generalize about the role the NSS might play under him and future premiers. Bennet at least, and his somewhat more experienced successor as premier, Yair Lapid who will take over as part of a two-year power sharing arrangement linked to their coalition government agreement, are likely to be even more dependent on the NSS for information and advice than the far more seasoned Netanyahu.

As one 'present at the creation',[7] serving on the NSS for its first five formative years, I opined at the time that if it took the American NSC fifteen years to become the highly influential body we know today, it would likely take closer to thirty years in Israel's case. An advisory mechanism designed for a hierarchical presidential system is not a natural graft for a fractious parliamentary coalition system. At the twenty-year point, this forecast does not appear to have been wide of the mark.

---

[7] The title of Dean Atchison's autobiography, including his account of the American NSA's early years.

11

Japan's National Security Council since 2013: The Abe and Suga administrations

Yasuhiro Matsuda

Introduction

This chapter examines the functions of the National Security Council (NSC) and National Security Secretariat (NSS) under the Shinzo Abe Administration (2013–2020), and his successor, Yoshihide Suga (2020–2021). Japan emulated the US NSC and established a Security Council (SC) within the Cabinet in 1986. Its nine major cabinet members met infrequently. A SC secretariat was also established in the Cabinet Secretariat.[1] Unlike its US counterpart, SC discussions largely addressed routine work related to the defence budget and defence planning, with some crisis management.

Administrative reforms under the Ryutaro Hashimoto Administration in 1996 strengthened the Cabinet's power. These allowed Prime Minister Junichiro Koizumi to use the SC as a power centre for crisis management and security policy after the 9/11 terrorist attacks in the United States, such as sending Ground Self-Defence Force units to Iraq for post-conflict reconstruction.[2] Abe gained experience under Koizumi as Deputy Chief Cabinet Secretary, Director-General of the ruling Liberal Democratic Party, and Chief Cabinet Secretary. He believed Japan needed the US-type NSC to deal with Japan's difficult security challenges. Becoming Prime Minister in 2006, Abe tried to establish a new NSC

---

[1] Yasuhiro Matsuda and Hideki Hosono. 'Nihon: anzen hoshō kaigi to naikaku kanbō' [Japan: Security Council and Cabinet Secretariat], in Yasuhiro Matsuda ed. (2009). *NSC kokka anzen hoshō kaigi: shuyō koku no kiki kanri anpo seisaku tōgō mekanizumu* [*NSC: Integration System of Crisis Management and National Security Policy in Major Countries*] (Tokyo: Sairyusha), 285–298; Mayumi Fukushima and Richard J. Samuels (2018). 'Japan's National Security Council: Filling the Whole of Government?' *International Affairs*, vol. 94(4), 1–6.

[2] Matsuda and Hosono, op. cit., 287–289.

within the Cabinet; however, his deteriorating health forced him to step down, and the initiative failed.

Abe returned as Prime Minister in 2012 and established the current NSC and NSS. His renovated NSC has been highly regarded for improving policy coordination through its whole-of-government approach.[3] Prime Minister Suga used the same arrangements, which his successor, Fumio Kishida, currently has continued. This chapter considers the NSC's power, major functions, and whether it has improved Japan's crisis management and national security decision-making.

Legislation and establishment of the NSC

The National Diet passed the Act establishing the NSC in December 2013, amending it twice as of October 2021.[4] Article 2 describes thirteen missions, including drafting, amending or discussing Japan's Basic Defence Policy, National Defence Program Guidelines (NDPG), major defence issues, and major issues in UN peacekeeping operations. There are three types of NSC ministerial meetings.

- The 'Nine-Minister Meeting' (NMM) considers long-term strategies. It consists of the: Prime Minister (Deputy Prime Minister, if necessary); Chief Cabinet Secretary; ministers for: Internal Affairs and Communications; Foreign Affairs; Finance; Economy, Trade and Industry; Land, Infrastructure, Transport and Tourism; Defence; and Chair of the National Public Safety Commission.
- The 'Four-Minister Meeting' (FMM), established as a core body of the NSC, is comprised of the: Prime Minister (Deputy Prime Minister, if necessary); Chief Cabinet Secretary; and Ministers of Foreign Affairs and Defence.
- The 'Emergency Ministerial Meeting' (EMM), whose membership depends on the nature of the emergency.

---

[3] Adam Liff, (2018). 'Japan's National Security Council: Policy Coordination and Political Power', *Japanese Studies*, vol. 38(2), 276–277.

[4] Prime Minister of Japan (30 September 2015). *Kokka anzen hoshō kaigi setchi hō* [Act for Establishment of the NSC].

The Prime Minister chairs all NSC ministerial meetings, which strengthens responses, coordination and political decision-making in major emergencies for which lower-level crisis-management mechanisms are insufficient.[5]

At ministerial level, there is a Contingency Response Expert Committee, with director-general level officials from relevant ministries, chaired by the Chief Cabinet Secretary. In addition, a Special Advisor to the Prime Minister on National Security was established in the NSC, reporting directly to the Prime Minister.

The NSS, established in the Cabinet Secretariat,[6] is headed by the Secretary-General of the NSS and the National Security Advisor (NSA). The first NSA, Shōtarō Yachi (2013–2019), was previously the Administrative Vice-Minister for Foreign Affairs. His successor, Shigeru Kitamura (2019–2021), the former Director of Cabinet Intelligence (from the National Police Agency), left on health grounds after twenty-two months to be replaced by Takeo Akiba. Like Yachi, Akiba is a former Vice-Minister for Foreign Affairs, and close to the Prime Minister. There are two Deputy Secretary-Generals, one from the Ministry of Foreign Affairs (MOFA) and the other from the Ministry of Defense, who direct and work with their parent departments.

Cabinet Councillors (*naikaku shingikan*) and Cabinet Counsellors (*naikaku sanjikan*) head the functional and regional policy teams, and come from key national security ministries, such as the Ministry of Defense, MOFA, and the National Police Agency. Most NSS staff come from government ministries and agencies rather than non-governmental organizations, such as think-tanks.[7] The NSS can respond rapidly to events: in April 2020, the Economic Security Team was established quickly within the NSS to deal with economic security issues mainly flowing from the US/China trade war, despite debate about whether to include economic security under the NSC.[8]

5   Liff, op. cit., 264.
6   Prime Minister of Japan. *Naikaku kanbō kokka anzen hoshō kaigi setchi junbi shitsu, 'Kokka anzen hoshō kaigi ni tsuite (setsumei shiryō)'* [About the NSC, Slides for Briefing], at www.kantei.go.jp/jp/singi/ka_yusiki/dai6/siryou1.pdf, accessed 30 August 2021.
7   (26 January 2014). 'NSC 67 nin no jitsudō butai' [NSC: Working Unit with 67 Staff], *Nikkei Shimbun* at www.nikkei.com/article/DGXNZO65888980V20C14A1NN9000/, accessed 30 August 2021.
8   (1 April 2020). 'Kokka ampo kyoku ni 'keizai han' hossoku, shingata korona taio mo kyumu' [Inauguration of 'Economic Security Team' in the NSS, COVID-19 Response Is Required in the NSC], *Nikkei Shimbun* at www.nikkei.com/article/DGXMZO57510630R00C20A4PP8000/, accessed 30 August 2021.

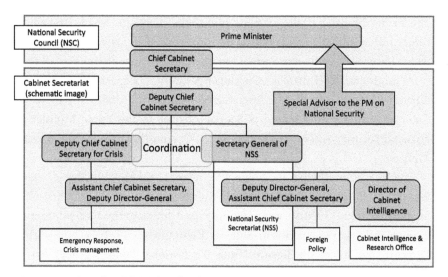

Figure 11.1 Japan's NSC, NSS and Cabinet Secretariat.[9]

Rise of the FMM; the NSC's new core?

The NSC met 268 times between December 2013 and October 2021 under Prime Ministers Abe and Suga; approximately every eleven days, significantly more often than the earlier SC. There was also a clear trend favouring use of the FMM (194 meetings against 53 NMM and 21 EMM) – see Table 11.1.[10]

In the first month (December 2013), the NMM met six times and the FMM three times. Discussions focused on meeting protocols, the situation in South Sudan where Self-Defence Forces were dispatched as UN peacekeepers, the NDPG and particularly developing the first National Security Strategy, which was the most important task at the time. The NDPG was largely concerned with budget planning for defence capability building, but the National Security Strategy goes beyond this, setting fundamental principles of national security based on broad 'national interests and national security objectives'. It covers traditional threats such as the Democratic People's Republic of Korea (DPRK)'s nuclear developments, non-traditional security challenges, e.g. economic, and coordinates non-military measures such as foreign policy and official development assistance, which are not covered by the Ministry of Defense. There

9   Source: Ministry of Foreign Affairs (27 October 2015). *Diplomatic Bluebook 2014 Summary*, Chapter 3.
10 Prime Minister of Japan. 'Kokka anzen hoshō kaigi kaisai jōhō' [NSC Meeting Information] at www.kantei.go.jp/jp/singi/anzenhosyoukaigi/kaisai.html, accessed 30 December 2021.

Table 11.1 NSC Meetings 2013–2021

Year	NMM	FMM	EMM	Total
2013 (December only)	6	3	–	9
2014	8	25	–	33
2015	10	25	–	35
2016	7	41	–	48
2017	4	42	–	46
2018	5	12	–	17
2019	6	13	–	19
2020	6	18	19	43
2021 (to October)	1	15	2	18
Total	53	194	21	268

is also a commitment to establish a new headquarters to dictate national security policy and crisis management.[11]

In 2014, the NMM and FMM discussed important security policies, such as changes in interpreting the Constitution concerning the exercise of collective self-defence, and lifting the arms export ban to countries other than the United States. However, the FMM started to engage more extensively with intelligence sharing and enabling discussions among core security ministers covering the situations in East and South Asia, the Asia-Pacific, Ukraine, Europe and the Middle East.

In 2015, NSC meetings drafted new Peace and Security Legislation authorizing the limited right of collective self-defence, allowing rear area support to US armed forces in major situations influencing Japan's peace and security, and widening the Self-Defense Forces' role in UN peacekeeping and other operations. Meetings also discussed hostage murder cases in the Middle East, cyber security, Japan–US security cooperation, arms sales, energy security, the North Pole and counter-piracy operations. In 2016, with the DPRK violating UN Security Council Resolutions and threatening Japan's security by resuming nuclear testing and ballistic missile launches around Japan, NSC meetings hit a record high. The FMM addressed the DPRK's ballistic missile and nuclear weapons tests, the intrusion of Chinese submarines into Japan's contiguous zone, and the Dhaka attack in Bangladesh in July.

[11] Prime Minister of Japan (17 December 2013). *National Security Strategy.*

2017 was also busy, the result of further DPRK ballistic missile and nuclear tests. Of sixteen ballistic missile launches over or near Japan, twelve were successful, as was a nuclear test conducted in September. The FMM met after every incident, sometimes with multiple meetings per day; it met twice a day for five launches and three times in a day on another occasion. The FMM became the top crisis management centre during the missile and nuclear crisis in 2017.

NSC ministerial meetings decreased in 2018 and 2019, reflecting fewer missile launches following a US–DPRK 'rapprochement' under President Trump, and a Japan–China rapprochement seeking to balance a deterioration in Sino–US relations from 2018. However, the reprieve was merely temporary. In 2020, despite Abe's attempts to upgrade Japan's ballistic defence capability with offensive capabilities, which required NSC authorization for a new missile defence policy, the FMM remained dominant. Abe held six FMMs to discuss plans for missile defence before leaving office on 16 September due to ill-health. Overall in 2020, six NMMs were held (four under Prime Minister Suga) against eighteen FMMs (three under Suga).

A new crisis arrived in early 2020 when COVID-19 broke out in the Chinese city of Wuhan. In addition to NMMs and FMMs, the EMM met nineteen times to deal with the pandemic, twice under Suga. The first pandemic-focused EMM, on 31 January, declared it an 'emergency' requiring inter-ministry/agency coordination. However, the Novel Coronavirus Response Headquarters (NCRH), not the NSC, became the centre of COVID-19 decision-making.[12] The NCRH membership mirrors the full Cabinet, reflecting the complex nature of the threat. Only border-control decisions were referred to the EMM for discussion, which happened twice. Otherwise, the EMM was held virtually, with documents sent to ministers for sign-off (*mochimawari*).

From January to October 2021, eighteen meetings were held, including *mochimawari* in the EMM, but FMMs dominated. There were two key themes. First, the 'Senkaku Islands' (Diaoyu in Chinese) issue was raised in the main FMM agenda twice. The islands are under Japan's administration, but China has claimed them since December 1971 and has sent coastguard ships to the waters near the islands to demonstrate its 'sovereignty' since December 2008. The frequency increased, even during the COVID-19 pandemic, and in January 2021 China passed legislation allowing its coastguard vessels to use weapons against foreign ships in water 'under Chinese administration', which includes the Senkakus and inside

---

[12] Prime Minister of Japan. *Shin gata koronauirusu kansen shō taisaku honbu* [Novel Coronavirus Response Headquarters], at www.kantei.go.jp/jp/singi/novel_coronavirus/taisaku_honbu.html, accessed 30 August 2021.

the South China Sea's nine-dash line.[13] Second, the 'Japan–US Alliance' was raised twice, while a Japan–US Security Consultative Committee (SCC/2 plus 2) meeting was held in Tokyo, and the Japan–US Leaders' meeting in Washington DC between Prime Minister Suga and President Biden discussed the regional security challenges posed by China.[14]

The FMM has gained prominence in dealing with Japan's most urgent threats, such as DPRK missile shots and nuclear developments. 'DPRK' appeared on NSC agendas fifty-three times, but 'China' only appeared once, even though it should have been discussed in NSC meetings looking at East Asia, Asia-Pacific and the Indo-Pacific. This reflects diplomatic consideration over wider Sino–Japanese relations. However, the priority afforded to the FMM also reflects a preference seen in the later years of Abe's Administration for small group decision-making that he, and his successors, could dominate.

The NSS

As the NSC's secretariat, the NSS conducts its staff work, but is not transparent: the staff work is confidential. However, the first NSS Secretary-General, Shōtarō Yachi's, public profile was very high. Yachi was Assistant Chief Cabinet Secretary when Abe was Deputy Cabinet Secretary in the Koizumi Administration. He was also the Administrative Vice-Minister for Foreign Affairs under the first Abe Administration. As a top diplomat extremely close to Abe, Yachi was seen as the most trusted and powerful diplomatic advisor. However, Yachi was a pro-US realist diplomat deeply rooted in history and realpolitik with a sober approach to China and Russia.[15] Abe on the other hand had a more romanticized right-wing idealism. Their relationship was compared to Henry Kissinger's NSA under President Richard Nixon.[16]

Yachi established strong relationships with NSAs in major countries, playing the role of Abe's diplomatic deputy by facilitating working-level communications with his foreign counterparts, particularly the United States.[17] Susan E. Rice, under President Barak Obama and Herbert R. McMaster and John Bolton under

---

[13] Kentaro Furuya (8 March 2021). *Challenges to the International Order: Implications for CCG Activity around the Senkaku Islands*, The Sasakawa Peace Foundation.

[14] David Brunnstrorm et.al. (16 April 2021). 'Biden and Japan's Suga Project Unity against China's Assertiveness.' *Reuters.*

[15] Giulio Pugliese (2017). 'Japan's Kissinger? Yachi Shōtarō: The State behind the Curtain', *Pacific Affairs*, vol. 90(2), 237–242.

[16] Pugliese, op. cit., 245

[17] Liff, op. cit., 269–270.

President Trump had frequent contact with him. John Bolton's memoirs mention close and frequent communication with Yachi, especially on DPRK and Iranian nuclear and missile issues.[18]

Yachi also worked with China and Russia. He established communication channels with State Minister Yang Jiechi, who was responsible for China's foreign and security policy. Sino–Japanese relations had become turbulent after the Senkaku Islands issue in 2012. Yachi organized a task force to achieve a 'détente' with his counterpart when Abe visited Beijing to join the Asia-Pacific Economic Cooperation (APEC) Leaders' Meeting in November 2014.[19] Yachi also initiated an annual 'Japan-China High-level Political Dialogue' with his counterpart, which continues under his successor.[20] With Russia, Yachi built a relationship with the Secretary of the Russian Security Council, Nikolai P. Patrushev.[21] Abe had ambitions to conclude the Japan–Russia Peace Treaty after 'solving' the issue of the Northern Territory of Hokkaido which, despite the Soviet–Japanese Neutrality Pact, was illegally invaded and occupied by the Soviet Union immediately before the Japanese surrender in August 1945. Yachi's remarks after his resignation, show he was not convinced that Russian President Vladimir Putin could return the islands that had been occupied by Russians for over seventy years. He felt Russia might simply benefit from economic cooperation with Japan and never return the islands.[22]

There were large differences between the NSC officials from MOFA, such as Yachi, and the *Kantei* officials,[23] who always accompanied Prime Minister Abe.

---

[18] John Bolton (2020). *The Room Where I Happened: A White House Memoir* (New York: Simon & Schuster), Chapters 4, 11, 12.

[19] Pugliese, op. cit., 248–250.

[20] Pugliese, op. cit., 250; (29 February 2020) 'Dai 8 kai haireberu seiji taiwa, Tokyo de kaisai' [The 8th Sino-Japanese High-Level Political Dialogue held in Tokyo], *Xinhua Net* at http://jp.xinhuanet.com/2020-02/29/c_138829722.htm, accessed 30 August 2021.

[21] (13 March 2014). 'NSC gaiko kappatsuni, Ukuraina kiki Yachi kyokuchō ga hōro'" [NSC Diplomacy is flourishing: Secretary Yachi Visits Russia When Ukraine Crisis Occurs], *Nikkei Shimbun*, at www.nikkei.com/article/DGXNASFS12036_S4A310C1PP8000/, accessed 30 August 2021.

[22] (24 January 2020). 'Yachi zen kokka anzen hoshō kyokuchō: Roshia wa mujoken teiketsu yokyu, heiwajoyaku kōshō de' [Former Secretary-General of the National Security Secretariat Yachi says 'Russia Requires Unconditional Conclusion of the Peace Treaty,' at the Peace Treaty Negotiations], *Sankei Shimbun* at www.sankei.com/politics/news/200124/plt2001240047-n1.html, accessed 30 August 2021.

[23] *Kantei* means Prime Minister's Office. *Kantei* officials are those who prefer to work at the Prime Minister's Office and have close personal relations with Prime Minister, rather than go back to their parent ministries and get promoted. They tend to work extremely long periods of time at *Kantei*. Aurelia George Mulgan, 'Kantei Diplomacy under the Abe Administration' in Lam Peng Er and Purnendra Jain eds. (2020). *Japan's Foreign Policy in the Twenty-First Century: Continuity and Change* (Lanham: Lexington Books). In the Abe Administration, reportedly, the *Kantei* bureaucrats were Takaya Imai (from MEITI), Hiroto Izumi (from MEITI), Eiichi Hasegawa (from MEITI), Shigeru Kitamura (from Police), Kazuhiro Sugita (from Police). There were no officials from the Foreign Ministry or Defense.

Abe's diplomatic goals included a peace treaty with Russia and Xi Jinping's state visit to Japan. However, both raised MOFA concerns, since Russia was sanctioned for its annexation of the Crimean Peninsula, and Sino–US strategic competition was about to break out. Xi's plan to visit Japan had been heavily criticized domestically, since China's Coast Guard was escalating intrusion into the territorial water and contiguous zone of the Senkaku Islands. Aware of MOFA's traditional pro-US viewpoints, sanctions-hit Russia, and China, suffering from a trade war with the United States, were attempting to use Japan to balance the United States. This could have triggered a negative reaction to Japan in the United States but the pro-Russia/China 'rapprochement' was promoted by the Executive Secretary to Prime Minister Takaya Imai (later, Special Advisor to the Prime Minister, 2019–2020) and Special Advisor to the Prime Minister, Eiichi Hasegawa, rather than the NSC.[24] Imai strongly supported economic cooperation with Russia and Xi Jinping's Belt and Road Initiative in China.[25] His pro-China/ Russia positions were criticized both at home and abroad.[26] Abe's diplomatic decision-making increasingly became inner-circle-oriented, while institutions such as the NSC began to be treated lightly by the Prime Minister.[27] Finally, Yachi left office in September 2019, and was succeeded by Shigeru Kitamura, who came not from the MOFA but the police intelligence community.

Conclusion

Japan's NSC mainly responds to external threats; the COVID-19 pandemic is not a major challenge; hence a separate system was used. It considers short-term threats and middle- to long-term planning, including preparation for future threats. In practice, however, its major mission has been to deal with crises, principally DPRK's missile launches and nuclear tests. Terrorist attacks and UN peacekeeping operations have also featured as major topics for the FMM. The frequency of NSC ministerial meetings drastically increased under the Abe administration, compared to the previous SC. The (small) FMM has become the core organization of the NSC, with intelligence on regional situations frequently

---

[24] Mulgan, op. cit., 80–81.
[25] Hiroshi Hoshi, (1 July 2017). 'Abe ikkyō wa kawarunoka' [Will the Situation of Abe-Commanding-Lead Change?], *Shūkan Tōyō Keizai*, 108.
[26] Devin Stewart (23 July 2020). *China's Influence in Japan: Everywhere Yet Nowhere in Particular*, Center for Strategic & International Studies, 16,
[27] Hoshi, op. cit., 108. Stewart, op. cit., 16.

shared in the meetings. The NMM mainly considers Defence planning and budgetary agendas. The NSA has also become one of the most important national security staff members in the Cabinet Secretariat. Shōtarō Yachi, the first NSA and NSS Secretary-General, played a significant role dealing with his counterparts in the United States and other nations thanks to his proximity to Prime Minister Abe, at first.

The current NSC was designed, established and operated under Prime Minister Abe, a rare politician with specific agendas concerning Japan's national security. Having created the system, however, even Abe began to slight NSC ministerial meetings after 2018, when his decision-making style tilted towards his personally closest staff in the *Kantei*. Prime Minister Suga was a more domestic-oriented politician, who appointed Takeo Akiba, a highly experienced career diplomat and former Vice Foreign Minister as the new NSS Secretary General. With Prime Minister Kishida being a former foreign minister, the MOFA appears to have regained a central role in foreign policy decision-making reflecting the deteriorating international security environment and ongoing Sino–US rivalry.[28] However, how the NSC functions in future national security and crisis management decision-making and coordination processes is unknown. Like Bismark, Abe's boots might be too big for ordinary feet; his successors must show similar political will to harness and utilize the NSC.

---

[28] Koji Sugimoto, Sankei Shimbun (8 July 2021). 'Takeo Akiba: What Does the Former Vice Minister Bring to Japan's National Security Secretariat?', *Japan Forward*.

12

Kenya's National Security Council: Balancing democratic control and executive power

Singo S. Mwachofi

Introduction

Kenya's National Security Council (NSC) has evolved significantly since independence from British colonial rule in 1963 through numerous political and constitutional changes. The most important developments were the security sector reforms beginning in 2009 through commissions of inquiry into the 2007/08 post-election violence.[1] The Commission of Inquiry by the UN Special Rapporteur Phillip Alston, the National Commission Report led by Phillip Waki, and the Kenya National Dialogue and Reconciliation process (which mediated peace) under former UN Secretary General Kofi Annan formed the basis of Kenya's security sector reforms. The cross-cutting principles behind reforming Kenya's security sector were the need for democratization, constitutional separation of political and security institutions, and safeguarding civilian control and oversight of security institutions to avoid overly powerful Executive control.

This chapter describes the threats Kenya faces before outlining the development of the current NSC, its functions, structure and processes, and then examines its effectiveness. In doing so, it charts a path from national security as a means of internal control, towards one whose design aims to safeguard the population from abuses by the state, accepting that in doing so, one form of (classic) security is sacrificed for another (democracy).

---

[1] The violence resulted in the deaths of over 1,000 people and the displacement of a further 600,000. See International Federation for Human Rights (FIDH)/Kenya Human Rights Commission (2017). *Kenya's scorecard on security and justice: Broken promises and unfinished business*, 6.

Kenya's security threats

Kenya takes a broad approach to national security, which covers, among others, corruption, terrorism, criminal activity (cyber, organized crime, drug trafficking etc.), climate change, gender-based violence and resource-based conflict. Unemployment, perceived marginalization, environmental degradation, technological advances, corruption, unhealthy political competition and negative ethnicity are all considered important.[2] While the threats are both internal and external, internal threats dominate routine NSC activity, even though few have the potential to cause state-wide instability in the short term. Corruption, inter-communal conflicts and proliferation of illicit weapons typically occupy the NSC's attention. Other internal threats only occasionally influence NSC meetings and decisions. The NSC thus appears to have mostly short- and mid-term focus on internal threats.

External threats, including military threats, terrorism and the threat to the country's territorial integrity occupy the NSC at a more serious level than internal threats. Military threats do not currently pose a high-alert risk, hence the NSC focuses mostly on terrorism (al-Shabaab) and the threat to territorial integrity especially the Kenya–Somalia maritime dispute, the Kenya–Uganda Migingo island dispute, the demarcation of the Kenya–Tanzania boundary, and the question of the Ilemi Triangle. Regional disputes also occupy its time, primarily the conflicts between Ethiopia–Sudan, the political crisis in Somalia, Rwanda, and the delicate transition and peace in Sudan and South Sudan respectively. Kenya has thus been a leading recipient of asylum seekers and refugees/internationally displaced persons, and constantly under threat of wars and the conflicts in neighbouring countries spilling over.[3] The NSC considers external threats over the short, mid and long term. Responding to the threats requires a multi-agency approach for coordinating and collaborating among security agencies, led by the NSC, which formally defines and measures national security threats annually.

Evolution of the NSC

Before independence, national security was the responsibility of the British Colonial government. Represented by the Governor, and, serving the interests of

---

[2] President of Kenya (2020). *Annual Report to Parliament on the State of National Security*, ix.
[3] Republic of Kenya (2017). *Defence White Paper*, Part II.

the Crown in London, it sought to exploit the country's resources. It was frequently brutal, abusive and intolerant of the rights and freedoms of the native Africans. National security depended on maintaining law and order, usually through subjugation, oppression and human rights abuses. Its primary goal, and that of the national security institutions, was to subdue and enforce compliance of the population.

The first post-independence constitution was adopted in 1963.[4] Article 158 created the NSC comprising the Security Minister, Chairs of the seven Regional Assemblies' Law and Order Committees, the Commissioner of Police and a representative of Nairobi Area. Regional Commissioners of Police could attend as advisors to the regional Law and Order Committee chairs. The Security Minister was responsible for summoning and presiding over the Council, whose decisions were arrived at through a majority vote. The Inspector General of Police, the Regional Commissioners of Police and the representative of Nairobi Area were not entitled to vote.

The new government moved quickly to amend the constitution, removing the authority of the British Crown and designing a presidential political system. An Office of the President was created and the regional assemblies abolished. Subsequent amendments replaced the decision-making NSC with a National Advisory Council to advise the President on the management of national security and national security policies.[5] The gradual emergence of a one-party imperial presidency, under President Jomo Kenyatta (1963–1978) then President Daniel Moi (1978–2002), consolidated power. All national security matters became the preserve of the President; while there were ministers in charge of internal security and defence, these were within the Office of the President.

The repeal of section 2A of the 1963 Constitution in 1992 paved the way for reintroducing multiparty politics and gave a sense that the country was ready to reform the security sector. However, it was only when President Kibaki was democratically elected in 2003 that Kenya began to enjoy sweeping democratic reforms. Kibaki rapidly embarked on an ambitious plan for reforming the security sector, first targeting the police. Recruitment was massively increased, salaries, remuneration and general welfare improved, equipment modernized, and the training curriculum reviewed to incorporate human rights' education

---

[4] Kenya Gazette Supplement No. 105 (10 December 1963). Statutory Instruments 1963 No. 1968. The Kenya Independence Order in Council 1963. Schedule 2, Constitution of the Republic of Kenya, 1963.

[5] Francis Omondi Ogolla (2014). *Determinants of Kenya's national security policy since independence.* Masters Dissertation, University of Nairobi.

and awareness. For the first time since independence, police officers began to respect citizen's rights and freedoms rather than being a tool of oppression. Other reforms included reviewing the 'use of force' provisions and the Police Act, creating an independent National Police Service (replacing the politicized National Police Force), and institutionalizing police accountability through an independent civilian oversight institution.[6] But while the Kibaki government started positively in terms of security sector reforms, corruption and nepotism persisted. A number of scandals erupted in the course of his first term in office,[7] and all key security institutions were filled by members of his Kikuyu tribe, which eroded his credibility as a president committed to instituting equality and equity in the public service.[8]

The constitution still conferred excessive power on security organs and the Executive, and increased their opacity, allowing interference with democratic processes by the security agencies under the president's control. Following the 2007–08 post-election violence, a power deal negotiated by the international community saved the country from collapse and ushered in a coalition government where power was shared between President Kibaki and Prime Minister Raila Odinga, 2002's opposition candidate whose supporters believed the Presidential elections had been rigged. The coalition government continued the path of security sector reforms. An important milestone was the 2010 Constitution. It democratized the NSC by placing it under civilian control, made its processes open and transparent, diversified its membership and ensured its accountability to Parliament.[9] Corruption scandals, however, plagued both sides of the coalition government.[10]

NSC functions, structure, composition and processes

The 2010 Constitution (Article 240) establishes the modern NSC to exercise supervisory control over the national security organs and serve as a coordinating body for integration of domestic, foreign and military policies regarding national

---

[6] ICTJ Briefing (2010). *Security Sector Reform and Transitional Justice in Kenya*.
[7] See: David McGuffin (14 February 2006). 'Corruption Scandals Rock Kenyan Leadership'. *NPR*; AP Nairobi (8 July 2004). 'Scandals Then and Now'. *The Economist*.
[8] National Cohesion and Integration Commission (2012). Towards National Cohesion and Unity in Kenya: Ethnic Diversity and Audit of the Civil Service, vol. 1.
[9] Republic of Kenya (2010). *Constitution of Kenya*, Chapter 14.
[10] Derek Kilner (2 November 2009). 'Corruption Charges Pose Latest Challenge to Kenya Coalition'. *VOA News*.

security for purposes of inter-agency cooperation. It is also charged with assessing and appraising the objectives, commitments and risks to the republic in respect of actual and potential national capabilities.[11] Accountability to civilian control and oversight is achieved by mandating the NSC reports to Parliament, which it does annually through the 'State of National Security Report'.[12] Parliament can also demand that the NSC reports on any issue or matter related to NSC functions or national security.[13]

The National Security Council Act 2012 also directs the NSC to:

- review policy matters relating to national security;
- develop priority programs for internal, defence and foreign interests;
- review security policy from time to time;
- identify strategies for security organs to respond to internal and external threats;
- review internal, defence and foreign focus areas; and
- receive reports from security organs on the implementation of the Council's policy directives.[14]

The NSC comprises: the President (chair); Deputy President; the Cabinet Secretaries for Defence, Foreign Affairs and Internal Security; Attorney General; Chief of Kenya Defence Forces; Director General National Intelligence Service; and Inspector General of the National Police Service. The largely civilian membership of top-ranking civil servants and their numerical voting power, ensures the NSC is firmly under civilian control. The NSC can also co-opt other experts as necessary, although they have no voting powers.[15] The representation of key government departments, while creating a large body with costly budgetary and procedural implications, allows for bargaining between departments to achieve rational decisions. The NSC must meet at least four times every financial year, not more than four months apart. The President, as chair, may convene special sessions in accordance with emerging developments of significance to national security.[16] The NSC is further allowed to establish committees to assist in achieving its objectives, as well as enhance the effectiveness with which the NSC works (see Figure 12.1).

---

[11] 2010 Constitution, op. cit.
[12] 2010 Constitution, op. cit., Art. 240(7).
[13] National Security Council Act 2012, s. 16.
[14] National Security Council Act, s. 4.
[15] National Security Council Act, s. 5(2).
[16] National Security Council Act, First Schedule.

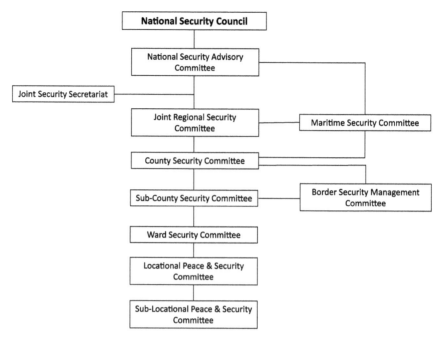

Figure 12.1 Kenya's NSC Structure.[17]

The NSC is supported by the National Security Advisory Committee (NSAC) which, because Kenya does not have a national security advisor, is headed by the Head of the Public Service. The composition of the NSAC is not clearly defined but includes top public servants in the security sector, especially at ministerial and departmental levels. The NSAC role is purely advisory and its resolutions are fashioned as proposals to the NSC and Cabinet. The NSAC receives information from the subordinate security committees, which it analyses to better advise the NSC on security policy decisions.[18] The NSAC also receives information on border and maritime security from the Border Security Management Committee and Maritime Security Committee. In essence, the NSAC acts as the nerve centre for information from all levels of the national government administration structure (formerly the Provincial Administration) that impact on the country's security policy. The NSAC is the NSC's internal think-tank, but lacks the mandate to exercise executive authority. When, in October 2020, the NSAC issued directives barring political gatherings as a

[17] Kennedy Mkutu, Martin Marani and Mutuma Ruteere (July 2014). *Securing the Counties: Options for Security after Devolution in Kenya*. Centre for Human Rights and Policy Studies, 23.
[18] Mkutu, op. cit.

measure to contain the spread of COVID-19, the High Court quashed the directives as illegal and unconstitutional.[19]

Looking at the NSC's composition, functions and role, it is clearly designed to be the most powerful security organ in the country, with access to the most senior decision-makers in government. It shapes, defines and coordinates the country's security priorities, strategies and policies – at least since the National Security Council Act 2012 took effect to operationalize the NSC. Other government departments implement the security directives from the NSC and report to it on progress, which then reports to Parliament. The NSC thus monitors performance in other departments and by so doing seeks to provide a coordinated approach and action across departments charged with national security matters. The NSC, however, also seeks the input of civilian experts and external think tanks to allow it to access diverse knowledge as well as acting on synthesized intelligence and security analysis by government agencies.

The NSC is in charge of a broad spectrum of threats, which ordinarily would be difficult to manage effectively in the four meetings it must hold annually. However, the NSC's structure allows it to function and respond to threats on a daily basis through a Secretariat, the NSAC, the Border Security Management Committee, Maritime Security Committee and Security Sub-Committees at various levels. The NSC thus functions through the national government administrative structures until the NSC meets ordinarily or when a significant national security matter arises warranting a special meeting. Other committees can also be set up for specific purposes. For COVID-19, a National Emergency Response Committee on Coronavirus was created under the Cabinet Secretary for Health. Its membership included those on the NSC and also brought in other relevant departments.[20] Nevertheless, the NSC retained executive authority, approving lockdowns and other key measures.[21]

The NSC also controls the information accessible to the public on matters of national security and the Council's affairs through the Oath of Secrecy and regulations developed by the Council allowing the respective Cabinet Secretary (for Defence or Internal Security) to 'classify and declassify' government documents.[22] However, civilian oversight and control over how the NSC manages

---

[19] Kamau Muthoni (18 August 2021). 'Police should not take orders from National Security Advisory team, court says'. *The Standard Media*.
[20] President of Kenya (28 February 2020). Executive Order No. 2 of 2020: National Emergency Response Committee on Coronavirus.
[21] President of Kenya (26 March 2021). Fifteenth Presidential Address on the Coronavirus Pandemic.
[22] National Security Council Act, ss. 13(1) and 14.

information subjects the Council's regulations for classifying documents to Parliamentary approval.[23]

The NSC, however, does not have budgetary powers over other departments, and is itself restricted to utilizing the budget allocated to the Office of the President. This means that it depends on others to allocate the resources needed to deliver its decisions.

Efficiency of the NSC

It is clear that concerns remain over the risks of too powerful a security system that could oppress Kenya's citizens; a legacy of colonial rule and the first two Presidents. Consequently, the power given to the NSC to react to threats is constrained. While it has performed relatively well in holding the delicate balance between security goals, human rights and the democratic space, it has performed poorly in dealing with security issues such as the long-running territorial questions, countering al-Shabaab, and addressing mega corruption.

The NSC is seen by the public as weak in defending Kenya's territorial integrity. The Kenya–Somalia maritime dispute and Migingo Island dispute with Uganda remain unresolved after thirteen years and public anxiety is growing. Kenya's decision in March 2021 to prematurely withdraw from the International Court of Justice final proceedings against Somalia over the maritime boundary has created worry among the public. The Migingo dispute still has no end in sight. Since 2009, the Ugandan military has asserted sovereignty over the Island but there has been no active diplomatic or political engagement by either country to find a lasting solution to the contested ownership of the tiny island. Migingo appears to be a matter that neither the leadership in Kampala nor Nairobi has been keen to resolve. This could be that neither government sees it as a serious territorial issue between them – every time it flares up, usually in the arrest of Kenyan policemen by Ugandan authorities, it soon fizzles out – but the public do not appear as relaxed.

Success against al-Shabaab is also limited. Al Shabaab is resurgent in Somalia and continues to carry out attacks inside Kenya and invaded Kenya's Boni Forest near the Kenya–Somalia border. The NSC deployed the military to Boni Forest in 2015 (*Operation Linda Boni*) with the initial goal of removing al-Shabaab in ninety days. Nearly six years later, the operation is still underway, and the Kenyan

---

[23] National Security Council Act, s. 13(2).

military appears to be struggling despite the NSC's efforts, including deploying the military to Somalia as part of the African Union Mission (AMISOM).[24]

Corruption remains a serious concern, with Kenya estimated to lose about 30 per cent of its annual budget to corruption,[25] in which key security organs represented in the NSC are implicated as among the most corrupt institutions.[26] Such a scale of corruption bears significant long-term implications on the country's security and economic development. It also hinders attempts to address other security issues, such as counter-terrorism.[27] With high levels of corruption in the police, the military is increasingly being used in domestic security, but with less democratic oversight.[28] Despite the threat, it is argued that some of those in power do not take the fight against corruption seriously enough and are among those who benefit most.[29]

Conclusion

Kenya's NSC is a necessary coordination, supervisory and decision-making body on national security matters. The fact that the constitution creates, defines and provides for civilian control and oversight of the NSC protects the democratic space and individual rights and freedoms of citizens from being trampled by 'national security' exigencies or an overbearing Executive. The current NSC is institutionally accountable to the public for its conduct, performance and powers, which has helped to democratize the security sector and make national security decisions inclusive. This has increased openness and transparency in the affairs of national security and promotes the public image and trust in the most powerful security organ in the country. However, problems remain. In attempting to protect the public from abuses of power, the NSC remains constrained in its ability to deliver security. The absence of a dedicated National

---

[24] Andrew McGregor (27 October 2017). 'How Kenya's Failure to Contain an Islamist Insurgency is Threatening Regional Prosperity.' *Terrorism Monitor*, vol. 15(20).

[25] The East African. (15 November 2020). Theft of public funds by Kenya govt officials doubles to $1.4b. *The East African*.

[26] Kenya Corruption Report (August 2020) at www.ganintegrity.com/portal/country-profiles/kenya/, accessed 30 August 2021.

[27] Narrelle Gilchrist and Norman Eisen (22 August 2019). *Corruption and Terrorism: The Case of Kenya*. Brookings Institution.

[28] FIDH/Kenya Human Rights Commission (July 2017). *Kenya's Scorecard on Security and Justice: Broken Promises and Unfinished Business*, 6.

[29] Rael Ombour (11 December 2019). 'Is Kenya's Government Fighting Corruption or Just Conducting Political Theatre?'. *VOA News*.

Security Advisor is part of this, although the Head of the Public Service is supported in their security role by the NASC and a secretariat. The NSC's transparency is still limited, although the degree of secrecy is subject to approval by Parliament. Corruption too remains a weakness, with the police widely seen as among the most corrupt institutions in the country. Aside from undermining confidence in national security, it also leads to greater domestic use of the military, even though civilian oversight of the military is weaker. The NSC needs to establish mechanisms for building the capacity of national security institutions to effectively respond to national security threats, improve their performance and achieve short-, mid- and long-term security goals.

13

New Zealand: Small but integrated

Jim Rolfe

In the beginning

Until 1987 New Zealand had an almost completely ad hoc approach to dealing with national security issues, then primarily focused on defence, intelligence and terrorism matters. A Defence Council integrated defence-related advice for the government, an Intelligence Council did the same on intelligence matters, and an officials' terrorism committee coordinated preparation for and responses to terrorism. Natural disasters were managed by a separate Ministry of Civil Defence.[1]

Following the 1985 attack on the Greenpeace vessel *Rainbow Warrior* in Auckland Harbour, and a 1986 exercise testing terrorism responses, the cabinet approved a paper recommending a centralized mechanism that would 'review and coordinate domestic and external security policy'.[2] There would be a coordinating mechanism responsible to the Prime Minister and a security-focused cabinet committee. Eventually, this would sit within what is now the Department of the Prime Minister and Cabinet (DPMC) and would prepare for a range of issues, ranging from military threats and threats of espionage, sabotage or subversion, through threats to public order to various physical hazards, both from within (such as seismic activity) and of external origin (for example, pandemics). The defined threats and hazards were quite conventional in their depiction, although expansive for the time.

The paper also defined the principles behind the new national security system. It was to be: comprehensive (beyond defence and terrorism); afforded

---

[1] When established in 1959, the Ministry of Civil Defence's main focus was protection from nuclear attack as a consequence of global war, but the focus turned to natural disasters from 1964.
[2] New Zealand Government (13 May 1987). 'A National Security Policy for New Zealand'. Office of the Coordinator of Domestic and External Security, *Domestic and External Security Policy and Objectives*, a paper for the Cabinet Committee on Domestic and External Security.

reserve emergency powers (e.g. to quarantine people or places in bio-security or medical emergencies); allocated resources in a timely manner; and centrally coordinated. The coordinating mechanism was small: three or four including the Coordinator. This fitted the prevailing approach of light-handed oversight and lasted until 2014–15 when a significant build-up of capabilities began reflecting a new philosophy requiring active and centralized management.

Much of the system remains in place with today's operating processes and principles recognizably descended from 1987. There are also many differences. The range of issues considered and scope of central coordination are vastly greater, as too is the size of the coordinating structure. Numerous reviews of DPMC's role as the focal point of the national security system, of the secret intelligence agencies and their authorities and relationships with other components of the system, and of the management and governance of security emergencies and natural disaster led to significant changes to structure and process between 2010 and 2019.[3]

The national security system

National security has been formally defined since 2011 as:

> the condition which permits the citizens of a state to go about their daily business confidently free from fear and able to make the most of opportunities to advance their way of life. It encompasses the preparedness, protection and preservation of people, and of property and information, both tangible and intangible.[4]

This definition has two parts. First, an enabling approach to security, and second a protective one. These might be described as 'business as usual' on one hand, with actions focused on making the country a better place for its residents and preparing for future emergencies, and 'emergency management' on the other, where routine processes are discarded for emergency ones. The system's structure, processes and work plans must be able to operate across the full range of likely conditions, including sovereignty, public safety, economic prosperity and protection of the natural environment.

National security requires both that citizens be protected and their lifestyle preserved. This leads to a continuum of security activity of risk reduction,

---

[3] The author estimates between thirty and forty 'security-related' reviews were conducted in this period. The number varies according to the definition of 'security-related'.

[4] DPMC (August 2016). *National Security System Handbook*, 7.

readiness, response and recovery (the '4Rs'), in which a 'lead agency' has 'the primary mandate for managing the hazard or risk' across the 4Rs spectrum.[5] Lead agencies are those with a statutory role (e.g. the Ministry of Health for public health events, or the Ministry for Primary Industries for food safety) or those identified as a matter of policy (and logic) to take the lead, e.g. the Ministry for Primary Industries for drought management.[6]

Central management

Today, the central management system has between forty and fifty people at its core, which is not large by most international standards. It has two distinct but equally important roles in achieving the enabling and reactive components of national security: governance and crisis response.[7] Overall, the system aims to support ministers under all circumstances by providing 'consistent advice', whether during business-as-usual periods or emergencies.[8] That advice is based on the routine working and preparation of the system and its agencies.

Underpinning the system is legislation that authorizes the activities of the intelligence agencies, the National Emergency Management Agency,[9] and specific agencies (such as Defence, Police, Health or Primary Industries) to deal with security within their own areas of responsibility. This legislation covers both routine activities and emergency powers and actions for which specific triggers are established.

Political direction and system oversight is given by the External Relations and Security Committee of Cabinet (Cabinet ERS). The Committee's mandate is to give:

> Oversight of the national security and intelligence sector…, resilience, and significant hazards. Coordinate and direct national responses to major crises or circumstances affecting national security (either domestic or international).[10]

The Cabinet Committee is supported by senior officials in the Officials' Committee for Domestic and External Security Coordination (ODESC), which

---

5   DPMC Handbook, 19.
6   DPMC Handbook, 22–23.
7   DPMC (20 October 2017), *Briefing to the Incoming Minister for National Security and Intelligence*, 8.
8   DPMC, *Briefing*, 11.
9   Until 2019 called the Ministry of Civil Defence and Emergency Management.
10 DPMC (December 2020). Cabinet Office Circular CO20(9). Cabinet Committees: Terms of Reference and Membership at https://dpmc.govt.nz/publications/co-20-9-cabinet-committees-terms-reference-and-membership-html#section-7, accessed 30 August 2021.

has the system-wide governance role and takes the lead in advising the government on responses for national security events. Chaired by the Chief Executive[11] of the DPMC, its standing membership comprises chief executives from across the state sector.[12] For specific issues ODESC co-opts other agencies as necessary. The chair of ODESC is, in effect, the government's national security adviser. ODESC meets as required: seventeen times in 2018–19.

Alongside ODESC are two senior boards, the Security and Intelligence Board and the Hazard Risk Board. These boards are responsible for ensuring resilience within the system for 'traditional' (normally state-based threats) and less traditional security matters respectively.

Supporting ODESC is a 'National Security Group' within DPMC, and a range of working groups, committees, watch groups and boards, each focusing on a specific security requirement and responding to and helping formulate ODESC requirements.[13] The structure and the related mechanisms are analogous to the National Security Council adopted by many countries. The central structure is shown at Figure 13.1.

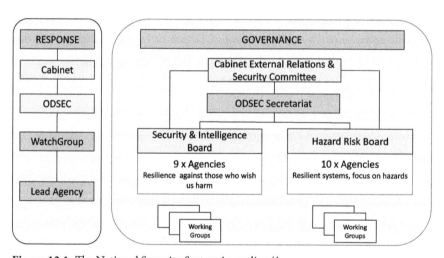

Figure 13.1 The National Security System in outline.[14]

[11] The term 'chief executive' for a public agency or department equates to 'permanent head', 'permanent (under) secretary', 'secretary', or similar in other jurisdictions.

[12] ODESC membership is described in the DPMC *Handbook*, 15.

[13] DPMC Handbook, 15–18 gives more detail.

[14] Source: DPMC *National Security Governance System* at *https://dpmc.govt.nz/our-programmes/national-security-and-intelligence/new-zealands-national-security-system/national-1*, which amends the diagram in the DPMC Handbook, op. cit.

Working together: lead agencies and the centralized system

The centralized system enables and supports detailed activity by the lead agencies and agencies supporting the lead agency.[15] During business as usual, lead agencies work with supporting agencies to promote security in the areas for which they are responsible, develop risk reduction measures and prepare for security events. The results of their planning are seen in a range of reports and plans for possible events.[16]

In 2018 the government approved sixteen national intelligence and security priorities.[17] These range alphabetically from 'bio-security and human health' to 'transnational organized crime' and cover, as with the hazards identified in 1987, both domestic and external potential threats.[18]

Supporting the preparedness and readiness activities, a national exercise programme practises agencies in specific facets of security management in emergency conditions. In 2019–20, exercises were held dealing with terrorism, regional insecurity and bio-security. Two or three major exercises with different scenarios are scheduled annually.

Issues become immediately important for the national security system if one of the core objectives faces a hazard that 'might adversely and systemically affect' sovereignty, people, the economy, the environment, or the effective functioning of the community, against set criteria.[19] During emergencies, or concerns about future emergencies, 'watch groups' are initiated by the lead agency or DPMC. These function normally at deputy chief executive level and have authority to commit their agency. Their role is to support the lead agency in developing and initiating plans to respond to emergencies and to act as a filter for ODESC activity. In 2018–19, watch groups met fifty-four times.

Some emergencies require an immediate response, which might have to be provided by whichever agency is closest to hand. For this, a Coordinated Incident Management System (CIMS – similar to systems in North America and Australia) is used to provide 'a framework of consistent principles, structures, functions, processes and terminology that agencies can apply in an emergency response'.[20] CIMS is the basis for a response by any agency in any form of emergency at any level of activity, and all emergency services are trained in its practices and procedures.

---

[15] DPMC Handbook, 19–20 and 38.
[16] DPMC Handbook, 47–49.
[17] DPMC (2019). *Annual Report 2018/19 for the year ended 30 June 2019*, Appendices, 85.
[18] DPMC *Handbook*, 15. By September 2021, the national risk register had still not been approved for publication.
[19] DPMC, *Handbook*. 11.
[20] New Zealand Government (2019). *The New Zealand Coordinated Incident Management System*, 3rd edition. (Wellington: Officials' Committee for Domestic and External Security Coordination).

Who rules, who controls?

Almost without dissent the centre, through the ODESC, controls the agenda (to the extent that events don't overtake it), the priorities accorded to issues and processes and in some cases, resources. This control is not all-encompassing. ODESC has no mandate to make explicit budgetary trade-offs between choices, e.g. over new military equipment or schools or hospitals, each of which could be considered a 'security matter' given New Zealand's expansive definition of security. Budget setting is a separate issue managed within Cabinet and between the Treasury and individual agencies. This centralization is reinforced culturally by widely accepted notions of 'all of government' and 'joined-up' activity that make independent action by any one agency against the group almost unthinkable.[21]

Although central control is a given, the ODESC chair cannot rule by fiat. He or she is just one (although clearly first) among equals. The other chief executive members of ODESC have their own legislative mandate and minister with whom they can raise issues if they believe the system itself is heading in the wrong direction or if they believe their own agency is being unreasonably disadvantaged. Political resolution of differences is possible, but the strong preference is to be able to resolve inter-agency conflict at the ODESC official level rather than through political processes.

Ultimately, politicians not officials make the substantive decisions. This is seen during non-emergency periods when contingency plans are prepared and formally agreed by ministers. During emergencies, when ODESC and watch groups may meet daily, significant decisions are, again, made by ministers on the advice of ODESC.[22]

Responding to COVID-19

New Zealand's national security system was formally watching the pandemic's development overseas from January 2020 and preparing contingency plans. By

---

[21] The terms 'all of government' and 'joined up' are used throughout the *National Security System Handbook* in a variety of contexts, all reinforcing the notions of collegiality and cooperation rather than bureaucratic competition between agencies.

[22] Seen most recently during the COVID-19 pandemic: major decisions around quarantine, border controls and economic consequences were made and announced by the Prime Minister supported by Health and Finance ministers, and senior officials. These decisions were debated exhaustively within ODESC before advice was given to the government.

February, officials had determined that any outbreak in New Zealand would be complex, would involve all elements of the economy and society, and would have a significant international dimension. They concluded that if a New Zealand response were to be necessary, the 'standard' model of ODESC working through a single lead agency responsible for coordinating the response would need adaptation or replacement.

Once the country was placed in lockdown from late March, the pandemic response built on the standard emergency management model rather than replacing it. An all-of-government controller (with wide statutory authorities) was appointed, supported by four senior functional positions: the Director-General of Health; the Director of Civil Defence and Emergency Management; an operations commander (a Deputy Commissioner of Police, later replaced by the newly retired Commissioner) and a strategy and policy leader – also a senior civil servant. Known as the Quint, this group was responsible for day-to-day management of the response. Beneath them, work-streams covered all aspects of governmental activity, each with a lead agency controller.

The Quint reported, depending on the issue, through the ODESC system, or directly to a COVID-19 Ministerial Group, which was empowered by Cabinet to act without further reference to cabinet. The ODESC system itself remained in place to carry on the routine, non-pandemic security-related business of government.

For the immediate response and in the months following, the system worked. There were several reasons for this. The first was the government's prudential response, privileging public health advice as being directly related to national well-being, including the well-being of the economy. This was encapsulated in the 'go early, go hard' catch phrase. The second was because the concept of 'all-of-government' approaches with an emphasis on agreed outcomes, cooperation and coordination is an approach that has been central to New Zealand's public policy processes for some time and is well understood. Within the all-of-government concept, the security sector (the core of the pandemic response) has trained and exercised together for the best part of a decade.[23] The senior people generally know each other, have worked with each other and implicitly

---

[23] However, an independent committee highlighted how the Ministry of Health had not worked as effectively as possible within the system: '*Without exception government agencies we spoke to expressed concern at their inability to be "heard" by the Ministry of Health*'. New Zealand Government (28 September 2020). *Report of Advisory Committee to Oversee the Implementation of the New Zealand COVID-19 Surveillance Plan and Testing Strategy*, 8. Notably, the Ministry of Health is not a core security sector agency and consequently less familiar with the norms of collaboration developed within the sector.

understand and accept the system. Finally, as part of its national culture, New Zealand is a law-abiding country by inclination, tending to put the needs of the group ahead of those of the individual; that approach was memorialized in the idea of the 'team of five million'.

Of course, the pandemic response was not perfect; it was a new issue, in the detail at least, and officials had not explicitly thought through the needs of a response that had to provide security for the whole country. Decisions were made pragmatically, with the question 'will it work?' always hanging. Where specific decisions were not working, they were changed. Normally, the second iteration worked, although the long-term consequences of many decisions, for example almost universal wage subsidies lasting six months, will take time to play out. They are, in any case, a political rather than security system issue.

Does the system work?

New Zealand's national security system has been in place since 1987, and largely in its current form since 2014. It is designed and structured both for long-term readiness and sustainability and for immediate or short-notice response, and works in the background continually. It has been activated for emergencies or potential emergencies many times (in 2018–19 some seventy-one times),[24] and is exercised regularly. We should note that an 'activation' could be limited to a watch group convening and deciding that no further central action is necessary, although individual agencies may well be working in the field.[25]

Not all activations have gone smoothly and sometimes claims have been made that if the system had worked properly it would not have had to be activated.[26]

---

[24] E.g.: 2011 Christchurch earthquake; 2015 threat of malicious poison contamination of infant formula; 2015 Ebola viral disease readiness and possible Ebola case; 2016 contamination of a small town water supply and consequent campylobacter outbreak; 2017 Disruption of fuel supplies to Auckland; 2019 terrorist attack on Christchurch mosque.

[25] DPMC *Handbook*, 31.

[26] E.g., following the 2019 terrorist attack on a Christchurch mosque, claims were made that the national security system should have been aware of the possibility and prevented the attack. Royal Commission of Inquiry (26 November 2020). *Report of the Royal Commission of Inquiry into the terrorist attack on Christchurch masjidain on 15 March 2019*. Of 40+ recommendations, several relate to the national security system and surrounding machinery of government. The most significant for this chapter is a recommendation that a 'new national intelligence and security agency' be established (Recommendation 2, p. 732). Although there is a list of suggestions about its roles, the agency is not discussed within the broader context of the national security system. The government, in its formal response, has indicated that it agrees in principle with the recommendation but further consideration is required: Department of the Prime Minster (8 December 2020). *Documents Relating to the Government's Response to the Royal Commission of Inquiry into the terrorist attack on Christchurch masjidain*.

Whether or not a specific emergency response is considered successful, a lessons-identified exercise is conducted for all significant system activations. Sometimes this is done by the lead agency and supporting agencies, sometimes by an external and independent auditor and sometimes a formal inquiry will be held, perhaps taking evidence from the public. These reports directly impact on the system's operations by being incorporated in structures or processes.

The 'all hazards' approach to planning is important. This does not mean a 'one size fits all solution' is necessary; instead, it requires lead agencies' to consider what might affect their component of the system and develop sensible plans to prepare and respond. This involves working collectively with counterparts in other affected agencies. However, analysis of all hazards can tend to concentrate on the more probable (in New Zealand, earthquakes for example) rather than on the less probable (invasion or nation-wide drought), which may have equally devastating or long-term effects. It may also be that there is more emphasis on protective and responsive security than on positive or enabling security, or on risk reduction. Managing these tendencies, to the extent they are a factor, is a function of the central system.

In general, the system is one that all participants are happy with and, if it were not already extant, would have to be developed. In 2016 the Auditor-General found that 'in my view, the governance arrangements for responding to national security events and emergencies are well established, fundamentally sound, and fit for purpose'.[27]

---

[27] Controller and Auditor General (15 November 2016). *Governance of the National Security System*, Report B.29, 3.

14

Disjointed security: Assessing Norway's national security sector

Anders Romarheim

Norway's national security architecture lacks a clear top node. Adding a National Security Council, a National Security Advisor and a shared understanding of what 'national security' constitutes would improve matters, but to succeed the political will for reform must markedly exceed the bureaucracy's inherent inertia and opposition to cross-sectoral change.

To Norway, 22 July 2011 (22/7) is a date tarnished by bloodshed and terrorism. In history's worst act of solo-terrorism, carnage was brought to Oslo's streets and the remote island, Utøya. While the macabre shooting spree on Utøya was quite sophisticated and innovative, a car-bomb against Norway's foremost symbol of power was both foreseeable and preventable. The tragedy forced Norway to ask painful questions and thoroughly reassess its national security.

A grand public inquiry was established to examine what happened, why, and crucially, to prevent anything similar happening again.[1] 'Never again' became an auto-therapeutic phrase used across society. Historically loaded, it came from the Norwegian experience of foreign invasion in 1940.[2] The Gjørv Commission duly delivered, explaining in meticulous detail the horrific events that unfolded on that rainy summer's day. As a diagnosis of a partly dysfunctional security system and its preparedness, the report brought much-needed clarity. However, the Commission had little impact in changing the upper echelons of Norway's security sector. Indeed, it argued such reform was unlikely to improve national security. In its view, the overarching problem lay in a feeble security culture and

---

[1] The Gjørv Commission's Report (2012) states the inquiry was to establish 'What happened on 22 July? Why did it happen? And more fundamentally: How could our society have let this happen?', 13. At www.regjeringen.no/no/dokumenter/nou-2012-14/id697260/, accessed 6 December 2021.
[2] Nina Berglund (9 April 2010). 'Never again the Ninth of April', NewsinEnglish.no.

poor leadership.[3] These, it felt, could be addressed without significant structural change to the security architecture.

My conclusion is the opposite; the nation missed its best chance to overhaul a security apparatus that failed to protect its populace and leadership. A structural overhaul would add value and is badly needed: Norway lacks a sector-independent impartial arbitrator to overcome gridlocks, assuage security concerns and forge cross-sectoral and holistic national security policy. The interagency in-fighting that left the Office of the Prime Minister vulnerable to attack still exists. Furthermore, structures, and the formal apportionment of political power and resources are tools by which security culture and leadership can be enhanced. Institutions and structures may themselves help create the culture the Commission recognized was absent.

Norway regularly adopts security measures adequate to the task, yet as the Gjørv Commission found, decisions tend to take too long.[4] This is exacerbated because there is no government body that exercises horizontal authority to leverage broad security policy across departments, other than the Prime Minister. Needless to say, the PM has limited time for the demanding task of running the national security apparatus and needs support.

The term 'national security' itself is unclear, and was little used in government before Norway's main security law was re-labelled as a law on national security in January 2019.[5] The phrase in vogue is '*Samfunnssikkerhet*', meaning societal security. It is a very – arguably too – broad concept of security, including safety and security dimensions, e.g. safety regulations for ferries, and fire protection. However, it has state security at its core, and bears some resemblance to the US concept of homeland security. In a recent white paper on societal security, national security is defined as state security plus essential aspects of societal security.[6] The absence of a broadly accepted and precise notion of national security hampers understanding and action.

Sometimes it appears that advances in national security occur *despite*, rather than because of, the system. As Magnus Håkenstad observed: 'Norway's security

---

[3] Gjørv concludes 'In the opinion of the Commission, these lessons learned are to a greater extent applicable to leadership, interaction, culture and attitudes, than to a lack of resources, a need for new legislation, organisation or important value choices.' Op. cit., 16.

[4] '22/7 exposed formidable vulnerabilities that were a result of inadequate or slow implementation of already adopted measures, and of plans that were to some extent highly germane, not being used', Gjørv, op. cit., 17.

[5] 'Act relating to national security' (2019), at: https://lovdata.no/dokument/NLE/lov/2018-06-01-24, accessed 6 December 2021.

[6] Societal Security White Paper (2020). *Samfunnssikkerhet i en usikker verden: Melding til Stortinget No.5 (2020–2021)*, 11. At www.regjeringen.no/no/dokumenter/meld.-st.-5-20202021/id2770928/?is=true&q=#match_0, accessed 6 December 2021.

system should not in theory work well. Yet, in practice it does.'[7] Norway's security sector has capable people working an imperfect system diligently. This chapter examines Norway's security architecture, how the system works, including some of its shortcomings, before considering Norway's COVID-19 response.

Norway's government and security sector

Norway's system of government and its underlying public sector are notoriously compartmentalized;[8] occasionally, as on 22/7, dangerously fragmented. Parliament primarily treats the Cabinet in a segregated manner too. For troublesome issues, it looks for the one minister bearing constitutional responsibility. Misinforming parliament or sub-par performances may trigger hearings and reprimands, even replacement of the minister in question.

Naturally, government business needs to be delegated, rendering each subject to the competent department, but in Norway this is taken to a level that hinders effective coordination. Since public servants belong to one department and 'serve' only one master, they are not incentivized to make another minister look good or succeed. The team dimension is weak; inter-departmental strife is commonplace as civil servants care about and tend to their own department's business.[9]

This tribal nature of the Norwegian public sector is particularly conspicuous and problematic in the security realm because the preservation of national security requires a concerted effort from police, military, intelligence and a variety of other agencies. Aggravating the problem is the fact that Norway lacks a Home Office. Domestic – societal – security is provided by the Department of Justice (DOJ), whose remit includes coordination across all non-military parts of government. At this, as public inquiries have routinely observed, they seldom succeed.[10]

---

[7] Anders Romarheim (2019). 'Totalforsvaret – en uunnværlig umulighet' in Per Norheim-Martinsen ed., *Det Nye Totalforsvaret*, (Oslo: Gylendal), 151.

[8] Eivind Smith (2015), 'Ministerstyre: et hinder for samordning?', *Nytt Norsk Tidsskrift*, vol. 32(3).

[9] Government investigations reach similar conclusions. In a refreshing admission of such shortcomings, the Norwegian Digitalisation Agency's (DIFI) 2014 Report 7 is titled: '*Against all odds: paths to coordination for Norway's public sector*'.

[10] The Office of the Auditor General (Riksrevisjonen) is Norway's highest authority for investigating shortcomings in the public sector. Appointed by, and answering directly to, Parliament, it has been deeply sceptical of DOJ's security coordination, criticizing it in reports from 2008, 2015, 2017 and 2018. The main report (2015) is at www.riksrevisjonen.no/globalassets/rapporter/no-2014-2015/justisogberedskapsdepartementetsarbeidmedsamfunnssikkerhet.pdf, accessed 6 December 2021.

The coordination of civil preparedness is too demanding for any single department as one minister rarely succeeds in directing another. Moreover, this daunting task comes on top of the rest of the DOJ's vast portfolio, which includes running the entire justice system of police, courts, prisons and immigration. It also handles Arctic affairs and cyber security.[11] The DOJ's Law Department is also the Executive branch's primary interpreter of law, working hard on government legislative proposals. The outcome is that security for the civilian sector remains a small part of the DOJ's undertakings, and the Law Department remains 'the place to be'.

Before 22/7, the size and professionalism of the DOJ's security section was not impressive. However, a considerable overhaul took place and DOJ's Societal Security section gained in size and formal security competence.[12] Evidence of the section's improved standing came with the appointment in early 2019 of a Minister for Public Security, Ingvil Smines Tybring-Gjedde.[13] However, as with other attempts at structural reform of Norway's security architecture, the change did not work well and was short-lived. In January 2020, a cabinet reshuffle abolished the post.

Norway's highest forum for national security is at ministerial level. The Government Security Council (RSU) is led by the Prime Minister and meets at least monthly. 'Meet' is a key word, because the RSU is as much a meeting as a fully staffed government body. The meeting is very high-level, which has benefits, but means there is little time to go into the finer details of running the security sector. The issues discussed are not public as it regularly includes intelligence briefings. Its permanent members are the Ministers of Justice, Defence, Foreign Affairs and Finance.[14] Other ministers are invited depending on the issues being discussed. In a coalition government, the party leaders attend all meetings, regardless of which department they hold.

Since July 2015 a permanent secretariat at the Prime Minister's Office (SMK) has prepared the RSU agenda and facilitated meetings.[15] Currently, this secretariat only employs six civil servants, which complicates developing a

---

[11] Cyber Security Strategy (2019) at www.regjeringen.no/en/dokumenter/national-cyber-security-strategy-for-norway/id2627177/, accessed 6 December 2021.

[12] One of the Gjørv Commission's main findings concerned negligence and bureaucratic paralysis in the DOJ's security work. In particular, coordination was deemed unsystematic. op. cit., 458.

[13] www.regjeringen.no/en/aktuelt/changes-in-the-government/id2626334/, accessed 6 December 2021.

[14] Total Defence Concept Manual. MOD/DOJ (2018). *Støtte og Samarbeid: En beskrivelse av Totalforsvaret i dag*. 66–68.

[15] www.regjeringen.no/no/aktuelt/nytt-sekretariat-for-regjeringens-sikkerhetsutvalg-rsu/id2427856/, accessed 6 December 2021.

distinguishable Cabinet Office voice in national security, as staff tend to be on loan from other government agencies. However, RSU does hold the highest authority the Executive branch of government has to offer and, if determined enough, can get its way.

Below the RSU, the top layer of the bureaucracy has its own crisis management council. Kriserådet (the Crisis Council) with five permanent members: the top civil servants from the SMK, and departments of Justice, Defence, Foreign Affairs and Health. It is expanded depending on the nature of each crisis. Its permanent secretariat is the Crisis Response Unit (KSE) located in the DOJ,[16] which is more removed from the PM than in other countries. A key recommendation of the Gjørv Commission was a demand that the RSU and Kriserådet meet regularly, which speaks volumes about the sporadic and ad hoc nature of their work before 22/7.[17]

Another cross-sectoral arrangement is the Depstrat Group. Established formally in October 2019, it includes heads of communication from all three security and intelligence services, SMK, DOJ, Defence and Health. The Ministry of Local Government and Modernization and the Directorate for Civil Protection are also included. Depstrat has eluded public attention thus far but seeks to cohere strategic communication across government. During COVID-19 it tackled disinformation, thus contributing to widespread acceptance of national health policy that limited COVID-19's spread.

System shortcomings

The difficulties of cross-sectoral coordination are revealed in the ill-fated appointment of a Deputy Minister for Security and Preparedness in 2013. Although situated in the Prime Minister's Office, Deputy Minister Laila Bokhari's chances of influencing national security policy quickly deteriorated. The bureaucracy – particularly the DOJ and SMK – opposed the position vehemently and she was not even afforded a small personal staff before the post was abolished.[18]

Further evidence of disjointed security was revealed in early 2019. The Solberg government had strong parliamentary support and could push

---

[16] www.regjeringen.no/en/dep/jd/organisation/Departments/Department-of-Public-Security/id677820/, accessed 6 December 2021.

[17] Op. cit., 458.

[18] www.tv2.no/a/7012094/ and www.vg.no/nyheter/innenriks/i/pz1Wo/byttet-parti-i-siste-liten-gjorde-lynkarriere, accessed 6 December 2021.

legislation through along party lines, yet, its attempt at getting a new intelligence law through Parliament fell flat. Some opposition to the law was legitimate, but other criticism during the round of hearings looked like partisan turf-wars. Moreover, and unprecedentedly, the government's long-term Defence plan was also rejected. The most surprising opposition to the intelligence law came from the Police Security Service (PST). It speaks volumes that the domestic intelligence service was crucial in blocking the main law governing foreign intelligence. Moreover, it is astonishing that no one in Cabinet or government had discovered the PST's considerable animosity to the proposed law before sending it to Parliament. This reflects poor political craftsmanship; one a fully operational cross-sectoral National Security Council should avoid. A revised law was eventually passed in summer 2020, followed by a new long-term Defence plan.[19]

A discernible pattern is that coordination problems are left unaddressed. It is unusual to see two closely cooperating government agencies, best evidenced in the nation's two large intelligence services openly at odds in a government-run legislative process. The lack of even basic coordination is also observable in the fact that the two annual open threat assessments from PST and the foreign intelligence service are released only weeks apart. In 2021, their annual threat assessments were presented together,[20] which suggests coordination, but greater benefit to the public would accrue by releasing them six months apart. While in-fighting will not disappear merely by introducing new bodies, it may decrease, and simple coordination problems should occur less often.

Still, the overall picture of Norway's security system is not all negative. The COVID-19 pandemic demanded massive efforts across all layers of government and society, and showed how, in the face of certain types of crises, the system can perform well despite its limitations.

COVID-19: an effective ad hoc response

In 2020, most countries in Europe and America were hit harder by COVID-19 than Norway, whose initial response was effective. By year's end the death toll was just above 400, and 800 by August 2021, still far below many countries. Sweden, a comparable country in terms of geography, political culture, public

---

[19] www.regjeringen.no/contentassets/3a2d2a3cfb694aa3ab4c6cb5649448d4/long-term-defence-plan-norway-2020---english-summary.pdf, accessed 6 December 2021.

[20] At www.regjeringen.no/no/aktuelt/trusselvurderinger21/id2831242/, accessed 6 December 2021.

health and national traits, counted more than 9,300 COVID-19 deaths in 2020, and fared worse in the OECD's initial assessment of national responses.[21] While the initial acquisition of vaccines was slow, by Spring 2021 the national vaccination programme accelerated so as the Delta variant surged in the summer, it affected healthy, unvaccinated younger cohorts, causing fewer casualties and hospitalizations. Overall, Norway's health authorities also performed particularly well in external communications. The Assistant Health Director, Espen Nakstad, was 2020's Person of the Year in Norway's main tabloid newspapers, *VG* and *Dagbladet*.[22] This was impressive as he was hardly the bearer of good news. In contrast, international counterparts such as epidemiologist Anders Tegnell from Sweden and American Dr Fauci received death threats.[23]

It is hard to establish any single factor leading to a relatively low death toll for Norway. Yet, as government is responsible for national security and public health issues (that conflate in COVID-19), containing the virus's spread and keeping the death-toll low was an accomplishment regardless. Their response involved a new cross-sectoral body, the RCU, modelled on the RSU. The 'S' for security was simply substituted with a 'C' for COVID-19.[24] Like the RSU, the Prime Minister headed the RCU, which included Ministers for Foreign Affairs, Health, Finance, Justice, Industry, and the Minister for Children and Families. Unlike the RSU, the Minister of Defence was not a permanent member. This shows the new Committee did not just include the usual suspects but built on the RSU. This also underlines that the pandemic was more of a public health and safety matter than a traditional state security matter, the latter dealing more with strategically adaptable adversaries.

The RCU met weekly in 2020, in addition to RSU meetings, which ensured the traditional national security system remained focused on security without being hi-jacked or side-tracked by the COVID-19 response. Similarly, the weekly government cabinet meetings, called 'R-conferences' continued as the Solberg government strived hard to not let the COVID-19 response eclipse other government activity. When the Støre government took office in October 2021, the RCU stopped and top health officials were no longer invited to government conferences, probably because the Solberg government had (prematurely?) declared the COVID-19 crisis over in September 2021.

[21] ECD/European Union (2020). *Health at a Glance: Europe 2020: State of Health in the EU Cycle*, OECD. Also www.aftonbladet.se/nyheter/a/EplVwa/stockholm-tredje-hardast-drabbade-huvudstaden-i-europa, accessed 6 December 2021.
[22] www.dagbladet.no/meninger/veiviseren-ble-arets-navn/73199654, accessed 6 December 2021.
[23] www.aftonbladet.se/nyheter/a/pLzmg6/anders-tegnell-har-tagit-emot-dodshot and www.bbc.com/news/world-us-canada-53677866, accessed 6 December 2021.
[24] Societal Security White Paper (2020), op. cit., Chapter 5.5, 43–44.

Disjointed security

Norway's security sector is at times disjointed. Ministries and strictly applied vertical government rule the day, and the planning bodies for ensuring cross-sectoral coordination are thinly staffed. These bodies typically borrow people from other functions, such as police and military, thus, no distinct agency identity is developed. One result is that simple matters of coordination remain unresolved: one hand knows not what the other is doing.

However, if Norway struggles with coordinating long-term security issues, it nevertheless performed well during the COVID-19 crisis. The pandemic highlighted Norway's ability for effective governing in the face of a mortal but prolonged threat. The flexible ad hoc arrangements at cabinet level were part of a response that was lauded even by Norwegian media, which shows a nation content with its response.[25] In August 2021, Norway topped Bloomberg's 'Covid Resilience Ranking', recognizing the effective and flexible crisis response.[26]

Success partly relied on effective strategic communication, a precondition for social control directing behaviour limiting the contagion. It is, however, significant that many severe national crises are likely to involve thinking and adaptive opponents and thus are security, rather than public health and safety, matters. Against the former, Norway's disjointed system has struggled, particularly faced with quickly unfolding attacks such as 22/7. In 2020 the timescale allowed development of an effective crisis response, whereas the 22/7 attack was over within hours.

The quickly unfolding crisis of 22/7 also suggests Norway has a sub-optimal security architecture for dealing with long-term security planning. Following suit with our closest allies in the UK and USA, formalizing the coordination of security actors may help. A bespoke Norwegian National Security Council, led by an authoritative National Security Advisor, could address some shortcomings by providing a vehicle for long-term security planning, streamlining national security decision-making internally, and serving as a point of contact with counterparts from other NATO countries for international threats. Another structural overhaul should include a standing capacity for responding to short-duration security crises under the Prime Minister's Office. This was a main

---

[25] Astrid Meland (24 November 2020). 'Derfor er Norge best i corona-klassen' [Therefore Norway is top of the class on corona], *VG*. Also, Societal Security White Paper (2020), *47*.

[26] www.bloomberg.com/graphics/covid-resilience-ranking/, accessed 6 December 2021.

recommendation of a previous Defence Commission,[27] and the original plan for the KSE, but it ended up in the DOJ. In Norway's public sector, all things must belong to one department.

One major hurdle is to ensure the political will to deliver changes and make them work in practice exceeds bureaucratic inertia. While civil servants provide advice, it must be subordinate to political direction. Finding ways to plug the hole in Norway's horizontal security architecture is much needed. This was illustrated in spring 2021 when an engine-maker in Bergen delivering to Norway's surveillance-ships was sold to a company with strong Russian interests.[28] The sale was later overturned but served as an eye-opener for Norway's Parliament, which realized that government was unable to adopt the new national security law as intended. An expert group was appointed to report to parliament on the inadequacies of the Norwegian national security sector. The group's mandate is to: map formal security competence in all departments; analyse the lack of cross-departmental coordination; and evaluate how to establish a shared understanding of security across departments.[29] This is welcome and overdue.

The Solberg government had the appetite for fixing the problems and tried different approaches, but the right formula eluded them. This is a grave indictment on a matter of such importance as national security. Hopefully, the Støre government elected in 2021 will fare better. They may be aided by a new grand Defence Commission and an expert group on national security. At the time of writing, precise details of the Commission were yet to be determined.[30] It could add significant value if it addresses the challenge of horizontal coordination the Gjørv Commission did not. It must, however, preserve the flexibility displayed in Norway's effective COVID-19 response.

---

[27] Expert Commission on Norwegian Security and Defence Policy (2015), 'Unified Effort', 100, at www.regjeringen.no/globalassets/departementene/fd/dokumenter/unified-effort.pdf, accessed 6 December 2021.

[28] Thomas Nilsen (26 February 2021). Engine supplier to Norwegian spy ship bought by Russian-controlled company. *Barents Observer*.

[29] Parliament strongly criticized handling of the Bergen Engines sale. See www.stortinget.no/nn/Saker-og-publikasjonar/publikasjonar/Innstillingar/Stortinget/2020-2021/inns-202021-503s/?all=true, accessed 6 December 2021.

[30] The call for a Defence Commission is at www.stortinget.no/no/Saker-og-publikasjoner/Publikasjoner/Innstillinger/Stortinget/2020-2021/inns-202021-087s/?all=true, accessed 6 December 2021.

15

South Africa: In search of both security and process

Abel Esterhuyse

From the Union's creation in 1910, South Africa has had to balance threats emanating from: beyond Africa; within Africa; and within South Africa's borders. Historically, the domestic security domain has dominated and shaped national security structures.[1] This chapter considers how South Africa went from a highly structured approach to national security essential to the apartheid regime, to an emphasis on human security. Though well conceptualized, the human security approach lacked operational and structural foundations, processes and structures, leaving the security forces without clear direction or capacity. A growing sense of insecurity, adhocracy and strategy of desperation followed. The chapter then considers attempts to mature the coordination of national security before looking at some of the challenges.

Before democratization, regime survival made security the government's primary focus. The approach was thorough, deliberate and comprehensive; informed by André Beaufre's ideas of total onslaught and total strategy.[2] The State Security Council (SCC), a cabinet within the cabinet, was the central coordinating body of the National Security Management System (NSMS). Bureaucratically, the NSMS was well-supported by staff officers from the security services, especially the military. Together, the SCC and NSMS turned South Africa into a national security state and society.[3] The NSMS relied on committees and commissions and a five-tiered structure for the management and coordination of national security: the SCC, SCC Working Committee, SCC

---

[1] Ian van der Waag (2010). *The Military history of modern South Africa* (Johannesburg: Jonathan Ball), 2.
[2] André Beaufre (1963). *An Introduction to Strategy* (London: Praeger).
[3] Chris Aldan (1996). *Apartheid's last stand: The rise and fall of the South African security state* (London: Macmillan), 1.

Secretariat, Interdepartmental Committees, and Joint Management Centres. The Joint Management Centres were a nation-wide system of eleven regional committees that bridged central and local government structures in coordinating security, economic, social and political affairs. They also provided reverse feedback of information.[4] The security forces were mostly professional, well trained and experienced, even though delivering the regime's tough internal control and suppressing dissent. The NSMS and security forces were critical to regime stability and were well-resourced. The strong control and discipline they exerted, also meant that despite high levels of political violence, they did not intervene in the process of democratization in the 1990s.

Redefining national security post-apartheid

The post-apartheid regime in 1994 dismantled the security processes and tools that had been used to oppress them, with human security providing a way to demilitarize security. Throughout the early 1990s transitional period, the 'Military Research Group' with its roots in the Copenhagen School's broad understanding of security and the ideas of Barry Buzan, Ole Wæver and Jaap de Wilde,[5] shaped the African National Congress' (ANC) views on security. The 1994 elections coincided with publication of a UN report on human security[6] that dovetailed with the ANC's views on South Africa's future and provided the conceptual tool for dismantling apartheid security thinking and structures. While well conceptualized, it lacked detail about how human security should be operationalized. Two ideas were implicit: that security forces were not to be instrumental in the security process; and, security should be a by-product of good governance.

The Mandela administration took a highly principled approach, and the 1996 Constitution provided guidelines on national security and the role of the security forces.[7] Chapter 11 delineated several 'governing principles' around three key issues. Firstly, security as the responsibility of a single defence force, single police service, and those intelligence services established under the Constitution. Secondly, security should not benefit or prejudice any party-political interests; it

[4] Aldan, op. cit., 71–75.
[5] University of Witwatersrand. Historical Papers. *The Military Research Group*, www.historicalpapers. wits.ac.za/inventories/inv_pdfo/AG1977/AG1977-A10-7-4-002-jpeg.pdf, accessed 30 August 2021.
[6] UNDP (1994). *Human Development Report 1994: New dimensions of human security.*
[7] South African Government (1996). *Constitution of the Republic of South Africa, Act 108 of 1996.*

must be non-partisan. Thirdly, security should be transparent and accountable through multi-party parliamentary committees that entrenched the role of parliament and parliamentary oversight.[8]

The 1996 White Paper, 'Defence in a Democracy', formally introduced human security as a policy framework,[9] tying security to the well-being and interest of society. In practice, however, security was overwhelmed by societal demands. By including everything that might affect society negatively, the debate and search for solutions became too broad and theoretical to be of practical value.[10] The White Paper did not help with how to operationalize human security; a gap that remains unfilled. The disconnect between concept and process, and security and strategy, typifies South African security since 1994.[11]

National security coordination – a domestic matter

The demilitarization agenda saw the military withdraw from domestic deployment in the 1990s. The domestic military command, control, and intelligence structures were dismantled, ending the military's central role in the management and practice of domestic security. The ANC government adopted a clustered approach to governance, with security within the 'Justice, Crime Prevention and Security' (JCPS) Cluster – Figure 15.1. JCPS includes the Departments of Police, Home Affairs, Justice and Correctional Services, Defence, and Military Veterans. Its role is '[to] streamline resources to achieve its objectives of reducing crime, improving the efficiency of the criminal justice system, dealing with corruption, managing South Africa's borders, improving our population registration system, and prioritizing the fight against and prevention of cyber-crimes'.[12]

The National Joint Operational and Intelligence Structure (NATJOINTS), through the National Joint Operational Centre (NATJOC), coordinates all security and law enforcement operations throughout the country. The South

[8]   Ibid.
[9]   South African Government (1996). *Defence in a democracy*. National Defence White Paper.
[10] John Baylis and James Wirtz. 'Introduction: Strategy in the contemporary world'. In John Baylis, James Wirtz and Colin Gray eds. (2018). *Strategy in the contemporary world* (Oxford: Oxford University Press), 13.
[11] Abel Esterhuyse and Benjamin Mokoena (2018). 'The need for progress in an era of transformation: South African professional military education and military effectiveness'. *Stability: International Journal of Security & Development*, vol. 7(1), 1–17.
[12] Republic of South Africa, Department of Social Development. *Justice, Crime Prevention and Security Cluster (JCPS)* at http://gbv.org.za/jcps/, accessed 30 August 2021.

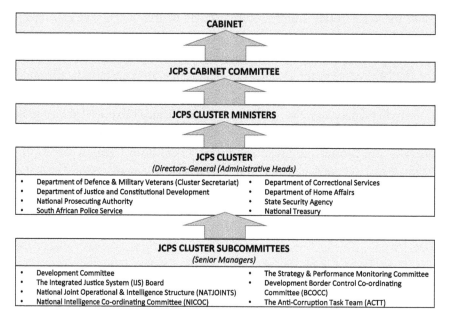

Figure 15.1 JCPS Cluster structures and reporting lines.[13]

African Police Service chairs the NATJOINTS, but operationalizing it remains a challenge.[14] Given the prominent role of the police, and high levels of crime – Police Minister, Mr Bheki Cele, described the murder rate as having turned South Africa into a place that 'borders on a war zone'[15] – the focus on justice, law and order is unsurprising. Traditional national security and its coordination is not paramount, and the JCPS has no national security strategy or equivalent document.[16] The government's inability to foresee, manage and coordinate the 2021 uprisings in KwaZulu-Natal Province,[17] confirmed the system's weaknesses in integrating and coordinating security – and intelligence – at the highest levels.

President Cyril Ramaphosa's February 2020 State of the Nation Address[18] announced the re-establishment of a National Security Council (NSC) to 'ensure better co-ordination of the intelligence and security-related functions of the

[13] Lebogang Mphahlele-Ntsasa (2021). *A strategic management framework for intragovernmental collaborations*. PhD thesis. University of South Africa, 110.

[14] South African Police Service (30 August 2019). *Annual Report*, 23.

[15] Staff Writer (18 September 2018). 'Here's how South Africa's crime rate compares to actual warzones'. *BusinessTech*.

[16] South African Government (December 2018). *Report of the High-Level Review Panel on the State Security Agency*, 3.

[17] Rebecca Davis, Greg Nicolson and Bheki Simelane (8 August 2021). 'South Africa's three bloodiest days: 342 dead and we are still in the dark'. *Daily Maverick*.

[18] Parliament of the Republic of South Africa (13 February 2020). *State of the Nation Address by President Cyril Ramaphosa*.

state'.[19] On 6 August 2021, he announced further measures 'to strengthen our security services and to prevent a recurrence of such [KwaZulu-Natal] events'. The first removes the Ministry of State Security and places political responsibility for the State Security Agency (responsible for the intelligence services) in the Office of the Presidency. This seems motivated by three considerations: better control of the intelligence agencies; increased effectiveness; and presidential responsibility to safeguard the nation's security and integrity.[20] Second, appointment of a National Security Advisor – Dr Sydney Mufamadi – to improve support to the President and NSC in strategic management of national security. Third, appointment of an expert panel 'to lead a thorough and critical review of our preparedness and the shortcomings in our response [to the] orchestrated campaign of public violence, destruction and sabotage'.[21] These changes led to widespread speculation about the growing centralization of security functions and decision-making.[22] How this will impact the functioning of the JCPS remains to be seen. There is no doubt, though, that the President has prioritized improving security and its coordination, which may also indicate a shift from human to a more traditional approach to security.

No security and no structure

Budgetary neglect and increasing entanglement of the security services in the ANC's factional struggles has precipitated a comprehensive decline in capacity and professionalism in the security sector.[23] Its effect was particularly evident in the failure to predict and respond to the 2021 uprising.[24] South Africans increasingly take responsibility for their own safety and security, with preventative law and order almost exclusively delivered by the private security industry: five registered private security personnel are deployed for every

[19] Pieter van der Merwe (11 March 2020). 'President re-establishes National Security Council'. *Business Day.*
[20] High-Level Review Panel on the State Security Agency, op. cit., 3.
[21] South African Government (5 August 2021). The Presidency, *President Cyril Ramaphosa: Changes to the national executive.*
[22] See, for example, CapeTalk (6 August 2021). 'Ramaphosa centralises power: 'He's now the de facto spy chief'. Charlotte Kilbane interview with Professor Jane Duncan of the Department of Journalism, Film and Television (UJ). Marianne Merten (9 August 2021). 'South Africa a step closer to a super Presidency after Ramaphosa's master class in consolidating power'. *Daily Maverick.*
[23] Thanduxolo Jika, Sabelo Skiti, Sibongakonke Shoba and Sam Mkokeli (25 July 2021). 'Inside Ramaphosa's security crisis: Why SA did not predict the threat'. *Sunday Times.*
[24] Farouk Araie (13 July 2021). 'Intelligence failure on co-ordinated insurrection will cost South Africa billions'. *Mail & Guardian*; Jane Duncan (14 July 2021). 'South Africa's tipping point: How the intelligence community failed the country'. *Daily Maverick*; Karabo Mafolo (16 July 2021). 'Parliamentary police committee accuses SAPS of "failing South Africa"'. *Daily Maverick.*

policeman. In an extremely economically diverse society, the poor are increasingly vulnerable to the dysfunctional security domain.[25]

Security planning normally centres on three issues: strategic environment; security institutions' capabilities; and cost and affordability in human, technological and operational terms. However, security is not objective. Power provides security with content: political power interprets the strategic context and develops and funds the security forces.[26] South Africa, like many post-liberation African countries, is a dominant party democracy, and the ruling ANC has a defining influence on the interpretation, definition and practice of security.[27] The ANC and those in the bureaucracy, however, shy away from a comprehensive analysis of the strategic environment. They appear particularly uncomfortable with the idea of a threat agenda and analysing the threats facing the country. The 2015 Defence Review process, for example, was 'threat-independent' and 'budget-independent'. In the end, it was little more than a coffee table publication and wishful thinking.[28] The discomfort may reflect concerns about exposing corruption, involvement in transnational organized crime and the intelligence services' dysfunctionality.[29]

The ANC worldview balances security with three paradigms: Africanist; anti-imperialist; and democratic.[30] Africa assisted the liberation struggle, hence cannot easily be reconciled as a threat. In its regional dealings, South Africa is avowedly multilateralist, both as a goal and strategy in foreign policy, especially under Presidents Mandela and Mbeki.[31] Beyond Africa, the West, United Kingdom and United States in particular, were always slow responding to the ANC as a liberation movement and cannot be trusted, while balancing individual and group rights and responsibilities in a multi-ethnic and multi-racial democracy is difficult. The ANC, South Africa by implication, confronts the reality that the Africanist and anti-imperialist paradigms are occasionally in conflict with the democratic,

[25] Abel Esterhuyse. 'From Supply to Demand: South Africa and Private Security', in Edward Mienie and Sharon Hamilton eds. (2019). *Private Military Security Companies' Influence on International Security and Foreign Policy* (Dahlonega, GA: University of North Georgia Press), 64–102.

[26] Anette Seegers (2010). 'The new security in democratic South Africa: A cautionary tale'. *Conflict, Security & Development*, vol. 10(2), 267.

[27] Renske Doorenspleet & Lia Nijzink (2013). *One-party dominance in African democracies* (Boulder, CO: Lynne Rienner).

[28] Greg Mills (2011). *An option of difficulties? A 21st century South African defence review.* Discussion Paper No. 2011/07. The Brenthurst Foundation.

[29] Marianne Merten (1 June 2021). 'Dysfunctional SSA biggest threat to South Africa's security, EFF's Ndlozi tells Parliament'. *Daily Maverick*.

[30] Laurie Nathan (2005). 'Consistency and inconsistencies in South African foreign policy'. *International Affairs*, vol. 81(2), 363.

[31] Ibid., 365.

particularly so when dealing with President Mugabe's Zimbabwe.[32] Inherently, and from a security perspective, there can be no development and progression in the absence of security, and no security in the absence of democracy. These tensions make consensus and cohesion about security a challenge.

Human security underpinned the Mandela Administration, aligning with his commitment to promoting human rights and democracy, justice and international law, international peace, and international mechanisms for resolving conflict.[33] The Mbeki Administration's security outlook focused on Africa, and the military experienced severe budgetary and operational pressure to balance its African peace mission and domestic obligations. Towards the end of Mbeki's Administration, though, the South African National Defence Force became the leading instrument in South African foreign policy in Africa.[34] Although not explicit, the economic plundering, political infighting, legal fiascos, and lack of governance in the Zuma Administration increasingly led to security being synonymous with regime security. The security services' focus and capacity were profoundly influenced and damaged by the way party and government were intertwined. The growing contagion of the intelligence and policy community by ANC factionalism progressively worsened from 2009.[35] President Ramaphosa, by default rather than design perhaps, focuses on national security as a matter of urgency, especially given the events of COVID-19 and 2021's civil unrest, which reinforced the problems of not having effective means of coordinating national security. From a structural and process perspective, the ANC's dominant position became clearly visible in the practice of security.

Ad hoc. Security is managed ad hoc and through a strategy of desperation. Adhocracy abounds within the security services, focused on crisis management in the absence of appropriate and comprehensive contingency planning.[36]

Centralized. Security management is highly centralized within the Executive – the various ministers and Office of the President through the security cluster. Centralization is a widespread phenomenon forming part of the ANC philosophy given many ANC members have former Eastern Bloc governments as their frame of reference.[37]

[32] Ibid., 367
[33] African National Congress (1994). *Foreign policy perspective in a democratic South Africa*.
[34] Thomas Mandrup (2018). 'An uncertain future: South Africa's national defence force caught between foreign-policy ambitions and domestic development'. *Journal of Eastern African Studies*, vol. 12(1), 136–153.
[35] High-Level Review Panel on the State Security Agency, op. cit., 3.
[36] J. Brooks Spector (1 June 2015). 'Two of the most uncomfortable words: Contingency planning'. *Daily Maverick*.
[37] Thomas A. Koelble and Andrew Siddle (2013). 'Why decentralization in South Africa has failed'. *Governance*, vol. 26(3), 343–346.

Weak oversight. Parliament has become marginalized in both the process and oversight of security management. This reflects a growing disregard for Parliament in the Executive and security forces.[38] Senior members of the security forces are reluctant to appear in front of Parliamentary oversight committees,[39] and treat the committees with distain.[40] Oversight is also hindered by a growing tendency to cloud security in excessive secrecy.[41]

Lacking professionalism. The security services have been deprofessionalized, lacking in capacity and public trust, and experience large-scale corruption.[42] Consequently, the military has again become the primary platform for debate about security. Defence policy documents are the most conspicuous in the security arena, most recently the 2015 Defence Review. Without a clear threat agenda or national security strategy, however, the Defence Review had to hypothesize about South African national security to permit defence planning. The National Defence College is an important nexus between academia and the security forces for debate on security, with strategic studies, as an academic discipline, having declined in universities since democratization. As such, the security debate is bureaucratic and lacks diversity and depth.[43] As under apartheid, based on use during the COVID-19 pandemic and the violent uprisings in KwaZulu-Natal, the military has again become the government's stop-gap security service.

COVID-19

A national state of disaster was declared for COVID-19, with a lockdown announced on 27 March 2021 under the Disaster Management Act 2002.[44] Inevitably Executive-driven, announced by the Minister for Cooperative

[38] Janse van Rensburg (2019). *Twenty years of democracy: An analysis of parliamentary oversight of the military in South African since 1994*. PhD dissertation. Stellenbosch University.

[39] defenceWeb (19 June 2019). *CSANDF non-appearance at Parliament 'disrespectful'*, at www.defenceweb.co.za/sa-defence/sa-defence-sa-defence/csandf-non-appearance-at-parliament-disrespectful/, accessed 30 August 2021.

[40] Jan Gerber (23 April 2020). 'You're not our clients. We take instructions from the president' – SANDF to MPs amid brutality claims'. *News24*; defenceWeb. (22 June 2020). 'Parliamentary committee takes "strong exception" to CSANDF absence', at www.defenceweb.co.za/featured/parliamentary-committee-takes-strong-exception-to-csandf-absence/, accessed 30 August 2021.

[41] High-Level Review Panel on the State Security Agency, op. cit., 2.

[42] Jakkie Cilliers (21 July 2021). 'South Africa's security sector is in crisis – reform must start now'. *ISS Today*.

[43] Lindy Heinecken. 'Reflections on insider-outsider experiences of military research in South Africa'. In Helena Carreiras, Celso Castro, and Sabina Frederic eds. (2016). *Researching the military* (London: Routledge), 36–48.

[44] Disaster Management Act: Regulations relating to COVID-19, Government Notice 318. (2020)

Governance and Traditional Affairs and placing responsibilities on other departments, confusion nevertheless surrounds the process of coordination below Cabinet-level, parliament's role and the budgetary processes for the COVID-19 responses.[45] The whole of the Defence Forces were placed on standby; though the number of deployed soldiers never exceeded 7,000.[46] Generally respectful and professional, others abused their authority, and the brutality was widely shared on social media.[47] The killing of Collins Koza by soldiers angered many South Africans,[48] highlighting that the military was not prepared for the mission.[49] Security leadership,[50] command and control structures and interoperability between the security forces were critical issues that underpinned the 'iron curtain ... falling on our freedom'.[51] That the security sector is in crisis is clear from COVID-19 and 2021's violent unrest.

Conclusion

History, geography and politics matter: apartheid and the ANC's liberation history have had a defining influence. South Africa is part of Africa with its many security legacies, dominant-party democracies, and developmental challenges. South African security reflects the preferences of the ruling elite, moving from regime to human security, regional and continental security and (perhaps inevitably?), regime security again.

The security structures lack functionality, strategic focus and coordination. They are centred on justice, law and order, rather than traditional national security with its understanding of wider threats and a cohering national security strategy. Security management is increasingly centralized under the Office of the

---

[45] Marianne Merten (23 April 2020). 'SA'S Constitutional Democracy? The path of Ramaphosa's letter for major SANDF deployment raises serious concerns around separation of powers'. *Daily Maverick*; Minutes of the Portfolio Committee of Parliament at https://pmg.org.za/committee-meeting/30107/, accessed 30 August 2021.

[46] Keegan Leech (13 July 2021). 'No, South Africa didn't deploy 70,000 soldiers during Covid-19 lockdown'. *Africa Check*.

[47] Poloko Tau (31 May 2020). 'Cele calls for cooperation amid allegations of police brutality during lockdown'. *City Press*.

[48] Minutes of the Portfolio Committee of Parliament at https://pmg.org.za/committee-meeting/30107/, accessed 30 August 2021.

[49] Craig Bailie (28 May 2020) 'South Africa's military is not suited for the fight against COVID-19. Here's why'. *The Conversation*.

[50] Craig Baily (24 August 2021). 'The SANDF's ingrained culture of secrecy and non-communication is counter-productive and anti-democratic'. *Daily Maverick*.

[51] Ray Hartley and Greg Mills.(30 April 2020). 'An Iron Curtain is Falling on our Freedom'. *Daily Maverick*.

President with the Executive growing in scope and importance, while Parliament's role and oversight is marginalized by a dominant ruling party.

The military is prominent in the debate and practice of security – despite demilitarization efforts after 1994's democratic elections – and of growing importance compared to the police and intelligence services. This reflects the absorption of the police and intelligence communities into the ruling party's corruption, factionalism and infighting; and unlike the overburdened police and intelligence communities, a peacetime military has time for planning and debate.

Society itself seems to have lost interest in the security debate, fixated on the general lack of security and need for self-help. The distrust and divide between the public and security services were prominent features of COVID-19 and the 2021 unrest. Although the state remains responsible for security, primarily through its security services, the social contract between South Africa's citizens and government is strained by a reliance on privately funded security. The security debate, currently marginalized, bureaucratized and lacking in diversity, comprehension and depth needs to be reinvigorated. This may, however, change with the recent crises and government attempts to reinvigorate national security coordination.

16

The National Security and Defence Council of Ukraine: Responding to state aggression

Hanna Shelest

The National Security and Defence Council (NSDC) plays a central role in Ukraine's state security and defence system. Its role has developed, becoming more comprehensive following the Russian Federation's illegal annexation of Crimea in 2014 and the start of the war in Donbas. Ukraine had to reshape its security sector, make its state institutions more resilient and upgrade most of its strategic security and defence documents. Where the 2007 National Security Strategy focused on softer security issues, such as economic, social and political security, the 2015 Strategy emphasized classic hard security involving military and defence threats. Still prioritizing hard security, the 2020 Strategy demonstrated a slight shift towards human security issues. The NSDC's main priorities have also changed since 2014, to be:

- Threat response. Decisions on: martial law; countering Russian Federation information aggression; countering national security threats through migration policy; full-scale anti-terrorist operations in Donetsk and Lugansk regions; securing national interests in the Black Sea and the Azov Sea, sanctions against Russian and Ukrainian individuals and organizations etc.
- Strategic industries. Decisions on state policies for: developing strategic industries; protecting national interests in aeroengine construction; military equipment testing; improving international cooperation in complex military equipment production; national supply of key equipment to the Armed Forces.
- Defence capabilities. Decisions on: defence budget and defence orders; strengthening cybersecurity; counter-terrorism; security and defence sector planning; and improving defence capabilities.

- Other security matters. Decisions on: energy security; withdrawal from treaties signed within the CIS and with Russia; sanctions, resilience, etc. COVID-19 also received the NSDC's attention.

This chapter explores the NSDC's evolution, its legal background, functions and influence, derived not from formal authority but personalities and the frameworks the President sets. Finally, it considers how flexibility in the definition of security has allowed Ukraine to respond to threats since 2014.

History

Between gaining independence in 1991 and adoption of the 1996 Constitution, there were two consultative institutions for national security: the Defence Council and National Security Council.

The Defence Council was established in October 1991[1] to define and coordinate defence strategies and exercise effective command and control to guarantee national security, territorial integrity, and the constitutional order. It comprised the President as chair and senior political, defence and security figures. The National Security Council, created in July 1992 as an advisory body to prepare Presidential decisions relating to national interests and national security, reported directly to the President.[2] The 1996 Constitution combined them into the NSDC, but it took two years before the role, functions, principles and composition were enshrined in law.[3]

NSDC

The NSDC is led by the President and includes the Prime Minister, Ministers of Defence, Interior and Foreign Affairs, and the Head of the Security Services. The President can appoint other members of the Council through Presidential Orders. The current composition (August 2021) also includes: Heads of the Presidential Office, Foreign Intelligence Service, General Staff, State Service of

---

[1] Постанова Верховної Ради України 'Про утворення Ради оборони України' [Parliamentary Decision on Creation of the Defence Council of Ukraine] 11 October 1991.

[2] Указ Президента України 'Про Раду національної безпеки України' [Presidential Order on the National Security Council] 1 July 1992.

[3] Закон України 'Про Раду національної безпеки і оборони України' [National Security and Defence Council Law] 5 March 1998.

Financial Monitoring, National Bank, and National Academy of Science; Vice Prime Ministers on European and Euro-Atlantic Integration, and Strategic Industries; Vice Prime Minister/Minister for Reintegration of the Temporarily Occupied Territories; Ministers of the Economy, Energy, Finance, Veteran Affairs, and Digital Transformation; Speaker of Parliament; and the General Prosecutor. The President can invite additional officials, including members of Parliament, to participate in meetings where necessary (without voting rights). NSDC decisions require two-thirds of the members voting in favour before being confirmed by Presidential Order.

The NSDC is served by a Secretary, appointed by the President without the need for confirmation by Parliament. This powerful position is responsible for daily management and agenda setting, and leads the NSDC Secretariat. However, frequent changes of Secretary have deprived the NSDC of stability; there have been fourteen NSDC Secretaries since 1999.

The NSDC was tested in 2014 during the Crimean occupation by Russian forces. After President Yanukovych fled, the NSDC led the security discussions, but failed a crucial decision to introduce martial law. The verbatim record of the 28 February 2014 NSDC meetings demonstrated the problems that can occur when taking decisions during crises, and highlighted the dominant role of personalities in the failure to declare martial law.[4] Decisions adopted in March–October 2014 were reactive rather than preventive or strategic, but reflected the threats. However, many decisions were not implemented within the deadlines set[5] because ministries and agencies hesitated or were incapable of implementing them. The NSDC had failed to consider the capabilities and resources of the state's executive bodies,[6] which led to many sensible decisions being ineffective.

In 2015, at the peak of Russian aggression, urgent steps were taken to improve national security. Among others, a Military Cabinet was created as a working body of the NSDC[7] focusing on defence matters, including: force deployments, mobilization, materiel and personnel resources and transiting the national

4   Чому не втримали Крим: стенограма РНБО від 28 лютого 2014 року [Why Crimea has not been saved: Transcripts of the NSDC, 28 February 2014] at www.radiosvoboda.org/a/29794488.html, accessed 30 August 2021.

5   Дацюк А., Полтораков О. Аналіз державної політики у сфері національної безпеки і оборони України [Analysis of the State Policy in the Sphere of National Security and Defence of Ukraine]. Reanimation Package of Reforms] (2015), 21 at https://rpr.org.ua/wp-content/uploads/2018/02/Analiz-polityky-NB-pravl-final.pdf, accessed 30 August 2021.

6   These are the Ministries and government Agencies.

7   Указ Президента України 'Про рішення Ради національної безпеки і оборони України від 18 лютого 2015 року 'Про додаткові заходи щодо зміцнення національної безпеки України' [Presidential Order on the Decision of the National Security Council 'On Additional Measures to Improve National Defence of Ukraine'] 18 February 2015.

economy during a 'special period'.[8] The Military Cabinet comprised the President, NSDC Secretary, Prime Minister, the Ministers of Interior, Foreign Affairs and Defence, the Heads of the Security Service, General Staff, State Border Service, Presidential Administration, the National Guard Commander and, where necessary, the Speaker of the Parliament. While a powerful body, the five years during which the Military Cabinet operated demonstrated that the NSDC still took most of the decisions; it has met only a few times since. One of the reasons for this was the lower intensity of the military activities in the country's East. However, in a sign it has been reinvigorated, July 2021 saw the composition expanded to include: Vice Prime Minister/Minister for Reintegration of the Temporarily Occupied Territories; Vice Prime Minister of Strategic Industries; Heads of the Foreign Intelligence Service and Defence Intelligence Directorate; the Deputy Head of Presidential Administration responsible for national security and defence; and the First Deputies to the NSDC Secretary.[9] It remains subordinate to the NSDC but can gather more quickly during crises for rapid decision-making.

In March 2021, it was decided to establish a Centre for Countering Disinformation under the NSDC responsible for monitoring information security, including Ukraine's international electronic presence, strategic communications and cooperation with civil society, etc.[10] However, clarity is needed on its relationship with the Ministry of Culture and Information Policy's pre-existing Disinformation Centre, and although there should be fifty-two staff members, by August 2021 little progress had been made with only the director having been appointed.

Functions and powers

The 1996 Constitution describes the NSDC's functions as being to coordinate and control activities of state executive bodies in relation to national security and defence.[11] National security is defined in 2018's National Security Law as:

---

[8] Under the Defence Law, this covers periods of mobilization, martial law or post-war reconstruction, which has been in force since March 2014 when a Presidential Order announced partial mobilization.

[9] Указ Президента України 'Про внесення зміни до Положення про Воєнний кабінет Ради національної безпеки і оборони України' [Presidential Order 'On Changes to the Military Cabinet of the National Security and Defence Council'] 18 February 2015.

[10] Указ Президента України 'Про рішення Ради національної безпеки і оборони України від 11 березня 2021 року «Про створення Центру протидії дезінформації»' [Presidential Order on the Decision of the National Security and Defence Council 'On establishing the Centre for Countering Disinformation'] 19 March 2021 .

[11] Конституція України [Constitution of Ukraine] 28 June 1996, Article 107.

'the protection of state sovereignty, territorial integrity, the democratic constitutional order and other national interests of Ukraine from real and potential threats'.[12] The term 'state security' is also used, but only against non-military threats and in relation to Ukraine's National Guard and Security Services activities. The 2020 National Security Strategy adopts these definitions but gives a more detailed explanation of the threats and national interests.[13]

The Constitution, however, leaves further defining the functions to separate law. Article 3 of the respective NSDC Law (1998) defines three functions:[14]

- Advising and making proposals to the President concerning domestic and foreign policy in relation to national security and defence.
- Peacetime coordination and control over activities of the state executive bodies dealing with national security and defence.
- Coordination and control over activities of the state executive bodies dealing with national security and defence in time of war and emergency, and in crises that threaten national security.

In practice, the NSDC can discuss any question concerning national security and defence its members are interested in, including the National Security Strategy. These include political, economic, social, energy, financial, information and cybersecurity matters, through to the imposition of martial law and the declaration of war. It has wide-ranging powers to define national strategic interests and develop security strategies, doctrine, state programmes and legislation. It can also propose the state budget for national security. Not just a strategic body, it can also discuss topics at an operational level, conduct research and monitor the implementation of policy. De facto, however, crisis coordination and monitoring have been prioritized, with the advisory role often neglected.

Crucial though foreign policy is in generating international support for Ukraine and putting pressure on Moscow, the coordination of foreign support and managing relations with allies are mostly addressed outside the NSDC. The President, Minister of Foreign Affairs, and Vice Prime Minister for European and Euro-Atlantic Integration lead on matters of foreign policy. However, this means that there is no single vice-prime minister in charge of defence and security, and so the point at which it comes together is the NSDC.

[12] Закон України 'Про національну безпеку України' [National Security Law] 21 June 2018.
[13] Указ Президента України №392/2020 'Про рішення Ради національної безпеки і оборони України від 14 вересня 2020 року «Про Стратегію національної безпеки України»' [Presidential Order on the Decision of the National Security Council 'On National Security Strategy of Ukraine'] 14 September 2020.
[14] National Security and Defence Council Law (1998), op. cit.

The 2018 National Security Law[15] defined the functions of the state bodies responsible for national security and defence, established a system of command, control, and coordination, and introduced a comprehensive approach to planning and civilian democratic control. Several important articles cover the NSDC.

Article 4 describes the NSDC as part of the system of democratic civilian control over the security and defence sector that also includes the President, Parliament, and central and local authorities. This control is more about monitoring and supervision, however, in which it receives reports and proposes legislation, rather than having a powerful vertical prerogative.

Article 14 gives the NSDC the leading role in coordinating national security and defence, both in peace and crisis. This includes the power to impose sanctions or other restrictive measures (e.g. embargoes, martial law, restrictions to sell certain goods abroad, etc.).

The 2018 National Security Law requires each President to present a new national security strategy within six months of inauguration, developed by the NSDC. Previous legislation had not required this, and the value of the document had been undermined. Since 2018, the importance of a national security strategy in prioritizing domestic and foreign threats, defence and foreign policy visions etc. has increased and, being the basis for legislative action, it has reinforced the NSDC's central role. The NSDC is also responsible for approving the Military Security Strategy (developed by the Ministry of Defence), the Strategy for Human Security and Civilian Protection (developed by the Ministry of Interior), the Strategy for Military-Industrial Complex Development (developed by the Cabinet of Ministers), Cyber Security Strategy (developed by the National Coordinating Centre of Cybersecurity), and the National Intelligence Programme (developed by the respective ministries and agencies).

Support to the NSDC

The 2018 National Security Law identifies the NSDC Secretariat as part of the state security and defence sector (Article 12). In this regard, it is equal to the state's executive bodies, but a question remains whether it is equivalent to the other institutions or sits at a higher level to allow it to enforce coordination. Capped at 237 people, the Secretariat's composition reflects the National Security Strategy's wide-ranging priorities, including departments on: foreign policy,

---

[15] National Security Law (2018), op. cit.

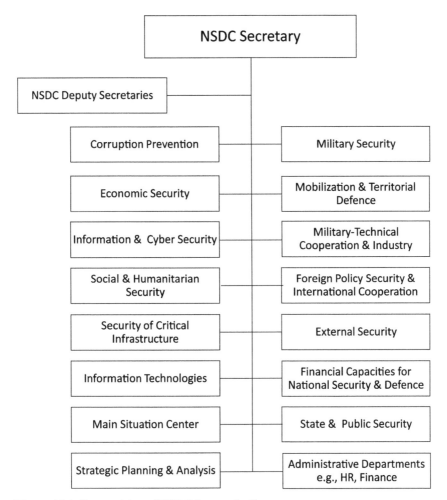

Figure 16.1 Composition of NSDC Secretariat.[16]

information and cyber security, state and public security, military security, mobilization and territorial defence, military–technical cooperation and development, economic security, social and humanitarian security, critical infrastructure security etc. (see Figure 16.1). However, the Secretariat does not have the same capacity for implementation as the other executive bodies, so it concentrates on coordination at decision-making level. Its effectiveness depends on the ability to set and inform the agenda, coordinate activity and monitor implementation by others. Despite this, the NSDC Secretariat's daily work priorities have not always been reflected in the Council's decisions.

---

[16] Source: Указ Президента України (Presidential Decree) 76/2021, 26 February 2021.

Several state advisory institutions (think tanks) covering security for many years informed the agenda, two of which were directly under the NSDC. Before 2010, three parallel structures existed: the National Institute for Strategic Studies, established in 1992 and reporting to the President; the National Institute of the Problems of International Security established in 2001 and operating under the NSDC; and the National Institute of the Problems of National Security, established in 2003 also under the NSDC where, since 2005, its director combined the post with that of the Deputy Secretary of the NSDC. In 2010, the NSDC's two think tanks were closed and all functions concentrated under the National Institute for Strategic Studies reporting to the President. Its director became the Presidential Advisor, providing analysis to both the Presidential Office and NSDC, although the Office of the President remained the primary consumer of their expertise.

The NSDC Secretariat is now increasing its use of the Institute, but its role is ambiguous. Its influence depends on the personality and personal influence of the Director in charge, as well as the reputation of its individual experts. Intended to cover all aspects of how the state functions, despite having between 200 and 300 staff, it struggles to cover the breadth of its responsibilities. Its ability to attract experts is also compromised because, despite being a state institution financed from the general budget and working to the President, its staff lost their status as state servants in 2015, and its financing has been reducing.

The NSDC during COVID-19

The response to the COVID-19 pandemic could become a crash-test for the NSDC effectiveness and in confirming its role for coordinating cross-government responses. In January 2020, the NSDC was the only institution trying to draw attention to the pandemic and the upcoming challenge, however this got little attention from the government.[17] In March, an NSDC decision was adopted, and confirmed by Presidential Order, 'On urgent measures to ensure national security in the conditions of an outbreak of acute respiratory disease COVID-19 caused by coronavirus SARS-CoV-2'.[18] This reactive response covered crisis

---

[17] Олексій Данілов: Між 'голубами' і 'яструбами', я завжди реаліст [Oleksiy Danilov: 'Between doves and hawks I am always a realist'] 6 July 2020 at www.pravda.com.ua/articles/2020/07/6/7258262/, accessed 30 August 2021.

[18] Указ Президента України Про рішення Ради національної безпеки і оборони України Від 13 березня 2020 року 'Про невідкладні заходи щодо забезпечення національної безпеки в умовах спалаху гострої респіраторної хвороби COVID-19, спричиненої коронавірусом SARS-CoV-2', [Presidential Order 'On urgent measures to ensure national security in the conditions of an outbreak of acute respiratory disease COVID-19 caused by coronavirus SARS-CoV-2'] 13 March 2020.

management activities in the health sphere, the return of Ukrainian citizens from overseas, extra financing for hospitals and the domestic production of medical supplies. Still the NSDC has not become the coordinating body for the state agencies in Ukraine's pandemic response. It has continued to hold numerous working-level meetings within the NSDC and with other agencies, created the e-map with the spread of COVID-19 and produced regular statistics.[19] It has also made recommendations on how to respond. Nevertheless, all these are advisory, rather than an indication of the NSDC leading or coordinating the security response. COVID-19, at the time of writing, has not yet enhanced the role of the NSDC among the state institutions in Ukraine.

NSDC effectiveness

Legally, the NSDC has a wide-ranging remit and powers, and significant support through a Secretariat and think tank. However, the immediate and overwhelming threat to Ukraine has narrowed the Council's focus and consumed its capacity. Unlike countries that do not face existential threats and who have broadened their definition of security beyond defence towards other threats, Ukraine has faced aggression and partial occupation. It has evolved its NSDC to deal with classical security, but within the construct of hybrid warfare that brings in all aspects of the state's power. Since 2014, it has traded its strategic advisory functions for crisis-reaction, inevitably (and understandably) focusing on managing immediate security and defence needs and slowed down the long-term development of security strategies.

The NSDC has continually adapted to threats as they emerge, but this remains more dependent on personalities than process. While the NSDC occupies a strong position in Ukrainian law, its real influence depends on the personality of the President; their interest, support, preparedness to listen, willingness to accept the Council's recommendations and support implementation by holding executive bodies to account. The personality of the NSDC Secretary, how influential and respectable they are and how close to the President, is also important. The President has significant control over the NSDC's membership, and the appointment of the Secretary is important in shaping the agenda and the quality of the support the NSDC receives.

---

[19] Електронна карта поширення захворюваності на коронавірусну інфекцію COVID-19 у світі та в Україні [COVID-19 E-map] 4 November 2020 at https://covid19.rnbo.gov.ua/, accessed 30 August 2021.

The new President took office in May 2019 and the NSDC's role initially reduced. The Council was not called on several occasions when it was expected and the NSDC and the Presidential Office did not speak in unison on many strategic issues, such as reintegrating separate districts of Donetsk and Lugansk regions. Even during the COVID-19 crisis, the role of the NSDC was not amplified. The situation started to improve in 2021 with the NSDC's decision-making role increasing, especially concerning sanctions, export control, terrorism and cyber security. However, arguably the NSDC is being overused by the President, with almost weekly meetings in spring–summer 2021 and adopting decisions on sanctions on individuals, both foreign and Ukrainian citizens, closing pro-Russian media, sanctioning smugglers, etc. Some of which are clearly within the Criminal Code rather than a NSDC task.

The personalities of those in charge of the NSDC (both the President and the Secretary) have a significant impact on its institutional power. To become fully effective, it needs a clearer definition of its place and broader sources of power that connect it to, and reinforce its position within, the national security system.

17

The British National Security Council:
It takes a village

Catarina Thomson

It all comes down to the fact you don't have a written constitution, you don't write anything down, or that which you do write down is only part of the story.[1]

The introduction and functioning of the United Kingdom's (UK) National Security Council (NSC) illustrates a central hypotheses of this volume quite neatly: a NSC needs to reflect (and build upon) the wider security system it serves. The UK's first national security advisor (NSA), Lord Ricketts, observed that establishing a NSC was not a revolution.[2] It built on centuries of effective defence coordination. Just a decade old, fewer than half of Britons even knew the UK had a NSC,[3] experts underlined its perceived pitfalls,[4] and some argued that the formal re-structuring of Whitehall that created the NSC hadn't improved national strategy.[5] However, examining the effects the creation of the NSC had through formal, codified documents and outcomes, and considering non-written patterns of behaviour, it has improved the coherence and adaptability of national security. To capture both dynamics, this chapter relies on published material and interviews with serving or recently retired high-level members of

---

[1] Anonymous interview.
[2] Peter Ricketts (2020). *Speaking truth to power: the problem with Prime Minister Johnson's new national security advisor*, RUSI.
[3] Author survey with a representative sample of 2,000 UK adults, fielded in April 2017 by YouGov. Project was funded by the Economic and Social Science Research Council (ES/L010879/1) and a University of Exeter's ADR Strategic Fund. When asked if the UK had a NSC, 45 per cent replied affirmatively, 6 per cent said no, and 49 per cent stated they didn't know. For methodological details refer to Catarina Thomson (2018). *Mind the Gap: Comparing Foreign Policy Attitudes of Security Elites and the General Public*, RUSI Whitehall Report.
[4] House of Lords and House of Commons Joint Committee on the National Security Strategy (JCNSS) (2012). *First Review of the National Security Strategy 2010*; Joe Devaney and Josh Harris (2014). *The National Security Council: National Security at the Centre of Government*, Institute for Government.
[5] David Blagden (2009). 'Strategic thinking for the age of austerity', *RUSI Journal*, vol. 154(6), 60–66; Timothy Edmunds (2014). 'Complexity, strategy and the national interest', *International Affairs*, vol. 90(3), 525–539.

the Ministry of Defence, the Foreign and Commonwealth Office, the Department for International Development,[6] the Cabinet Office, Home Office, National Security Secretariat, defence think tanks and academics,[7] as well as expert and public opinion survey data.

NSC origins

> When we think about security policy, the lines begin to get a little bit blurred around the edges of the policy domain. I think it's a fundamentally fuzzy policy domain.[8]

In the post-Cold War period, the UK security system evolved from a narrow focus on defence (primarily geared for state-on-state conflict), to a broader security machinery that involved new government and non-government actors. Broader participation required ways to bring together departments that could now include, for instance, the Department of Transport or Department of Health. Slowly but surely, changes were implemented to improve inter-departmental coordination,[9] which culminated in the institutional formalization of the 2008 National Security Strategy (NSS) in a standing NSC and the replacement of the Strategic Defence Review first by a Strategic Defence *and Security* Review (SDSR) in 2010 and then, an *Integrated* Review in 2021. The NSS constituted one of the most significant reforms to the sector since the Second World War.[10] It reflected a broadening view of security where citizens and security experts were concerned with varied threats requiring multi-departmental responses. Recently the top threats for UK security experts were cyber-attacks, climate change and Russian territorial ambitions while for the general population it was international terrorism, Islamic fundamentalism and cyber-attacks.[11]

---

[6]   Now combined in the Foreign, Commonwealth & Development Office.
[7]   For an in-depth analysis of the relationship between formal and informal institutions surrounding the NSC and the Strategic Defence and Security Review (and for details on interview sampling methodology) see Catarina Thomson and David Blagden (2018). 'A Very British National Security State: Formal and informal institutions in the design of UK security policy', *The British Journal of Politics and International Relations*, vol. 20(3), 573–593.
[8]   Anonymous interview.
[9]   For more details see Thomson and Blagden op. cit.
[10] Edmunds, op. cit., 525–539.
[11] Respondents classified issues as: critical threats to the vital interests of the UK in the next ten years; important but not critical threats, or; not important threats. Critical threats for security experts were: cyber-attacks to UK computer networks – 73 per cent; climate change – 43 per cent; Russia's territorial ambitions – 42 per cent. For members of the public, critical threats were: international terrorism – 70 per cent; Islamic fundamentalism – 64 per cent; cyber-attacks – 53 per cent. Thomson (2018). op. cit.

The UK's experience in Afghanistan (2001–2021) and Iraq (2003–2011) highlighted the importance of a whole-of-government approach. Intervening wasn't just about military confrontation but included providing basic goods and services as well as seeking internal political change. Government departments had related but distinct objectives which required improved coordination mechanisms. One interviewee noted that, 'we didn't really have comprehensive approaches and we learnt hard lessons in Iraq and Afghanistan about how you actually do this and how difficult it is to link up humanitarian aid and hard security elements in a successful way, but that is the concept.'[12] The domestic political environment was also changing: the 2008 financial crisis was a critical time, creating an environment where defence could not be funded as before.

Although it was Gordon Brown who first published a NSS, creating the NSC allowed David Cameron to claim he was moving away from the overly-informal and unaccountable approaches for which the Tony Blair government was widely criticized. Domestically, 'the NSC was shorthand for saying, "it's not these chaotic people, it's not Tony and his friends sitting on a sofa and it's not Gordon Brown who doesn't know whether he's coming or going"'.[13] Introducing a NSC also helped manage relations between the Conservative and Liberal Democrat parties governing together in coalition, which was unusual for the UK.[14]

The 2021 Integrated Review of Security, Defence, Development and Foreign Policy provides the most recent conceptualization of national security. It is a broad one indeed – the objective is to defend 'our people, territory, critical national infrastructure (CNI), democratic institutions and way of life – and by reducing our vulnerability to the threat from states, terrorism and serious and organised crime.'[15] As well as traditional security interests, priority areas include health, science and technology, the economy, and the environment as key issues. Such a broad definition of national security underlines the criticality of effective coordination.

---

[12] Anonymous interview.
[13] Anonymous interview.
[14] George Jones and Andrew Blick (21 May 2010). 'The PM and the Centre of UK Government from Tony Blair to David Cameron', *LSE British Politics and Policy Blog*.
[15] HM Government (March 2021). *Global Britain in a Competitive Age; the Integrated Review of Security, Defence, Development and Foreign Policy*, CP403, 11.

The Whitehall Village

> Brits wouldn't say anything if somebody didn't conform to something that wasn't written down, but that individual would probably know that they had failed, and so I think there is something about our strategic culture.[16]

Shared norms that lead to convergent expectations of what is (and isn't) appropriate conduct can be enforced formally (laws, rules, courts, etc.) or informally (social patterns).[17] As long as their violation is expected to generate some sort of external sanction, both can generate 'game rules for a society'.[18] As any visitor to the UK can attest, just because a norm isn't explicitly stated doesn't mean one isn't expected to behave accordingly! This is perhaps especially true in the foreign policy and security community, which despite becoming more diverse, remains rather remarkably quite narrow. One interviewee noted, 'There is a certain clubishness in the foreign policy establishment of 150–200 or so people; they go to lunches, dinners, clubs, "old pals"'.[19]

Despite the American security system being derived from the UK's Second World War structures,[20] 'some are trying to copy the American model, but the British tradition is that things aren't written down. We don't have clear roles like the U.S. because things aren't written down'.[21] This does not, necessarily constitute a limitation to a NSC functioning in a security system such as the British one. It just means that when analysing the effects of the NSC, one should consider whether it optimizes existing informal mechanisms (which are historically relevant in the British system) to aid security decision-making processes or tries to forcibly replace them. Introducing structural changes should be helpful not only due to new elements being introduced, but also to improve what was previously there.

One Whitehall trait that concerns some in the system is the tendency to seek consensus. A shared understanding of a problem is crucial, but while having consensus on approach can be a national asset at critical junctures, it also poses challenges. One interviewee noted that, 'the way the British system encourages

---

[16] Anonymous interview.
[17] Gretchen Helmke and Steven Levitsky (2004). 'Informal institutions and comparative politics: a research agenda', *Perspectives on Politics*, vol.20(4), 725–740.
[18] Douglass North (1990). *Institutions, Institutional Change, and Economic Performance* (New York: Cambridge University Press), 3.
[19] Anonymous interview.
[20] Franklyn Johnson (1961). 'The British Committee of Imperial Defence: Prototype of U.S. security organisation'. *The Journal of Politics*, vol. 23(2), 231–261.
[21] Anonymous Interview.

consensus might supress dissent … that, I think, is the great danger',[22] while another lamented, 'from what I've seen there's an aversion to bringing the debate into the room; there's a sense that everything needs to sorted before it gets to the NSC'.[23] The main lesson from the UK for consensus-seeking security communities in other countries would be to monitor what occurs *around* the formal NSC meetings. Inter-departmental discussions where different points of view are argued take place at the margins of UK NSC meetings.

The NSC

The informal relationships are what make the system work. You don't get things decided in informal relationships, but it's those that actually generate new thinking.[24]

The NSC, chaired by the Prime Minister (PM), and operating as their 'strategic brain',[25] is the main forum for collective discussion of the government's objectives for national security and about how best to deliver them. Members include: Chancellor of the Exchequer, Attorney General, Chancellor of the Duchy of Lancaster and key departmental Secretaries of State from: Home Office; Defence; Cabinet Office; and Foreign, Commonwealth and Development Affairs.[26] Other ministers or officials attend depending on the issue being discussed.[27] It is supported by National Security Ministers (NSM), and NSC (Officials) Meetings. There is a variable number of ministerial sub-committees dealing with specialized policy areas. Currently these include: Nuclear Deterrence and Security, Domestic and Economic Strategy, Climate Action Strategy, Crime and Justice Task Force, EU Exit Strategy and COVID-19 Strategy (although this sub-committee has been criticized for not meeting).[28] The NSC and NSM ordinarily meet monthly, with the NSC (Officials) supporting both.

Unlike its American counterpart, the UK NSC is restricted to discussing topics relevant to the PM. One interviewee stated, 'the structure of government depends on the personality of PM, because roles aren't formally written down.

---

[22] Anonymous interview.
[23] Anonymous interview.
[24] Anonymous interview.
[25] Anonymous interview.
[26] Joint Committee on National Security Strategy (JCNSS) (13 September 2021). *The UK's National Security Machinery*. HC231/HL68, 8.
[27] Thomson and Blagden, *op. cit.*
[28] https://assets.publishing.service.gov.uk/government/uploads/system/uploads/attachment_data/file/896093/Cabinet_Committee_list_and_public_ToRs.pdf, accessed 30 August 2021.

We don't have clear roles like in the U.S. so in a way the PM's power is less constrained that the President'.[29] Typically, the NSC functioned as a crisis response body, although there is now an intention to make it more strategic.[30] Another interviewee stated, 'we don't have very much national security policy. We've got a NSC but because we have been busy and in crisis after crisis it has been focusing predominantly on managing crises on an inter-departmental basis rather than necessarily producing a body of national security policy'.[31]

The informality means the personality of the NSA is crucial: 'the NSC needs a NSA who is politically significant and also independent, someone the PM would listen to, someone who could direct the NSC, work out policy and then present it to the PM or Home Secretary.'[32] As pointed out by the first NSA, Lord Ricketts, in the hands of the right person, the role entails 'setting the agenda – including persuading the prime minister to accept a balanced diet of subjects on the NSC agenda'.[33] Recent controversies regarding the appointment of NSAs highlight the role's importance, and expose tensions between the will of individual PMs and the broader national security community. When (then) Sir Mark Sedwill remained NSA while also becoming the Head of the Civil Service (following his predecessor, Jeremy Hayward's illness), many questioned Theresa May's decision and whether this dual-post hampered the distinctiveness of each role or downgraded the key role of NSA.[34] However, following Sedwill's retirement, the roles reverted to separate incumbents. The Johnson government also recently challenged convention, by attempting to make the first-ever political appointee to NSA who was also a minister. This was later abandoned, arguably influenced by the significant concerns raised over the effects such an appointment could have on the nature of the role. Opposing views included many from the governing party, including former PM Theresa May, and former officials.[35] This opposition shows both the importance of the role, and how the broader network, including retired senior officials, acts through formal and informal means to protect the national security system. The new NSA, Sir Stephen Lovegrove, the former civil service Permanent Secretary at Defence is considered better placed to be the independent voice many want.[36]

[29] Anonymous interview.
[30] JCNSS HC231/HL68, op.cit., 9.
[31] Anonymous interview.
[32] Anonymous interview.
[33] Ricketts, op. cit.
[34] James Blitz (25 October 2018). 'Critics question dual role for Britain's new top civil servant'. *Financial Times*.
[35] Richard Johnstone (29 June 2020). 'O'Donnell: Frost's appointment as national security advisor "risks civil service politicisation"'. *Civil Service World*.
[36] Cristina Gallardo (29 January 2021). David Frost appointed UK's Brexit policy representative, *Politico*.

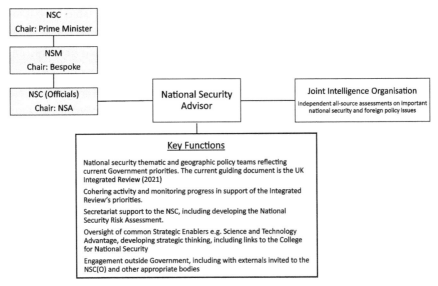

Figure 17.1 Support to the NSA.

The NSA is supported by a recently reduced team, now fewer than 180 people, in the Cabinet Office. The team provides thematic and geographic policy advice against national priorities, monitors how well the UK is delivering its priorities, and provides the Secretariat to the NSC, NSM and NSC(O). It includes the Civil Contingencies Secretariat that manages the National Security Risk Assessment (NSRA) and a new strategy cell to address the need for 'a strong strategy muscle' and improve relationships with academics, think-tanks and parliamentarians.[37] See Figure 17.1.

Despite the NSC being (thus far) strategically under-utilized, it contributes to the national security policy process in at least two distinct ways. First, it can present a unifying aim in times of national crises, including interventions abroad, to help achieve a comprehensive approach required in multi-department interventions. Second, it has optimized the informal structures so prevalent throughout the Whitehall Village by fermenting discussions in the margins of formal NSC meetings. 'Pre-NSC sessions' between representatives of different ministries and departments take place before the full ministerial NSC and sub-committee meetings.[38] Topics are varied and complex. As discussed previously, there has been a certain aversion to bring dissenting points of view to the NSC so it is these pre-meetings where different perspectives are discussed among those who support ministers. They help set the agenda and present ideas that should be,

---

[37] Sir Stephen Lovegrove, NSA, in evidence to the JCNSS (5 July 2021). Oral Evidence: National Security Machinery, Q125.

[38] Thomson and Blagden, op. cit.

if not fully acceptable to decision makers, at least in an acceptable bargaining range to begin formal discussions. In these sessions, 'we generated narratives or how we shaped it to what we thought, actually had to be focused on in the one hour session, saying, look, we totally get why you're interested in this, but there's a lot of challenges in this, but maybe if we shape it in a certain way, it becomes more feasible, more doable, more palatable'.[39] Importantly, however, the decisions themselves are minuted and taken within the NSC, thus increasing accountability which was one of the principal reasons for establishing the NSC in the first place.

COVID-19 and other shocks to the system

Although some criticized the government for the lack of formal NSC meetings as COVID-19 reached Europe and the UK,[40] the issue was being considered in the national security system from January 2020. However, it was quickly apparent that the crisis wasn't going to be a short-term issue, and the decision was made that COVID-19 needed a broader approach than the NSC could provide. Modelled on structures put in place to exit the EU, the Cabinet Office COVID-19 task force helped coordinate and deliver the government's response through two bodies: COVID-S (Strategic) and COVID-O (Operational). COVID-S, chaired by the PM, initially met daily, which reduced to twice-a-week. Operational COVID groups focused on health and care, international and economic matters, and other public services; they are chaired by senior Ministers.[41] Classified at a lower security level than the NSC, this facilitated meeting online during periods of lockdown. In addition to broadening the scope of participation needed to organize a whole-of-government response, these bodies have protected the NSC's capacity to focus on non-COVID-19 security issues in the National Security Risk Assessment.[42]

Some of the non-COVID issues requiring NSC-direction could hardly be more relevant as the UK defines what shape 'Global Britain' is to take. Having left the EU, key questions about the UK's national orientation – whether it will gravitate towards the United States or Europe – are being tackled in a heated domestic environment.[43]

[39] Anonymous interview.
[40] Defence Select Committee (22 April 2020). Oral evidence: Introductory Session with the Secretary of State, HC 295, Q3.
[41] JCNSS (8 July 2020). Oral Evidence: The Work of the National Security Advisor, Q7.
[42] JCNSS Oral Evidence (5 July 2021), op.cit., Q129.
[43] Michael Clarke and Helen Ramscar (2019). *Tipping Point: Britain, Brexit and Security in the 2020s* (London: Bloomsbury Press).

Conclusion

The NSC is a relatively new organization, headed by only three PMs, and its identity will evolve. Its ten years have been in extraordinarily tumultuous times. However, prominent voices within the Whitehall system are clamouring for further re-structuring of the UK security apparatus which is 'not enough because we still have a stovepiped system. Whitehall needs a complete overhaul, but no one's willing to commit to that, or convince the electorate this is needed'.[44] The JCNSS concerns include a lack of clarity in the NSC's role and remit, how issues are raised, and how cross-cutting issues are managed, including the NSM's ad hoc chairing arrangements, where the lack of clear ownership could complicate delivering integrated responses.[45] People are, however, listening. The Integrated Review urges a greater focus on being strategic, more flexibility and agility in how departments tackle cross-cutting challenges, and argues for clearer accountability for delivery.[46] The new NSA has also started to make changes; how successful they will be remains to be seen, and there is scepticism.[47]

For all its limitations, however, 54 per cent of UK security experts consider that the NSC makes a real difference to how security policy is designed in the UK. Forty-seven per cent think having a NSC makes the process of security policy design more transparent than in the past, while 40 per cent believe the NSC helps ensure individuals can be held accountable for decisions that lead to negative outcomes.[48] Its contribution to national security decision-making suggests that the NSC is here to stay. The interplay of international and domestic factors, including politics and personalities, will continue to shape its role, structures and processes. Getting it right, in both the formal and informal systems, is vital.

---

[44] Anonymous interview.
[45] JCNSS HC231/HL68, op.cit., 60–70.
[46] 'Global Britain', op. cit., 97.
[47] JCNSS HC231/HL68, op.cit., 4.
[48] Author survey with 64 members of the UK Defence Academy, and 533 members of the Royal United Services Institute (RUSI) and its extended network: Dec 2016–April 2017. Project funded by the Economic and Social Science Research Council (ES/L010879/1) and University of Exeter's ADR Strategic Fund.

18

Washington's 'Keepers of the Keys'

Frank Hoffman

The role of the US National Security Council (NSC) in the conduct of foreign policy is captured well, if hubristically, in *Running the World*.[1] Another historian saw the NSC staff as '*Keepers of the Keys*'.[2] That also sounds arrogant, but the importance of the NSC and supporting system to US foreign policy and strategy is difficult to overestimate. Effectively integrating America's diplomatic, military and economic instruments of national power into a cohesive strategy is a complex, even Sisyphean, challenge. NSC structures and processes have evolved to fulfil each President's needs and support their policy and decision-making requirements,[3] albeit within the boundaries of American strategic culture and government. The NSC and its staff represent the central policy-making process supporting foreign policy decisions, through integrating the diplomatic and military instruments of power primarily.

The US legislature does not ordinarily attempt to formalize the internal operations of the Executive Office of the President, but Franklin D. Roosevelt's seemingly uncoordinated conduct of the Second World War served to promote change. In 1947, Congress created the NSC to advise and assist the President to integrate domestic, foreign and military components of national security.[4] The NSC's statutory members are the President, Vice President, Secretary of State, Secretary of Defence and, since 2007, Secretary of Energy. The Chairman of the Joint Chiefs of Staff and Director of National Intelligence are statutory advisers.

---

[1] David Rothkopf (2006). *Running the World: The Inside Story of the National Security Council and the Architects of American Power* (New York: Public Affairs).

[2] *John Prados (1991). Keepers of the Keys: A History of the National Security Council from Truman to Bush* (New York: William Morrow).

[3] David Auerswald (2017). 'The Evolution of the NSC Process', in Roger Z. George and Harvey Rishikof, eds., *The National Security Enterprise: Navigating the Labyrinth,* 2nd ed. (Washington DC: Georgetown University Press).

[4] On the NSC's origins and National Security Act 1947, see Amy Zegart (2000). *Flawed by Design: The Evolution of the CIA, JCS, and NSC* (Stanford CA: Stanford University Press).

Each President organizes the Council and its major processes differently, inviting other senior officials to participate in NSC deliberations or join the major councils and committees.

Originally without its own staff, today the NSC has some 200, most of whom are career public servants seconded by their parent Departments/agencies for two- to three-year tours. Over time, the NSC staff has become a major actor in formulating national security policy: 'the intellectual engine of national security, fighting for policies that have been triumphs as well as terrible tragedies.'[5]

The head of the NSC staff, the National Security Adviser (NSA), plays a critical role in policymaking and strategic coordination. Uniquely in the US government, the NSA has no real source of power outside proximity to the President and the ability to manage the Council's agenda and staff. The NSA is not confirmed by the Congress, like the Cabinet members that sit on the NSC, and has a limited public role.

The NSC's organization and influence varies significantly between Administrations, from very process-oriented and transparent systems to those that are closed and operating with little structure to their policy-making. Cooperation between major agencies has often been difficult due to personalities, bureaucratic agendas and resource imbalances.

Strategy by Committee

Besides the full Council with the President presiding, the NSC employs two key committees to deliberate on options.

Principal's Committee (PC). This is the Cabinet-level senior inter-agency forum for policy issues affecting *important* national security interests. Created under President George H.W. Bush to free the President and Vice President from minor policy negotiations by agency heads, the PC does not include them but presents its work to the full NSC for high-level issues and implementation. It is convened and chaired by the NSA, or delegated to the Homeland Security Advisor. The Chair determines the agenda and schedule, and an Executive Secretary on the NSC staff ensures staff papers and estimates are prepared. Cabinet-level heads of executive departments and agencies, and other senior

---

[5]   John Gans (2019). *White House Warriors: How the National Security Council Transformed the American Way of War* (New York: Liveright), 9.

officials, can be included by the NSA.[6] Over the past two decades, the scope has been broadened beyond classical security and foreign policy to incorporate domestic security, sanctions, law enforcement and public health.

Deputies Committee (DC). Chaired by the Deputy NSA,[7] this the senior sub-Cabinet inter-agency forum for national security policy issues. The policy process' creative engine,[8] it monitors implementation of decisions, periodically reviews the Administration's major initiatives, and ensures issues have been properly analysed before being brought before the NSC, Homeland Security Committee and PC. The DC establishes Interagency Policy Committees (IPCs), which are the main day-to-day fora for inter-agency coordination. Chaired by NSC staff, the IPCs provide the senior committees with policy analysis and ensure timely responses to and coordination of Presidential decisions.

Current issues

While the security system's composition and basic processes have evolved, numerous issues reappear.[9] One insightful commentator observed: 'we have repeatedly witnessed the system's inability to integrate the capacities and expertise of departments and agencies.'[10] More recently, Robert Gates, who served on the NSC staff under Brent Scowcroft, and later as CIA Director and Secretary of Defence, commented, 'the structure itself is quite outdated.'[11]

NSA Neutrality and process transparency. Recurring issues involve the NSA's role and ensuring the NSC maintains a more strategic and coordinating

---

[6] Attendees are: Secretaries of State, Treasury, Defence, Energy and Homeland Security; Attorney General; President's Chief of Staff; Director National Intelligence; Chairman of the Joint Chiefs of Staff; CIA Director; Homeland Security Advisor; Representative to the United Nations. The Deputy NSA, Deputy NSA for Strategy, Vice President's NSA, and Executive Secretary also attend. When discussing international economic issues, the Secretary of Commerce, Trade Representative and Assistant to the President for Economic Policy attend.

[7] DC attendees are: Deputy Secretaries from the Departments of State, Treasury, Defence, Energy, and Homeland Security; Deputy Attorney General; Deputy Director of the Office of Management and Budget; Deputy Director National Intelligence; Vice Chairman of the Joint Chiefs of Staff; CIA Deputy Director; Deputy NSA for Strategy; Deputy Homeland Security Advisor; Deputy Assistant to the President; Vice President's NSA, and the Administrator of the U.S. Agency for International Development.

[8] Mark Wilcox (2014). 'The National Security Council Deputies Committee, Engine of the Policy Process'. *Interagency Journal*, vol. 5(1), 22–32.

[9] Shawn Brimley, Dafna Rand, Julianne Smith, and Jacob Stokes (2015). *Enabling Decision: Shaping the National Security Council for the Next President,* Center for a New American Security.

[10] James Locher (10 November 2015). *Statement before the Senate Armed Services Committee,* Washington DC.

[11] Robert Gates (2020). *Exercise of Power: American Failures, Successes, and a New Path Forward in the Post-Cold War World* (New York: Knopf), 60.

role.[12] The NSA's potential role is usually defined as an Honest Broker,[13] a neutral, refereeing competing Cabinet or Department views, refining options, drawing out debates and enhancing policy options.[14] More active or advocacy approaches, e.g. Henry Kissinger as NSA, are not seen as effective.[15]

The NSA should focus on getting multiple perspectives and options before the Council, vetting them, and stopping strong-minded Department heads from framing their preferred option isolated from the White House.[16]

> Being an 'honest broker' means running a fair and transparent process for bringing issues to the President for decision. It means maintaining a 'level playing field' in which ideas and views can compete with one another on an equal basis, without 'stacking the deck' in favor of one or another approach. It means in particular not using the privileged position accorded to the National Security Advisor in this process to 'tilt' the process in favor of the outcome favored by the National Security Advisor.[17]

While preferring the 'honest broker' function, Stephen Hadley cautions against its being neutered: 'The honest broker role requires producing the best options possible – developing a full range of options. Of course, you develop your own views. And when the president asked my opinion, I would tell him. You're not obliged to be a policy eunuch.'[18] There is widespread agreement that Scowcroft's open, transparent order is the Gold Standard for running the NSC.[19]

Centralization. The White House is frequently criticized for using NSC staff to centralize decision-making and doing work better done by experts inside functional Departments. Some accused the Reagan-era NSC staff of this after the Iran–Contra scandal.[20] A decade later, the Hart/Rudman Commission

---

[12] Ivo Daalder and I. M. Destler (2009). *In the Shadow of the Oval Office: Profiles of the National Security Advisers and the Presidents They Served–From JFK to George W. Bush* (New York: Simon & Schuster).

[13] John P. Burke (2005). 'The Neutral/Honest Broker Role in Foreign Policy Decision Making: A Reassessment,' *Presidential Studies Quarterly*, vol. 35(2), 229–258.

[14] John P. Burke (2009). *Honest Broker?: The National Security Advisor and Presidential Decision Making* (College Station: Texas A&M University Press).

[15] For comparisons of different models, see Bartholomew Sparrow (2015). *The Strategist: Brent Scowcroft and the Call of National Security* (New York: Public Affairs).

[16] Alexander George (1972). 'The Case for Multiple Advocacy in Making Foreign Policy'. *American Political Science Review*, vol. 66(3), 751–785.

[17] Stephen Hadley (24 August 2016). *The Role and Importance of the NSA*, Center for Strategic and International Studies.

[18] Colin Dueck (2014). 'The Role of the National Security Advisor', *Orbis*, vol. 58(1), 15–38.

[19] Robert Gates (13 August 2020). 'The Scowcroft Model, An Appreciation', *Foreign Affairs*; on Scowcroft and the Honest Broker paradigm, see James Mann (8 August 2020). 'Brent Scowcroft Didn't Always Follow 'the Scowcroft Model'', *New York Times*.

[20] Tower Commission Report of the President's Special Review Board (1987), https://archive.org/details/TowerCommission.

warned against the tendency for the NSC staff to evolve towards micro-management and becoming more operational:

> The NSC advisor and staff should resist pressures toward the centralization of power, avoid duplicating the responsibilities of the departments, and forego operational control of any aspect of U.S. policy. Assuming a central policymaking role seriously detracts from the NSC staff's primary roles of honest broker and policy coordinator.[21]

This problem remains unresolved: 'The NSC staff, originally envisioned as a coordinating body between departments and agencies has been continually remade but has not been consistently able to cajole or coerce inter-agency cooperation.'[22] While tied-up seeking information and striving to integrate disparate Departments and agencies following their own agendas, long-range strategic planning gets pushed aside.

The Obama Administration faced complaints about centralized decision-making and excessive control of government activity.[23] Mr Gates found the Obama White House 'by far the most centralized and controlling in national security of any I had seen since Richard Nixon and Henry Kissinger ruled the roost in the 1970s.'[24] His successor concurred, adding that: 'Far more than in previous administrations that I'd witnessed ... President Obama's decision-making apparatus was centralized in the White House'.[25]

Defenders of the Obama Administration, however, highlight the complexities of the issues being faced,[26] and the flaws in proper oversight earlier in the global war on terror when large problems in coordination were left unresolved.[27] They saw the Obama-era deliberations reflecting hard-learned lessons, reinforced by challenges during wars in Afghanistan and Iraq.

Long-range planning. Frequently, senior White House officials and NSC staffs are criticized for leaping from crisis to crisis. Reviewing events preceding the attack of 2001, the 9/11 Commission noted that, as 'the NSC staff is consumed

---

[21] U. S. National Security Commission/21st Century (2001), *Road Map for National Security: Imperatives for Change*, Government Printing Office, 49–52.

[22] Richard Weitz ed. (2012). *Case Studies, National Security Reform*, Strategic Studies Institute.

[23] David Rohde and Warren Strobel (9 October 2014). 'Micro-manager in Chief', *The Atlantic*.

[24] Robert Gates (2014). *Duty: A Memoir of a Secretary at War* (New York: Knopf), 566.

[25] Leon Panetta with Jim Newton (2014). *Worthy Fights, a Memoir of Leadership in War and Peace* (New York: Penguin).

[26] Derek Chollet (26 April 2016). 'What's Wrong with Obama's National Security Council'. *Defense One*.

[27] For an assessment of decision-making regarding the Iraq war, see Michael J. Mazarr (2019). *Leap of Faith: Hubris, Negligence, and America's Greatest Foreign Policy Tragedy* (New York: Public Affairs).

by these day-to-day tasks, it has less capacity to find the time and detachment needed to advise a President on larger policy issues.'[28] One proposed solution for improving longer-range planning was to re-establish the Eisenhower-era Planning Board, with Undersecretary or Deputy Secretary-level officials from each major department's strategic planning office.[29] Contemporary advocates of this model envision senior officers from the State and Defence Departments comprising the boards. 'Re-establishing a Planning Board could, along with persistent presidential involvement in the formulation of strategy, go a long way toward improving the quality of U.S. strategy.'[30] Eisenhower's planning process was quickly dismantled by President Kennedy in 1961. Former NSA Zbigniew Brzezinski, concluded, 'The Planning Board was a very important instrument, the elimination of which has handicapped the US government ever since.'[31] The Planning Board, in theory, devises longer-range plans for the PC and the President, so they can focus on the big picture. Evidence for its efficacy is mixed.[32] Some participants, including Acheson, Kennan and Nitze, found the Eisenhower model exhausting and ponderous.[33] Today's DC fulfils the planning board's role, now augmented by dedicated NSC staff for strategy development.

Implementation oversight. The emphasis on the NSC's policy development and Presidential decision-making dominates the literature, but its implementation, oversight and assessment roles are under-explored. Two 'Surge' debates – Bush (2006) and Obama (2009) – highlighted the importance of effective assessment of progress and continued adaptation.[34] Presidents Bush and Obama struggled to understand how effective their policies and strategies were. Stephen Hadley, NSA in the second half of Mr Bush's Administration observed, 'Implementation management is an area of deficiency in the NSC

---

[28] The National Commission on Terrorist Attacks Upon the United States (2004). *The 9/11 Commission Report*, 402.

[29] Paul D. Miller (2013). 'Organizing the National Security Council: I Like Ike's', *Presidential Studies Quarterly*, vol. 43(3), 592–606.

[30] Andrew F. Krepinevich (19 March 2009). *Testimony Before the U.S. House of Representatives, House Committee on Armed Services, Subcommittee on Oversight and Investigation*.

[31] Quoted by Krepinevich (2009), *op. cit.* Also Council on Foreign Relations (31 October 1997). 'The NSC at 50: Past, Present, and Future'.

[32] Robert R. Bowie and Richard H. Immerman (1998). *Waging Peace; How Eisenhower Shaped an Enduring Cold War Strategy* (Oxford: Oxford University Press), 91–92.

[33] Chris Lamb in Hans Binnendijk and Patrick Cronin, eds. (2009) *Civilian Surge, Key to Complex Operations* (Washington DC: National Defense University Press), 53.

[34] Frank Hoffman and Alex Crowther. 'Strategic Assessment and Adaption', in Richard D. Hooker and Joseph Collins, eds. (2014). *Lessons Encountered, Learning from the Long War* (Washington DC: National Defense University Press), 89–163.

system; we identified it; we tried a number of things and we probably got better over time.' Hadley graded NSC policy development in the Bush Administration as a pass ('B') but gave himself a nearly failing grade of 'D' for inter-agency implementation.[35] Implementation oversight should be the most important role the NSC Staff plays, a task assigned to the DC. Unless the President makes it explicit that the NSC Staff has authority to oversee implementation, it may fail this part of its mandate.

Functional integration of domestic security and economics. Given Russian threats in cyber, business interruptions and chemical attacks, integration is acutely needed. Ongoing trade issues with Beijing also suggest that thinking strategically about international economic is similarly important. However, the NSC system struggles to integrate domestic security and international trade and finance in responding to a globalized and interdependent economy. Incorporating these elements poses new policy and strategy challenges that are often firewalled in the White House; during the Clinton Administration, a National Economic Council was established separate from the NSC. Similarly, the COVID-19 response was initially handled by NSC staff from the Asia Directorate working in a small cell originally created in the Obama Administration during the Ebola crisis. However, as the crisis grew in the Trump era, a standing task force comprising a broad range of White House domestic advisors and public health officials coordinated international and domestic policy decisions.[36] The intense public and domestic political role the task force played would have been highly unusual for the NSC staff and may change how future Administrations adapt where institutional seams are blurred by globalization and transnational crises.

The Biden Administration

Consistent with historical practice, one of the Administration's earliest decisions formalized the structure and attendance of the major NSC committees, expanding the seating plan.[37] The CIA Director gets a seat at this much larger table and, recognizing the cross-cutting nature of many challenges, the regular and 'as needed' participant list is expanded to ensure expertise in homeland

---

[35] Stephen Hadley Interview by Joseph Collins and Nicholas Rostow (2015). *Prism*, vol. 5(3), 146–158.
[36] John Rogin (30 March 2020). 'NSC Sounded Early Alarms about Coronavirus', *Washington Post*.
[37] White House (4 February 2021). *National Security Memorandum 2, Memorandum on Renewing the National Security Council System.*

security, global health, international economics, environment, cybersecurity and science and technology is properly represented. Key additions to the PC included the White House's director of the Office of Science and Technology Policy and the Administrator of the US Agency for International Development. Experienced observers noted this 'presumably reflect[s] the Biden administration's renewed emphasis on science and global engagement.'[38] It also reflects the need to consider trade-offs and costs as the Biden team seeks to renew the domestic and economic foundations of US national power after two decades of counter-terrorism campaigns.

The President has articulated a broad conception of national security that goes beyond the NSC's past practice, noting that 'economic security is national security'. This recognizes that foreign policy must be perceived as serving national interests and those of the middle and working class.[39] Consequently, the NSC and staff must consider international trade, finance, technology policy, and manufacturing/industrial resilience as part of national security. This comprehensive conception, while not entirely absent in past administrations, was achieved outside the formalized and deliberative NSC decision-making process. New NSC staff directorships and appointments of key personnel, such as former Ambassador and former NSA, Dr Susan Rice, as Director of the Domestic Policy Council, will facilitate institutionalizing this more comprehensive and integrated national security construct.

The NSC staff structure while not formally published, appears re-designed from the Obama Administration (see Figure 18.1). President Biden also restored senior policy level expertise in homeland security and cyber matters that were diminished under the last Administration.[40] Other new offices include energy and climate policy. The National Economic Council, Domestic Policy Council, and White House Officer of Science and Technology Policy are outside the NSC staff, but now attend NSC meetings and contribute to the policy-making process. As the Directive's title suggests, the NSC is being renewed for the twenty-first century, not simply restored.

---

[38] John Bellinger (8 February 2021). 'National Security Memorandum 2 – What's New in Biden's NSC Structure', *Lawfare*, at National Security Memorandum 2—What's New in Biden's NSC Structure? – Lawfare (lawfareblog.com), accessed 30 August 2021.

[39] White House (March 2021). *Interim National Security Strategic Guidance*, 15.

[40] David Sanger (13 January 2021). 'Biden to Restore Homeland Security and Cybersecurity Aides to Senior White House Posts', *New York Times*.

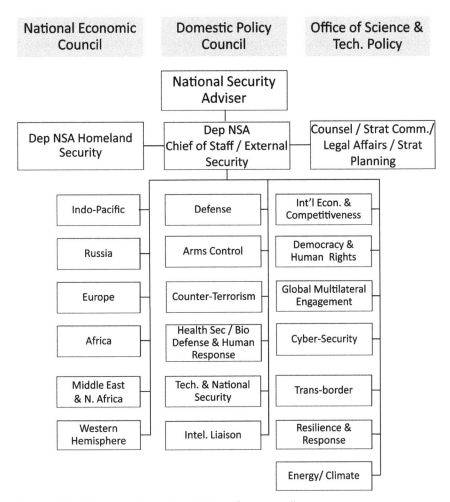

Figure 18.1 Biden Administration NSC staff structure.[41]

Conclusion

As government's principal integrating policy mechanism, the NSC has immense responsibilities in an increasingly complex world. Enabling the President and his Cabinet to better understand context, frame problems, and craft appropriate strategies, is increasingly important. The NSC's approach to integrated action has served Washington well, especially when the Cabinet deliberates in an open and disciplined manner supported by a neutral NSA and staff that focus on

---

[41] Source: Author.

major policy challenges and the strategic level. However, it is increasingly complicated by the interconnectedness of major issues like climate change or energy policy that impact both international and domestic policy. This is not new, but is challenging in the US government system where power and responsibility are distributed to large bureaucracies, coordinated by a small NSC staff that lacks legislative authority. The NSA, therefore, remains critical in managing the analysis of major policy actions, formalizing Presidential decisions and ensuring they are implemented efficiently.

19

Case study analysis

Paul O'Neill

National security challenges require effective horizontal management. The need for bodies to coordinate successful multi-agency security responses has grown as conceptions of what security means have expanded and appropriately integrated solutions are expected. Ironically, government attempts to improve their internal management systems through greater departmental specialization, budgetary structures and performance management regimes have reinforced the strength of vertical siloes.[1] These are efficient and cope well with clearly-defined problems, but high levels of specialization often result in fragmentation at a governmental enterprise level.[2] Such fragmentation is not well suited to national security's multi-dimensional problems.

NSCs are (often uniquely) placed to integrate government thinking and action across departmental siloes towards common goals. The case studies in this book show that, despite similarities in the design and functioning of NSCs, what works in one country does not necessarily work well in another. Some NSCs have executive authority (Japan), while others provide advice (Ukraine). Some prioritize internal security (Kenya, South Africa), while others focus on external threats (Georgia). A NSC cannot be directly transplanted from one body politic to another without risk of rejection and/or failure, as capacity building and security sector reform activity in Iraq and parts of Africa shows.

The principal lesson of this book is that the design of a NSC must be bespoke, reflecting choices made against three axes:

---

[1] Tom Christensen and Per Lægreid (November 2007). 'The Whole-of-Government Approach to Public Sector Reform', *Public Administration Review*, vol. 67(6), 1059.

[2] Paul Bracken, 'How to Build a Warning System', in Paul Bracken, Ian Bremmer and David Gordon (2008). *Managing Strategic Surprise: Lessons from Risk Management and Risk Assessment* (Cambridge: Cambridge University Press), 29.

1. the nature of the threat(s) and risks to national security;
2. the nature and structure of the government, its values, history and the bureaucratic habits that these create in the national security system (NSS); and
3. the specific role the nation and/or its leader expect of its NSC.

These axes operate within the context of, and are conditioned by, national, system and organizational cultures. Although these cultures are largely intangible, both individually and in their interaction, they profoundly affect how problems are framed and solved in practice; as Peter Drucker is reputed to have observed, 'Culture eats strategy for breakfast'.[3]

Characteristics

While their exact form differs depending on national assessments of the three axes, effective NSCs and staffs share common characteristics:

- **Horizontal**. They develop and support cross-government strategy/strategic responses to security challenges by coordinating functional departments. Typically, substantially smaller than those they are tasked to coordinate, they work with and through others.
- **Networked**. All sit at the centre of broad networks they are responsible for nurturing. Their principal role is to develop, at the highest level, cross-government strategies and responses to security threats and risks that cannot be managed in vertical siloes. They identify and convene partners from across government (sometimes wider) to build multi-dimensional and shared understanding of the problem(s) faced.[4] They have a core group of key ministers at their heart, supported by the most senior and experienced officials in the national security community. A wider periphery is engaged as necessary, including regional administrative bodies in federal or delegated systems.

---

[3] Boris Groysberg, Jeremiah Lee, Jesse Price and J. Yo-Jud Cheng (January–February 2018). 'The Leaders Guide to Corporate Culture', *Harvard Business Review*, 46. While the saying's originator is unclear, it is frequently attributed to management guru Peter Drucker; e.g. Paul Simpson in *Peter Drucker: the social and human value of work*, CIPD (21 July 2017) at www.cipd.co.uk/news-views/ changing-work-views/future-work/thought-pieces/peter-drucker-value-work, accessed 30 August 2021.

[4] Jeff Conklin (2008). *Dialogue Mapping: Building Shared Understanding of Wicked Problems* (Chichester: Wiley), 42.

- **Tiered**. The NSC sits at the top of a hierarchy of subordinate bodies that allows decisions to be taken at the lowest appropriate level. This maximizes the value of the time senior members of the Executive can devote to issues. Sub-groups are typically wider than the main group, allowing relevant but less invested departments/agencies to contribute without making the most senior body too unwieldy. Officials' groups also operate, usually involving a wider range of departments/agencies than the NSC, at which positions can be argued and adjusted to facilitate decision-making at the higher body. The different groups bring greater diversity of perspectives on the problem(s) and help spread knowledge and trust across the system.
- **Strong executive support**. They receive strong support from the Executive's political and bureaucratic elements. Often championed and chaired by the political head of the Executive, they also have strong relationships with the bureaucratic system through a NSA/equivalent to ensure cooperation despite the otherwise vertical organization of government responsibilities. Support varies as individuals or governments change, so governance and reward systems reinforcing desired behaviours enable outcomes to flow naturally from, rather than despite, the system design. The authority, role and influence of the NSA are important factors in the NSC's effectiveness, or otherwise, although the three are independent variables.
- **Staff Support**. All have access to administrative support, although the role of the staff differs substantially, as does its size. Larger secretariats can generate responses independent of departments, which can help overcome resource imbalances that typically favour larger departments, such as Defence. Others have small Secretariats that synthesize departments' disparate inputs to develop common positions.
- **Open**. All seek input from outside the polity to help understand complex issues and shape policy choices, but the degree to which the systems are open to engaging 'outsiders' in its core functions varies.

Design considerations

Galbraith's Star forces consideration of factors impacting on organizational design: strategy; structure; process; people and rewards.[5] These elements are

---

[5] Jay Galbraith (2014). *Designing Organizations: Strategy, Structure and Processes at the Business Unit and Enterprise Levels* (San Francisco, CA: Jossey-Bass).

shaped by, and help shape, organizational and system cultures. While each factor is considered separately below, they merge and interact. They also impact at different levels: the NSS; the combined NSC *and* Staff; individual organizations (the Council *or* its Staff, and individual departments). Successful NSCs find synergies in the interaction, making the whole greater than the sum of its parts.

Strategy

Strategy concerns how the NSS acts in response to national security threats/risks. NSCs sit within ecosystems of committees that ensure decisions can be made closest to the level of expertise and only the most important issues get elevated to the highest levels of central government. While Chan rightly asserts that clarity over the roles, authorities and responsibilities is important,[6] nodal clarity is not enough. System clarity is also needed; the relationships within the system, the processes by which the nodes interact, and how the escalation and de-escalation of issues is managed. Codifying this in a national security strategy helps. Even the process of developing the strategy helps, giving all parties the opportunity to collaborate. While the NSC may lead, understanding and ownership of security problems becomes shared across the system. Doing this transparently also allows society to become engaged (Ghana). While a strategy document is not essential where the threats/risks and roles and accountabilities are clearly understood – potentially even unhelpful where strategic updates are driven solely by the calendar[7] – its absence as a cohering force is felt in many countries, e.g. India and Norway.

Clarity over the meaning of 'security' is essential; it sets the parameters for threat definition and consequently to what the NSS should respond and how. The different definitions in this book reflect the diverse nature of the case studies, and the changing nature of the issues facing individual countries. Tensions between different understandings have often played out in Africa, seen in sometimes competing security systems: 'hard' security arrangements championed by strong military leaders, frequently in nations with a history of military-led liberation struggles, whereas human security is often driven by

---

[6]   Arthur Chan (2018). *Overcoming Challenges Arising from the Creation of National Security Councils: a Framework and Lessons from Sub-Saharan Africa*. RAND, 7.

[7]   Fixed schedules can lead to rushed analysis to meet the demands of the process, and/or decision-making inertia with important decisions delayed until the next scheduled review. House of Commons Defence Committee (2020). *In Search of Strategy – the 2020 Integrated Review*, 8.

international donors or an understandably principled response to regime oppression. However, grouping everything under 'security', as loosely understood human security can, does not make responses better. The desire to provide human security is not the same as having the capacity to deliver. Actor complexity increases, while the very act of securitizing can result in a loss of focus (societal security has arguably obscured national security in Norway) and limit debate, because raising the classification of information removes it from public access (South Africa).

The case studies generally highlight a shift from a classic (narrow) conception of national security to one that is broader, e.g. Colombia, United States, which bring more issues within its remit. This is not a one-way journey. A broad focus can narrow when circumstances warrant, for example in Ukraine when Russia annexed Crimea, or Georgia following its 2008 War. This broadening and narrowing of security's definition are part of an evolutionary process as the system adapts.

Countries face a wide range of threats: internal, such as poverty or crime in parts of Africa, or organized crime and a violent domestic insurgency in Colombia; external, e.g. Israel's external terrorist threats; or state-based military threats in Ukraine, Georgia and India. Some threats are best treated through government's civilian levers of power (e.g. New Zealand). Occasionally, however, the government itself can be a threat, through an over-powerful oppressive or corrupt regime (Ghana, South Africa). In this regard, history's hand shapes contemporary systems, and past oppression by NSCs makes societies unsurprisingly reluctant to grant them too much authority today (Iraq, Kenya). Inevitably, there are trade-offs between effective security and democracy (Canada, Kenya). COVID-19, and the ongoing climate emergency highlight another, increasingly important, kind of threat that comes from non-human actors. This distinction is significant because threats from pandemics and climate change cannot be deterred but must be treated, although human behaviour that frustrates or reinforces state strategies, against non-sentient threats is always amenable to influence. Different threats and *loci* of interest drive different structures, but all must retain the ability to cope with the unexpected. Even within a single polity, there is no evolutionary endpoint for an NSC: it must be able to adapt. This adaptation occurs within the framework of national values and history.

The NSC's role within the national strategy is crucial, whether primarily as a forum for discussing complex security issues – a counsel of the wise – e.g. Ukraine or for action, in either crisis-response (Japan, Georgia) or strategic planning (United States). The NSC function can also be delivered through a coordinated network rather than a single body, e.g. Canada. The role determines membership, hence education departments and those responsible for industrial strategy are more likely to be engaged when the focus is on long-term strategies. Crisis response bodies have more limited membership involving emergency response services such as police, fire and health. In reality, however, most countries' NSC and Staff cover crises and strategic planning at different times, adapting their basic approaches as necessary (Georgia). There is no neat delineation; immediate crises that endure can be placed on a (semi?) permanent footing managed as business as usual by a lead department rather than NSC, e.g. health departments for pandemics or police for counter-terrorism. When COVID-19's immediate crises became a long-term challenge, Argentina found it difficult to transition, especially where public consent had been sacrificed for speed at the start. Effective triggers and mechanisms for transition from crisis management to enduring problem, and from horizontal to vertical management, are needed.

Even long-term focused NSCs may have to respond in the short term. They should, however, balance being sucked into crises to demonstrate relevance against their (often unique) role in long-term planning of a nation's security posture. Failure to do so risks NSC capacity being consumed in reaction (Israel), and potentially exacerbating longer-term issues as second- or third-order consequences. This requires appropriate structures, processes and people bringing diverse perspectives to what are multifaceted problems.

Structure

Structure, under a systems-thinking approach, goes beyond the physical composition of the NSC. It includes the 'pattern of interrelationships among the key components' of the NSS,[8] including the NSC (and staff), the Executive, and government departments/agencies. While culture, manifested in the system's behaviours, is central to the challenges facing national security coordination, structures are still important. They act as planets, providing a gravitational pull that causes other actors (departments/agencies and individuals) in orbit to bend around them. In Kenya, for example, the NSC's existence helped democratize the security sector and made decision-making more inclusive.

---

[8]   Peter Senge (1994). *The Fifth Discipline Fieldbook* (London: Nicholas Brealey), 90.

The polity's nature and history impact on design. France's centralization of power reflects a fundamental principle of the Fifth Republic, hence its large staff is accepted; while in South Africa, increasing centralization raises fears about the oppressive use of national security that many suffered under apartheid. Other countries, such as New Zealand, for whom cooperation is second nature, have more diffuse and consensual decision-making mechanisms with smaller support structures. Ghana has a small structure but lacks the same tradition of cooperation, and government ambitions at coordination are undermined by competition between actors. Scope for competition is further exacerbated by ambiguity over the relationship between the National Security Coordinator and the President's NSA. This also affected Georgia before 2018, where rival Presidential and Prime Ministerial national security advisors lacked clear boundaries. Having a central figure cohering the system, such as an NSA, can help, provided they have both the capacity and credibility to deliver. In Kenya, the Head of the Public Service runs the National Security Advisory Committee, while in the UK concerns were expressed when the responsibilities of Cabinet Secretary and NSA were combined (briefly).[9] NSA capacity is also an issue in India.

Formal (legal) or informal (customary) systems affect structures. Formal systems can be transparent but slow to change, while customary systems are highly flexible but vulnerable to instability or confusion over lines of authority and accountability (India). Capacity, collectively or of individual actors, also impacts on structure. Strong central control may be needed where capacity is weak, but must be properly resourced to avoid staff, including the NSA, being forced to focus on administrative rather than policy matters and analysis, eroding overall effectiveness. Security sector reform efforts, particularly those driven by donors rather than the nation itself, need to guard against imposing solutions that are unsuitable and/or too ambitious in sophistication or timescales for the nation concerned, e.g. Iraq. Even where reform involves regional actors, it takes time for national security systems and individuals to adapt to accommodate and leverage the changes, e.g. Kenya; patience is essential.

Structures must reflect the role the NSC exists to perform.[10] While theoretically this might be crisis management or deliberate (long-term) security planning, in practice NSCs do both, (hopefully!) at different times. Typically, NSCs configure

---

9   Edward Elliott and Sam Goodman (14 July 2020). 'Global Britain'? Assessing Boris Johnson's major changes to national security and foreign policy. LSE BPP at https://blogs.lse.ac.uk/politicsandpolicy/johnson-natsec-and-fp/, accessed 30 August 2021.

10   Chan, op. cit., 7.

for one and adapt as necessary, but this can be difficult, e.g. Kenya's NSC is designed for, and clearly performs better against, internal than external threats. Another consideration is whether it is designed for all circumstances, or anticipates parallel systems being established for specific situations. Many countries (e.g. Japan, Norway) established parallel systems to manage COVID-19. In the United States, despite its NSC being structured to handle biological and pandemic responses, domestic policy and economic considerations overrode traditional response mechanisms, while New Zealand and Georgia chose to adapt existing NSC mechanisms, often with better initial outcomes. In Iraq, a separate body initially led on public health with the NSC focusing on mitigating the socio-economic impact of the pandemic. The NSC's involvement was subsequently broadened by a new Prime Minister who recognized ISIL's exploitation of security gaps resulting from the use of security forces in enforcing lockdowns and related restrictions.

The NSC and staff need sufficient capacity to allow for independent development of policy responses, but not so much that allows them to operate independent of or overwhelm other departments. The absence of the devolved administrations in the United Kingdom's national security decision-making is concerning because delivery involves them,[11] while in the immediate aftermath of Russia's 2014 invasion of Crimea, sensible decisions by Ukraine's National Security and Defence Council (NSDC) were sometimes ineffective because they exceeded the implementation capacity of other departments. Organizational maturity as much as individual competence is important to capacity. Argentina's Homeland Security Council, formed immediately after the fall of the military junta, lacked maturity as a democratic body and struggles to keep pace with the evolving security situation and the widely different views of security held by the left-wing (populist) and right-wing parties. Fundamental changes of emphasis with new governments or frequent ministerial reshuffles prevent organizations and systems from maturing, e.g. Georgia.

Most NSCs in this book are optimized for decision-making, which means significant activity occurs before a course of action is selected. Often, the staffs act as design authorities over positions prepared in individual departments,[12]

---

[11] Joint Committee on the National Security Strategy (JCNSS) (13 September 2021). *The UK's National Security Machinery.* HC231/HL68, 26.

[12] A Design Authority provides assurance that solutions are fit for purpose. It works to ensure that each component meets requirements and integrates and works within the complex enterprise architecture. See, Naomi Stanford (24 September 2018), 'Could We Use a Design Authority?', at https://naomistanford.com/2018/09/24/could-we-use-a-design-authority/, accessed 30 August 2021.

taking inputs and melding them into common positions. This avoids the problem Chan describes of NSCs becoming overly mighty bureaucracies taking scarce resources from elsewhere, but increases the risk of competition between departments' bureaucratic interests,[13] especially where departments are of unequal power. Those with the greatest resources and capacity to plan, typically defence departments, can disproportionately impact on decisions. Options, therefore, become an amalgam of one or two perspectives and not a genuinely inter-agency approach. Moreover, principals can sometimes come to meetings to protect their department's equity in a situation (United States), which makes finding solutions difficult; this is likely to be more of a problem in long-term planning because crises can create 'burning platforms' in which departmental ambitions may be subordinated to the greater good.

Post-decision implementation and management generally reverts to vertical structures. Departments deliver within their own siloes, although in Georgia the NSC staff developed an approach to monitoring the success of the COVID-19 response. This is less common, partly as a result of the size of most secretariats. While referring to the United Kingdom specifically, but of broader applicability, the Institute for Government highlighted 'the need for a well-resourced central secretariat and the difficulty of driving delivery from ... the small centre of UK government, as the secretariat – like any other part of the centre – suffers a capacity gap vis-à-vis departments'.[14]

Structures need to be designed with the ability to adapt, and all countries in this volume are on a journey of adaptation. Colombia and South Africa are still consciously on the path, but even those that feel themselves to be in equilibrium with today's security environment have to be able to respond to predictable or unpredictable (Black Swan) events.[15]

The NSS does not just comprise formal structures; it creates, reflects and sustains informal structures that allow issues to be aired widely and agreement gained about what is important for formal NSC meetings. This supports policy coherence. Aligning formal and informal structures is crucial, and part of the NSC's role is to nurture relationships as well as manage the system's activity. Formal and informal structures cannot become rigid, but require the ability to adapt, often at speed. New officials and/or ministers may need to be brought in

---

[13] Chan, op. cit., 3–4.
[14] Joe Devanny and Josh Harris (2014). *The National Security Council: National Security at the Centre of Government.* Institute for Government, 5.
[15] Nassim Nicholas Taleb (2007). *The Black Swan: The Impact of the Highly Improbable* (London: Penguin).

for new challenges, e.g. Ukraine's NSDC, with processes that give form to, but also accommodate, shifting structures.

Process

Processes as much as structures are shaped by the polity. The NSC has to fit culturally and processes work within the system and make the system work. Strongly federal structures pose different coordination challenges to more centralized systems. The complexity of governance in Argentina's federal system magnifies the need for coordination. Even more centralized systems require space for debate among different positions in a single Executive, let alone for coordinating political parties in coalition. In the United Kingdom, which does not have a tradition of coalition government, the transparency and predictability of a formal system was helpful in generating and sustaining trust.[16] In the United States, President Eisenhower's Solarium Project, while criticised by some for being little different to what went before and a compromise of all three options presented to the NSC,[17] enabled conversations over competing options. The compromise reached shows the value in having an NSC. NSCs can act as checks on particularly strong leaders seeking to move faster than the system can sustain. They also help protect against occasions where the head of government is weak, either through a weak mandate or in terms of their individual position, by providing collective authority.

Important though process is, bureaucracies need to resist the temptation to fixate on it: strengthening process in the wake of past failure, or applying more of the same process is not the same as improving outcomes.[18] However, transparency and clarity about the process helps. Having formalised doctrine that describes how the security system works can help in consistency and trust-building, both for those in the system and the public, and would benefit many countries, including India.[19] Transparency can help citizens distinguish between process and outcomes. While there is generally a positive correlation, bad outcomes do not necessarily mean bad processes, and even poor processes can occasionally get the right answer. Moreover, process transparency can help

[16] Author interview with United Kingdom NSC official, December 2020.
[17] John Lewis Gaddis (2005). *Strategies of Containment: A Critical Appraisal of American National Security Policy During the Cold War* (New York: Oxford University Press), 144.
[18] Fareed Zaharia (19 August 2021). Opinion: Here's Why the US National Security Apparatus Keeps Producing Failures'. *Washington Post*.
[19] Aaditya Dave (2022). 'India's National Security Council: Addressing a strategic gap'. *This volume*.

overcome confidence deficits in governments. Processes should be subordinate to outcomes, but fair processes help prevent abuses, create trust and enable better outcomes.

The basic NSC processes involve: information-gathering and filtering; problem analysis and option formulation by the staff working across departments; decision-making by the NSC or subordinate group; and monitoring and evaluating outcomes. Implementation of the decision tends to be the responsibility of individual departments and agencies rather than the NSC itself, although decisions are more likely to be implemented where those departments are represented in the process, even if only at subordinate boards.

- **Information-gathering**. Senior people on NSCs have little time to deliberate on complex issues, so administrative processes need to be good. Information-gathering requires access to a wide range of experts from inside and outside government to shed light and different perspectives on problems. This includes self-awareness to understand the nation's vulnerabilities and threat or risk tolerance, effective indicators and warning systems as well as understanding the threat or risk being faced.[20] India has formalized external input through its National Security Advisory Board comprising former bureaucrats, military and intelligence officials, academics and other experts. New Zealand's non-official advisory board supporting the Officials Committee for Domestic and External Security Coordination plays a similar role, as does Finland's Security Committee, which includes civil society, business leaders and NGOs.[21]
- **Problem analysis and option formulation**. Many countries have a dedicated staff supporting the NSC (Israel, Ukraine), but sometimes, this is too small to do all the analysis in-house, e.g. Norway, Argentina. In these circumstances, they use other government departments to generate the material. To avoid the risk of departmental positions dominating, special care is needed over the impartiality and quality of those in the secretariat. This requires the ability to present complexity in a balanced way and that helps decision makers understand the issues and trade-offs. The ability to share information is essential; elevating issues to high security classification levels should only be done where essential otherwise non-traditional

---

[20] Condoleezza Rice and Amy Zegart (May–June 2018). 'Managing 21st Century Political Risk'. *Harvard Business Review*.

[21] Turvallisuuskomitea Säkerhetskommittén: the Security Committee, at https://turvallisuuskomitea. fi/en/frontpage/, accessed 30 August 2021.

security actors without access to secure IT and communication systems can be excluded. The United Kingdom's decision to run the COVID-19 response from outside the NSC immediately reduced the classification and allowed a broader range of departments to engage during lockdown using non-secure communication means.[22] Producing material in a consistent and recognisable format also helps ministers/officials to assimilate it quickly and make decisions, as well as helping new members learn NSC processes. NSC subordinate committees, including those for officials, provide a means of quality control, refining papers to ensure they are suitable discussion and decision-making. There is a balance though between process and responsiveness, which can occasionally go too far towards elevating process, e.g. Prime Minister Olmert's Israel, or prioritize responsiveness over transparency (France or Japan).

- **Decision-making**. Formal decision-making generally occurs in the NSC, but often the subordinate groups, which may have a larger membership, are used to ensure the issues are aired widely and the problem is defined and presented appropriately. Smaller sub-groups of the NSC can be used for more directed action, e.g. the growing importance of the Four-Ministers Meeting in Japan against that of the Nine-Ministers Meeting.

  As well as the decisions themselves, transparency and accountability for the decisions are important, both within government and with the public. Where responses require changes in public behaviour, e.g. public health, or resilience against adversaries' attempts to undermine social cohesion, effective communication with the public is vital (Norway). Communication channels must be able to convey the complexity of the security environment without generating accusations of trying to securitize the population. Transparency, however, must be balanced by the need to create a safe environment in which participants can speak freely, including offering dissenting views on sensitive matters of national security. President Kennedy established the NSC Executive Committee after the Bay of Pigs incident, creating a safe space for challenge. The informal and confidential meetings, run without an agenda, authorized disagreements that improved national security decision-making[23] Confidentiality is important to effective decision-making, where openness is important in other parts of the process (e.g. Angola, Chad and Japan).

---

[22] Catarina Thomson (2022). 'The British National Security Council: It takes a village'. *This volume*.
[23] Tevi Troy (22 August 2021). 'All the President's Yes-Men'. *Wall Street Journal*.

- **Monitoring outcomes and lessons.** Most NSCs focus their efforts in the first three parts of the process, and a consistent theme in the case studies is a need systematically to monitor and evaluate implementation. Individual departments monitor their own activity, but successful delivery in each silo does not necessarily result in a coherent or successful outcome. 'Solutions' change the nature of a 'wicked' problem and effective monitoring of how departmental actions impact in aggregate is essential to identifying when responses should be adapted to reflect the changed situation. Of the countries in this book, New Zealand appears to have the most systematic monitoring process through lead agencies that cohere action on behalf of the whole government. Monitoring can also be provided by independent bodies scrutinizing the Executive, such as Parliamentary Committees or civil society. In jurisdictions like Canada, this is quite extensive. Where parliamentary capacity is less developed or marginalized, or civil society is weak, strong Executives or political parties can drive action in the name of national security without robust oversight, e.g. South Africa, Sierra Leone or Malawi. Whether formal monitoring (and evaluation) processes are robust or not, NSC's require the ability for self-reflection and learning to ensure the system develops and becomes more resilient.[24]

People

Creating a Council to talk about strategic issues does not make it strategic; it needs people who, individually and collectively, can think and act strategically.[25] This is nascent in the Indian political and bureaucratic leadership. NSCs can help develop habits of strategic thinking and collegiate working by exposing people to others operating in that way and giving them the opportunity to work together. Positive outcomes will reinforce the new behaviours. Anders Romarheim argues for such structural change to shape Norway's security culture, while acknowledging the challenges that imposing horizontal management may have on a strongly siloed system.[26]

---

[24] Chris Argyris (September–October 1977). 'Double-loop Learning in Organisations'. *Harvard Business Review*, 115–125.

[25] Peter Hennessey (1 October 2014). 'Lord Hennessey meets ... Lord Richards'. *Civil Service World*, at www.civilserviceworld.com/in-depth/article/lord-hennessey-meets-lord-richards (accessed 30 August 2021).

[26] Anders Romarheim (2022). 'Disjointed security: Assessing Norway's national security sector'. *This volume.*

Many NSCs remain highly dependent on personality, particularly post-Soviet states or countries making significant changes in approach, such as post-independence India or Japan's recent shift concerning use of the Self-Defense Forces. Strong personalities can make NSCs very effective, but this makes the system vulnerable to corruption (Iraq), appointment of party-political loyalists (South Africa) and/or rapid turnover (Ukraine) where authority waxes and wanes as key individuals change. This makes it harder to build trust within the system, even transparent ones with good processes.

The choice of NSA is particularly important. Not only do they play a vital role domestically, but they can be a focal point for engaging international security partners and diffusing tensions (India and Japan). The NSA must navigate competing interests as an honest broker, giving due voice and weight to smaller departments and the diverse groups whose input is needed. The individual needs to be close to the highest political levels of the Executive to understand the government's priorities and have the necessary authority to harness the bureaucracy effectively, but not so close that they cannot speak bureaucratic truth to power. Where they are brought in from outside the bureaucracy, such as in the United States, they also need to know how to work the bureaucracy to get things done. Clarity over whether they are a political or bureaucratic appointment is important because combining the two functions can be difficult, e.g. Israel, or the UK's flirting with appointing a political figure as NSA. Georgia's approach combines a political NSC Secretary balanced with an apolitical head of the NSC staff, an approach that has both benefits and risks.

The Secretariat also needs the right people, and in numbers appropriate to its role, with case studies ranging from approximately 1,000 for France to six for Norway, reflecting their very different functions. The United States makes extensive use of secondments into the NSC staffs from elsewhere in the NSS, which refreshes the talent pool but can bring parent department 'baggage'. However, the NSC staff must not become a mere stepping-stone to better things in which people do the minimum time to qualify for something else. A degree of staff stability is necessary for creating the relationships and networks essential to the system's effective running.

The US NSS is extremely open to bringing people in from outside. With many senior positions for officials being political appointments, a revolving door exists between the Executive and think tanks. This continually refreshes the organization, but externals may not understand how the bureaucracy works and struggle to get things done. Other countries, such as the United Kingdom and France are less (perhaps too little) open to recruiting external experts, but permanent officials offer continuity by serving administrations of whichever hue and possess tacit knowledge from experience that is not easily learned by those brought in from outside.[27] Education and experience are essential, and subordinate meetings can be training grounds for those who are part of the NSS during crises but not routinely (United Kingdom). Even permanent administrative staff who develop expertise in the vertical elements of the system need to learn horizontal working and behave beyond departmental stovepipes (Norway). The NSS works best when people have experience of working, or learning with each other. The United Kingdom is planning a cross-government College for National Security for strengthening a national security profession,[28] but must avoid this becoming closed to outsiders. President Macron closed the French *Ecole Nationale d' Administration* over criticisms that it lacked diversity and was out of touch.[29]

Effective NSS engage others outside government. An informed wider society can help conceptualize and indeed operationalize national security activity.[30] How the NSC engages with external specialists, such as civil society organizations, academics and think tanks etc., helps obtain the diverse views needed for fresh perspectives on wicked problems, promote healthy debate, reassure the public that the actions are necessary and compliance appropriate. Ghana's 2020 National Security Strategy involved a commendable willingness to incorporate a plurality of opinions, including academic challenge. This approach though is not universal. Civil society's involvement is often constrained, either through secrecy surrounding national security policies and strategies, or under-development of civil society; in Ethiopia, civil society organizations were banned for twenty-eight years.

Reward

The ability to incentivize the right behaviours is crucial to success. Coordinating bodies, such as NSCs, require the ability to 'overcome power structures and build a culture of cooperation'.[31] How they do this reflects different beliefs about

[27] Michael Polanyi (1966). *The Tacit Dimension* (London: Routledge).
[28] JCNSS, op. cit., 43–44.
[29] Kim Willsher (8 April 2021). 'Macron announces closure of elite school that hothoused French leaders'. *The Guardian*.
[30] Abel Esterhuyse (2022). 'South Africa: In search of both security and process'. *This volume.*
[31] United Nations (2012). *E-Government Survey. E-government for the People.* ST/ESA/PAS/SER.E/ 150, 63.

power and how it is wielded within government. Charles Handy[32] describes multiple power bases from which authority is drawn. NSCs may prefer, or depend on one primary source, but need more than one. 'Position Power', where authority comes from its formal, constitutional, position in the security ecosystem, is common.[33] Often enshrined in statute, e.g. Georgia, it can be less formal, drawn from custom or place in the system, e.g. the United Kingdom. There is, however, a danger in thinking only about formal authority. In Kenya, the misalignment between a horizontal and collaborative NSC sitting above strongly vertical siloes means each counters the other's preferred approaches. The NSC's dependence on formal authority can be like pumping water uphill; it takes considerable and constant effort to force the system to work counter to its natural state. Formal power may not reflect reality: Ghana highlights a disconnect between de iure and de facto authority, hence both formal and informal systems must be considered.

NSCs' real power often combines power bases: 'resource power' through controlling access to things others need; or 'personal power' of strong leaders with personal mandates or relationships. Typically, NSCs take three approaches:

- A vertical integrator, with a large and powerful secretariat acting as a design authority drawing authority from its position above other actors (e.g. France).
- A horizontal integrator, whose power comes from access to cross-cutting knowledge and its position in the centre of a knowledge web (e.g. United Kingdom).
- A network manager, enabling system-wide discussion and trust across organizational boundaries through common experiences and shared responsibility (e.g. New Zealand).

The vertical integrator is expensive in staff resource but can drive decisions and act swiftly, albeit at the cost of constraining debate and potentially being culturally challenging for nations without a strong tradition of, or imperative for, centralizing power. Position Power is its primary source of authority, requiring responsibilities to be clearly defined and understood by the NSS. It also harnesses 'Resource Power' by controlling access to senior levels of the Executive, funding or other valued commodities.

---

[32] Charles Handy (1986). *Understanding Organisations*. 3rd Edition. (London: Penguin), 124–126.
[33] Handy, op. cit.

Horizontal integration is less directive, where the NSC and staff use 'Expert Power' derived from their ability to see the security landscape from a different, more comprehensive position. They are the point at which individual departmental or agency perspectives come together. A convening authority, they set the agenda, bring others together and generate fresh understanding through the breadth of perspectives to which they uniquely have access. This involves access to government expertise, but also external experts free from the constraints imposed by being part of government.

The network manager relies on the ability to convene others. It often lacks staff capacity, so rather than reserving insights for itself, it diffuses power across the network of relationships it creates. The NSC (or the network itself, as in Canada) invests less in managing tasks than managing the relationships that deliver the tasks – akin to how joint ventures are managed.[34] This prioritizes building system capacity and may ultimately be more effective in dealing with long-term wicked problems. However, unless it is exercised and tested regularly, it may lack the decision-making immediacy needed in a crisis and struggle in larger systems when personalities change more quickly than trust can be generated. It might, therefore, be more suited to smaller governments, e.g. New Zealand.

In all three, 'Personal Power'[35] has an effect, positive or negative, and the status of the NSA (and head of the staff support function where separate) is vital. This is particularly important in new NSCs, before it can generate or harness other forms of power, but a NSC whose power depends solely on the NSA's personal authority is unlikely to remain effective. Personalities and allegiances change as part of the normal cut and thrust of democratic governance, e.g. Argentina, Colombia, India, Israel. The NSA, therefore, should embed the organization in the system, establishing alternative bases of power on which it can rely.

Power can also be used to stop things happening – 'Negative Power'.[36] Understanding how departments and agencies, especially those with the greatest political weight and/or resources, retain negative power is important. Overmatching the NSC, they can either impose 'prefabricated' policy position(s), potentially designed to different specifications, or force the NSC into challenging fiercely defended 'turf' positions rather than designing a genuinely integrated strategy (United States). This can result in lowest common denominator

---

[34] Rosabeth Moss Kanter (July–August 1994). 'Collaborative Advantage: The Art of Alliances', *Harvard Business Review*, 96–108.
[35] Handy, op. cit., 127.
[36] Ibid., 127–129.

decision-making that fails to respond to the challenges. Where fear of oppression remains high, negative power can be used to prevent actors becoming too powerful by limiting positional and resource power, and/or ensuring personal power is weak through rapid staff turnover.

Rewards cannot merely be negative (forcing compliance); incentivizing the right behaviour is more important over the long term, which depends on the NSC's ability to demonstrate value at three levels:

- **System.** The system needs to recognize the value of coordination. This might result from an exogenous shock for which the incentive is to: respond more effectively/prevent a recurrence (Colombia); mark a change from the past (Argentina, Iraq, United Kingdom), or; deliver security sector reform initiatives (Kenya, The Gambia). However, system incentives on their own are weak. Imposed coordination can be rejected, and external events, even ones that shock a nation, may not be sufficiently compelling (Norway or Israel's 2006 Lebanon War). COVID-19 could become a global burning platform for nations where departmental cooperation is not embedded in the culture by forcing diverse actors to work together. The challenge may be in sustaining the habit of security system management beyond the immediate crisis. This may also require organizational and individual incentives to overcome bureaucratic inertia.

- **Organizational.** Incentivizing at the organizational level is difficult if the NSC is seen as usurping existing departmental power or resource.[37] Where cooperation produces better outcomes, this can off-set perceived loss of departmental independence. While easier to achieve during crises, where the imperative to work together is greatest (Norway), crises are not the best training grounds. Trust cannot be surged in a crisis, so NSCs need to build up repositories of goodwill and the habit of cooperation before they are needed in earnest. This partly explains why separate structures for new emergencies may not be as effective as the bespoke nature of the response might otherwise suggest, e.g. Colombia. Exercises and rehearsals can demonstrate value and educate, including for those who might otherwise be marginalized in the security process (New Zealand).

- **Individual.** Attracting the right people and reinforcing the right behaviours requires appropriate rewards. This is not purely about remuneration, although Ukraine's experience shows its importance, but intrinsic elements,

---

[37] Chan, op. cit., 7.

such as purpose, opportunities to make a difference and status. These are powerful factors in attracting talent in Georgia, but are less evident in Norway.

Final remarks

The countries in this volume have different histories, political and bureaucratic systems, face a unique range of threats and have set different roles for their NSCs. Nevertheless, key themes and issues emerge. They are horizontal coordinators of otherwise vertical government structures. They are networked throughout the system, able to call on a broad range of actors and draw their authority from both the political and bureaucratic parts of the Executive. They have access to staff support, including from outside the polity to access diverse perspectives on the challenges. Beyond this, variations in strategy, structures, processes, people and rewards are substantial. The issue is achieving their alignment at the system, organization and individual levels, which is easier said than done. The environment is fluid, so the NSC must continually evolve to achieve this.

20

The orchestration of National Security Systems: The NSC as conductor

Paul O'Neill

The value of a NSC (or equivalent) derives from its unique position to act on and through a network of departments/agencies that allows coordinated action towards a common goal. This book sought to understand the factors influencing the need for, and the mechanisms used to, coordinate national security. Its starting hypothesis was that there is no universal structural solution to how a NSC should look, which the case studies confirm. The means of coordination need to be as unique as: the mix of threats and risks the nation faces; the government system and imperatives of national security culture(s) in which responses are generated and delivered; and the demands of the coordinating body's role. Form must follow function and NSCs are varied, and continually evolve as their environment changes. Effective NSCs help decision-makers consider options for responding to national security problems and enable others to make sense of the myriad choices facing nations as their security needs change over time and then act. Rarely are the issues simple or amenable to a definite 'solution'; they involve judgements about (often finely balanced) risks. The lessons from NSCs are equally relevant to other whole-of-government approaches and security sector reform.

While different in detail, effective approaches have some common characteristics. NSCs work *horizontally*, across traditional vertical departmental responsibilities, operating at the centre of a *network* they are responsible for nurturing. They require strong *support* and reinforcement from both the political and administrative parts of the Executive, and need access to an effective staff. The NSC itself is often merely the top *tier* of bodies that allow issues to be handled at the most appropriate level. Finally, the system is *open* to diverse views that generate shared understanding of the nature and dynamics of security's wicked problems.

Key lessons

Three key lessons for the coordination of national security are revealed from the case studies (the three Cs). The NSC must be:

- **congruent** across three axes of: threat/risk; system; and purpose or role;
- **capable** individually and as a part of a capable national security system; and
- **credible**, both to others in the system and to those outside.

In many respects, the NSC is like the conductor of an orchestra, seeking to create harmony among individually highly accomplished players. Congruence requires that the conductor's interpretation remains true to the composer's score and works with the character of the musicians and instruments. Capable reflects the skills of individual musicians (or sections of the orchestra), and the conductor's ability to liberate, synthesize and integrate them; it concerns how the music flows among the players and the effect this has on the sound. Credible is a multifaceted expression of trust; the trust between players and conductor that all will perform predictably and subordinate themselves to the music, which is learned through rehearsals and performing together, and in the audience's trust that the performance will repay the investment in attending.

Congruence

Congruence reflects how well the NSC works across the three design axes: the nature of the threat; nature of the national security system; and its purpose and role.

Threat. The threat(s), risks and opportunities must justify creating a horizontal coordination mechanism at the highest levels of government that is superimposed on otherwise vertical structures. Raising matters for coordination at national level increases the costs in terms of time, money, people and goodwill, and removes the issue from individual departments with expertise in delivery. As with other joint ventures, the relationship must be of strategic *importance* to all the parties to justify the costs.[1] This depends on the nature and magnitude of the threat(s) and opportunities, although often the focus is skewed towards threat reduction and less on exploiting opportunities. Where the threat, risk or ability to exploit an opportunity exceeds the capacity of any single actor, and greater

---

[1]   Rosabeth Moss Kanter (July–August 1994). 'Collaborative Advantage: The Art of Alliances', *Harvard Business Review*, 100.

value derives from cooperation than the loss of independence, partners are more likely to cooperate. Although where a population perceives its government to be part of the threat and fears a strong NSC may become a tool of repression, central coordination can be rejected.

While most countries have similar high-level national security aims, typically around protecting their territory and people, the concept of security itself is contested.[2] Not all problems are the same, and numerous variations about appropriate responses abound. Some require rapid action, others are longer term, requiring deliberate planning, e.g. climate change. Human threats are generally amenable to persuasion through deterrence, coercion or compellence, while others, such as natural hazards, are not. Some require nationally coordinated responses, others do not. Even where responses need national-level coordination, some may benefit from more localized variation in delivery, e.g. COVID-19 responses that allowed for local variations in delivery were often more effective than monolithic central approaches.

Recognizing and configuring for the nature of the threat(s) is crucial. However, a paradox in complex adaptive systems is that optimizing for one problem can increase fragility against others; there is a trade-off between specific efficiency and general adaptability.[3] Moving towards the presenting problem is wise, but in doing so it is important to preserve the ability to adapt as the problem itself does, and continue scanning the horizon for new threats while retaining capacity to respond to them. Where possible, optimization needs to be viewed at an output level and against long-term capability, not merely inputs. Congruence, therefore, considers a suite of threats, not just the immediate problem, although sometimes, the speed and scale of a threat precludes this (e.g. Russia's annexation of Crimea). This may justify taking specific issues off the NSC, protecting its ability to focus on wider or existential issues, as many countries did with their COVID-19 responses.

Many of the case studies identify a broadening range of issues for which action at the highest level of national security is demanded. Elevating issues to a NSC can help raise their importance and attract resources, but making everything a matter requiring a national security response can cause problems by insulating the topic and stifling wider debate.

[2]   Barry Buzan (1991). *People, States and Fear: an Agenda for International Security Studies in the Post-Cold War Era* (London: Harvester Wheatsheaf), 6.
[3]   Alexander Siegenfeld and Yaneer Bar-Yam (2000). 'An Introduction to Complex Systems Science and Its Applications', *Complexity*, 4, at https://necsi.edu/an-introduction-to-complex-systems-science-and-its-applications, accessed 18 July 2021.

An NSC is valuable for enabling broad debate, even if only within an exclusive security establishment but often more widely, which is essential for genuinely wicked problems that are best addressed through debate and challenge. A feature of wicked problems is the 'no-stopping rule'[4] – how much security is enough/ how much risk is acceptable – which requires fine judgements about the risk being faced and the costs of securing against them in terms of freedoms, resources and lost opportunity costs. Breadth and diversity of membership is needed to provide appropriate insights into, and authority over, the tools required to respond to the security challenges(s), but there is a trade-off between a proper appreciation of the problem and the urgency to respond.

Inevitably judgements about risks are shaped by the likelihood and impact of the event, with imminent and/or existential threats to homeland or people crowding out issues that may be longer-term or more concerned with quality of life. Governments tend to find it easier to deal with threats than risks, and opportunities are even harder to address for many reasons. Threats are more tangible than risks, and can focus the collective mind more sharply. Risks are infinite but resources are not,[5] while addressing opportunities is harder still because overcoming institutional and bureaucratic inertia is easier when problems are concrete and proximate.

How threats, risks and opportunities are viewed depends on understanding the referent object of security. There has been a general, though not universal shift from state to human security, with a broadening of issues, actors and thus relationships that fall within the purview of national security. This adds complexity, which can be particularly hard for fledgling systems lacking solid institutional foundations, such as those in post-independence/liberation nations in Africa, where it is not always clear if the beneficiary is intended to be the state, people or governing party.

National security system. The complex nature of the threats and risks requires a culture that values debate among diverse actors to uncover the dynamics of the problems being faced, where reactions depend 'less on probabilities than behavioural factors'.[6] The question of *who* should be part of this debate is not directly addressed in this book, but is a major issue for democracies generally,

[4]   Horst Rittel and Melvin Webber (1973). 'Dilemmas in a General Theory of Planning'. *Policy Sciences*, vol. 4, 162.
[5]   Mikkel Vedby Rasmussen (2006). *The Risk Society at War: Terror, Technology and Strategy in the Twenty-First Century* (Cambridge: Cambridge University Press), 7.
[6]   Paul Bracken, Ian Bremmer and David Gordon (2008). *Managing Strategic Surprise: Lessons from Risk Management and Risk Assessment* (Cambridge: Cambridge University Press), 6–7.

and points to the need for nationally bespoke processes and mechanisms that balance inclusion and responsiveness, debate and consensus, understanding of problem interdependencies and action. The NSC must fit within and be congruent with the wider system in which it operates, especially where that system is congested or has competing agendas. Creating and strengthening the networks through organizational and individual interaction that creates trust, habits and the ability to shortcut processes through familiarity across the system is crucial.

Often behaviours are problematic because the system reinforces vertical (departmental) structures and merely balances the NSC as a horizontal coordination layer over the top without embedding it or changing reward systems to incentivize cooperation. Without a culture of cross-function cooperation, the risk of rejecting horizontal working, or more likely 'consent and evade', is greatest, especially where the NSC's remit extends beyond decision-making and into delivery or holding other actors to account for delivering the decisions made. Regardless of where the NSC sits on the spectrum from coordination to control, it must be congruent with the wider system's traditions, aims and capacity if it is to coordinate effectively.

Effective control may be impossible, except in nations with a tradition of strong central control, otherwise coordination may be the best that can be hoped for, especially in federal structures where legal authority is reserved to regions. Alternatively, centralized models that allow local actors to shape outcomes also work. How nations conceive security, often determined by history, is highly relevant to the NSC's design. Some formally differentiate defence and security, but this muddies authority where threats straddle both. Others, often with strong colonial baggage, prioritize human security and civil liberties, and strengthen transparency and oversight, and/or constrain the system's power. History's shadow need not be permanent, and nations beginning with hard security have successfully become softer by diversifying Council membership; COVID-19 accelerated this for many, and new crises may provide further opportunities to respond differently by demanding the system adapt its size, shape or internal relationships.

Role. NSCs are designed by intelligent people and typically are appropriate to their role at the time, but that can change. The design needs to be *institutionalized*[7] so it is understood, not just by those inside the NSC, but by those forming the wider security ecosystem; all need clarity of their responsibilities, accountabilities, and when and how the NSC needs to act. Where the NSC has a wide remit, investment is needed in the wider polity so membership can be adjusted easily

---

[7]   Kanter, op.cit.

to match new security threats; this should include a broad range of cross-government departments and agencies (central, and where appropriate regional), ministers and the Executive's administrative function – the Civil Service or equivalent. COVID-19 responses show some countries using their NSCs, while others set up parallel arrangements. While not essential, or even desirable, for all national security matters to go through the NSC, the criteria for determining whether something is tackled through normal bureaucratic channels or the exceptional arrangements of an NSC need to be understood. NSCs should avoid being sucked into immediate activity that can be delivered by normal (vertical) government mechanisms, and that consumes long-term planning or horizontal management capacity that NSCs are best, even uniquely, placed to provide. Where national coordination is needed, however, governments should 'guard against creating parallel structures or institutions because these complicate the difficult job of coordination' unless they have prior experience of collaboration.[8] During COVID-19, new and untested non-NSC systems initially caused problems for those without experience of national-level coordination, until the habits were learned.

The challenge with remaining congruent is that while national security is dynamic, bureaucracies typically are not. Creative dissatisfaction is important to ensure NSCs remain relevant to potentially rapidly changing environments where past successes are no guarantee of future effectiveness of the structure, processes or outcomes. Embedding capacity to adapt within the NSC, both for itself and in its connections with other actors on a system-wide basis, becomes essential.

Capability

Sustainable systems dynamically balance what is wanted and their ability to deliver. The case studies suggest this is not always the case, e.g. strong and ambitious leaders set unrealistic demands that the system cannot sustain, or rely on (non-existent) credibility of institutional or individual actors within and outside government. This can also be because the nature or magnitude of new threats exceeds planning assumptions (COVID-19, Russian annexation of Crimea), or where well-meaning external actors demand security sector reform without working under local leadership or sharing ownership.[9]

---

[8] United Nations (2012). *e-Government Survey. Chapter 3. Taking a Whole-of-Government Approach*, 63.

[9] OECD (2007). *The OECD DAC Handbook on Security Sector Reform (SSR): Supporting Security and Justice*, 14.

Capability, akin to what Kanter calls '*individual excellence*', is required, but throughout all levels of the national security ecosystem: individual; organizational, and system.[10] All three are desirable, but where two exist they may be able to compensate for weaknesses in the third. Success is unlikely if capability exists in only one domain, or none. The NSC and/or wider security sector may need external help, including through donor-led initiatives as part of security sector reform programmes. In these situations, capacity-building efforts must consider all three elements, not narrowly focus on the NSC as a discrete organization. Too often, capacity-building is organizationally (department) focused, and efforts invested in developing the NSC fail to grow the capacity of other actors or the relationships between actors to the extent necessary to make the whole greater than the sum of its parts. Security sector reform can set unrealistic ambitions and timelines by not understanding the maturity of the different elements, or superimposing alien solutions out of context. This results in structures, processes and people that cannot sustain the changes, and become dependent on external help.[11]

Individual capability. System and organizational capability rest on a foundation of individual competence and relationships. A diverse talent pool with the right skills to develop strategies and get the system to deliver is needed. A sign of the *investment* in the NSC is the degree to which it attracts high-calibre people. This may require talent from outside government as well as developing those already in the system. There is, however, a Catch-22: talent and diversity are essential to understanding the problems but can erode capacity for action as alpha personalities clash and arguments proliferate. Building behaviours and the competence for working horizontally atop vertical expertise is vital for effective cooperation and applies not just to administrative parts of the Executive but its political members. HR practices that reward horizontal appointments and movement across government siloes are important, as are training and exercises. These should engage a wide group of ministers and officials, but it is impossible to predict with complete accuracy all who will need to be involved. Moreover, both politicians and officials can change roles quickly so investment in training and exercises etc. is needed to familiarize actors with the debates and processes and help spread the horizontal mindset but is a continuous process. It should be done before individuals are needed for a crisis because trust cannot be surged on demand. It needs building and strengthening before it is asked to bear the pressures of an emergency.

---

[10] Kanter, op. cit.
[11] Ann Fitz-Gerald (2022). 'National security structures in Africa'. *This volume.*

Organizational capability. The NSC and its staff are important actors and must be up to the task in terms of its structure, process, people and rewards, but it is not enough. The other departments/agencies (nodes in the national security web) must also be competent; effectiveness depends on all the organizational actors in the system and what they can and cannot do for themselves. An essential part of this is to be aware of the resource imbalance that often exists across government, with ministries of defence and homeland security often richer in resources and capacity to plan for contingencies. This can give them a dominant voice in security discussions that drowns others out. All partners must bring value to and seek positive benefits from the alliance if they are to cooperate successfully – Kanter's *interdependence*.[12] Each must be competent in their own role and competent in working together. Where the nation has come from is important, particularly how much time has elapsed since forming their national security bodies, and the degree to which the journey has been consistent enough to allow the organizations to mature. Institutions created rapidly, and those that experience fundamental changes of emphasis with new governments or frequent ministerial reshuffles can lack the institutional maturity necessary to deliver effectively. Time and practice are needed for organizational (and system) development.

System capability. Whereas organizational capability focuses on the nodes, system capability considers how the nodes are connected – the relationships. Paul Jackson describes security sector governance as 'best understood as a function of political networks', so the NSC cannot be considered independent of the system.[13] The strength of the network to cope with the demands placed on it is fundamental to overall effectiveness. Investing in communications, through both physical networks (the technologies for sharing information, especially that which is classified) and the human connections and relationships, creates and sustains the system. The flow of *information* needs to be open, enabling partners to share insights and perspectives.[14] Flexibility in information's passage around the system can change how structures perform; system processes can change even rigid structures and help them operate differently for different purposes. Knowing what needs to follow vertical rules and thus what can take horizontal (or diagonal) paths is important, but requires trust.[15] Trust leads to effective

[12] Kanter, op. cit.
[13] Paul Jackson, 'Security Sector Reform and State Building: Lessons Learned', in Albrecht Schnabel and Vanessa Farr, eds. (2012). *Back to the Roots: Security Sector Reform and Development*, Geneva Centre for the Democratic Control of Armed Forces, 252.
[14] Kanter, op. cit.
[15] Stanley McChrystal (2015). *Team of Teams; New Rules of Engagement for a Complex World* (London: Portfolio Penguin), 196.

integration, through the development of shared ways of working and horizontal connections in which peers can engage directly without always having to escalate information before it moves across the network.[16] The network bounds are conditioned by how security is viewed: narrow definitions involve smaller networks and are easier to create and nurture. Where the definition is broader, actor complexity increases and the effort required to create or sustain it is commensurately greater. Nations that have the luxury of narrower definitions of security or can develop models of cooperation before a crisis can find it easier to cope in emergencies.

The openness of African nations to external expertise for developing individual, organizational and system capacity is positive, even if the outcomes have not always been successful. But capacity building has typically worked in one direction – from the global North to the global South. Developed nations need to be more open to learning, for example from African nations whose experience of Ebola and AIDS helped many of them deal with COVID-19 with ingenuity.[17]

Credibility

Important though Congruence and Capacity are, the consent of the parties to being coordinated is important. That consent is most likely where the NSC, NSA and staff are credible – honest brokers that add system value because if working horizontally does not add value, there is little incentive for others to incur the cost of cooperating outside their vertical siloes. It is this credibility that creates their informal authority. It is underpinned by how they communicate, their ability to ensure an all-informed network by sharing relevant information and by the degree to which they can create shared values and goals that lower the costs of control.[18] Cooperation fails where it conflicts with the bureaucratic interests of sovereign departments or agencies, hence credibility in working *with* rather than *on* the system, organizations and individuals is essential. Credibility is fragile and can be damaged by difficult relationships, often resulting from unclear roles, authorities and accountabilities. But personal credibility may not be enough. Political support is vital from across the Executive, but it needs

---

[16] Kanter, op. cit.
[17] Maru Mormina and Ifeanyi Nsofor (15 October 2020). What Developing Countries Can Teach Rich Countries. *The Conversation*, at https://theconversation.com/what-developing-countries-can-teach-rich-countries-about-how-to-respond-to-a-pandemic-146784 (accessed 30 August 2021).
[18] Abdulkader Sinno (2008). *Organizations at War in Afghanistan and Beyond.* (New York: Cornell University Press), 74.

to be more than individual patronage; the system needs to have roots in the bureaucracy if it is to flourish and endure beyond an electoral cycle.

Generating credibility requires trust, and as with other whole-of-government approaches, 'how to get there is as important as getting there'.[19] The NSC and staff need to be able to forge and sustain constructive relationships and create new value by harnessing the diverse perspectives across the system. In Kanter's terms, *Integrity* is essential. An independent NSA builds trust and reassures the partners that the alliance is not a take-over. Christopher Shoemaker describes the NSA's importance thus:

> The entire national security system must have confidence that the [NSA] will present alternate views fairly and will not take advantage of propinquity in the coordination of papers and positions. He must be able to present bad news to the president [...] sniff out and squelch misbehavior [...]be scrupulously honest in presenting presidential decisions and in monitoring the implementation process. Perhaps most important, he must impart the same sense of ethical behavior to the Staff he leads.[20]

Opportunities are needed to build credibility: a history of success helps create a positive reputation, but crises are the most unpredictable and demanding of situations. Moreover, good processes do not automatically result in good outcomes, and governments must be realistic about what they can achieve. Trust and credibility have to be earned before they are given, so engaging across the polity through subordinate bodies with wider membership, exercises and other shared experiences in safe environments can help generate trust, ensuring it exists before it is needed. This should allow for easier transition of responsibility from the NSC to departments and agencies when the issue becomes normal government business.

Trust is also built when all parties' *investment* in the joint venture is clear, including ensuring the right people participate and find time for its activities, especially if it is not the sole role for many of those involved.[21] Politically independent administrative functions supporting the Executive should develop career paths that ensure people understand how to coordinate across departments. Where key players are tied to single departments or are political appointees who change with each administration, it can be harder to manage the transitions and more effort needs to be spent in creating trust and building credibility. However, if the NSC is made too broad, its composition can become too fluid to sustain trust among its members. Trust is highly individual, shared,

---

[19] OECD (2006). *Whole of Government Approaches to Fragile States*, 41.
[20] Christopher Shoemaker (1991). *The NSC Staff. Counseling the Council* (Boulder, CO: Westview), 115.
[21] Kanter, op. cit.

if at all, between people, rather than positions, so it must be refreshed when key players change; this increases the organizational cost of coordination.

If credibility within the system is based on trust in peoples' behaviour and intentions, those outside, unless they understand the process, can only judge the NSC's credibility based on its outcomes or independent verification of how the system behaves. As outcomes are uncertain, engaging the wider polity in the process through clarity over accountability and transparency is important for gaining and sustaining credibility. This can be compromised where dominant political parties bypass the normal bureaucracy, placing too much power in the hands of the Executive without effective checks by the legislature. But transparency must be balanced against the need for confidentiality when dealing with sensitive matters of national security. Having vetted bodies, such as the UK's Intelligence and Security Committee, helps because NSC members must feel confident about expressing their views, including dissent, freely. Open and transparent processes, and external scrutiny may be slower, but are important for building long-term trust and commitment among the population whose security the system seeks to ensure.

The dangers of a shortfall in connectivity between national security and the population is recognized in the United Kingdom's integrated Review, which asserts a need to 'become better connected to, and fully representative of, the people'.[22] This reflects similar language in UN Security Council Resolution 2553(2020), that urges 'efforts that enhance the trust and confidence between national security actors and institutions, and the population'.[23] More than merely an exercise in communications, it requires appropriate oversight, and a commitment to rooting out all forms of corruption, which is highly corrosive of trust.

Credibility both inside and outside the system requires that the system learns from its experience. The NSC and staff need the ability to monitor and evaluate the impact of its decisions and reassess the collective response to ever-changing security challenges. Feedback loops and the ability to learn from experience are vital. This requires: systematic problem solving; experimentation with new approaches; learning from experience and past history; learning from others' experiences and good practices; and transferring knowledge quickly and efficiently throughout the system.[24] It is also enhanced through independent, objective scrutiny and transparency. Being at the centre of the network, the NSC is uniquely placed to enable the generation and passage of information essential to system learning.

[22] HM Government (2021). *Global Britain in a Competitive Age*, 98.
[23] United Nations Security Council Resolution 2553 (2020), 5.
[24] David Garvin (July–August 1993). 'Building a Learning Organization'. *Harvard Business Review*, 81.

Conclusion

The bodies coordinating responses to national security challenges operate as part of a dynamic environment of risks, threats, government structures and public expectations of how governments should respond. This ecosystem is in a state of permanent flux. As the context changes, so too must the national security system. As a (even *the*?) key part of that system, the NSC and staff have to adapt. This requires 'flexibility and agility [...] in the way in which departments tackle cross-cutting challenges, with clearer accountability for delivery'.[25]

Collectively, the national security system seeks to bring risks and threats below the level needed for coordinated state-level action requiring coordination through an NSC. Understanding when not to act, and whether to act quickly or slowly, is essential. As is knowing what the NSC can or must engage with, what is best left to other parts of the system and when to transition between horizontal and vertical arrangements (and vice versa). A starting point is to reflect on whether the situation requires coordinated action by the national security system – Figure 20.1.

Assuming a need for coordinated action, the body responsible for this needs to ensure it is: congruent with the threats, how government works and its role; capable at the individual, organizational and system levels; and credible to other parts of the system and the wider polity, including the population. The following

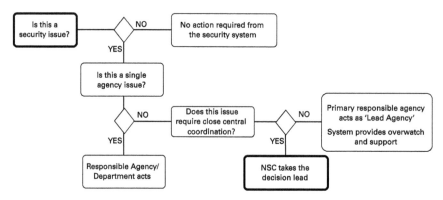

Figure 20.1 Decision tree for taking action against a threat/risk.[26]

[25] Global Britain in a Competitive Age, op. cit., 97.
[26] Developed in collaboration with Dr Jim Rolfe, Victoria University of Wellington.

questions might be asked of any national security system – Table 20.1. Whatever answers result are not necessarily right or wrong, but should demand a follow-up question: 'Is this the way we want it to be?'. If the answer is 'no', change is needed.

Table 20.1 Evaluating the National Security Systems' fit

Congruence

Overarching question: *Does the country have a clear understanding of what constitutes national security and how to achieve it?*

1   What does 'security' mean for the country? Do all agencies follow the same definition?

2   Do all agencies work to a common understanding of the risks to national security?

3   Are roles and responsibilities clear and understood?

4   How do agencies receive direction on security issues? Is that direction mandatory?

5   To what extent do agencies work with each other as a matter of routine? What are the obstacles to working together?

6   Is there a clear understanding of the relationship between career and elected or politically appointed officials in security matters?

7   How do officials work with political leadership to achieve a common understanding of threats and the necessary responses?

Capacity

Overarching question: *Do the system and the organizations within it have the capacity to deliver the outcomes expected of them?*

1   Is the network of organizations robust for the task and resilient? How extensive and how strong are the relationships? How dependent are they on one or a small group of individuals?

2   Are there sufficient resources (people, materiel, access to information etc.) to meet the identified tasks and risks?

3   Do the system's processes allow regular and timely meetings between responsible agencies to examine risks and determine the most appropriate responses?

4   Are the nodes, and the relationships connecting the nodes strong enough to deliver what is needed?

5   Do the members of the system have experience of working together, e.g. exercises, training, etc.?

6   Is there a means for bringing emerging risks to the attention of senior politicians and managers?

7   Is there a means for determining trade-offs between different forms of security threats and response?

8   Do actors in the system have the individual and collective capacity to deliver the outcomes anticipated?

9   Does the NSA have the trust of the political and administrative elements of the system?

10   Does the staff attract high-calibre people: is it seen as career enhancing?

Credibility

Overarching question: *Does enough trust exist to enable effective working within the system, and is the system itself sufficiently trusted?*

1   Do those in the system share the same values and goals?

2   Are there agreed principles against which security activity is conducted?

3   Does the system allow for regular dialogue between political and non-political officials?

4   Do the NSC and staff have a reputation as honest brokers?

5   Is the system capable of learning and adapting to events? How does it determine the effectiveness of the decision (not just how actions are implemented)?

6   Is the system suitably transparent and subject to appropriate oversight by the Legislature, in particular committees overseeing aspects of security?

7   Are all the elements within the system sensitive to the needs of other groups with security responsibilities?

The answers may change over time, and the NSC must change with them. This changes the rest of the system in a permanent cycle of evolution. The capacity to undertake effective organizational design, therefore, is crucial. However, the ability to manage relationships may be more important to security outcomes than the structure itself; as John Kania and others argue, 'transforming a system is really about transforming the relationships between people who make up the system'.[27] For some nations, especially those that mistrust strong national security coordination or for whom departmental cooperation is not part of the culture, COVID-19 offers an opportunity. It has forced diverse actors to cooperate; the challenge now is to sustain the habit beyond the immediate crisis.

As the national security system's conductor, the NSC interprets the score, determines the allocation of tasks, sets the tempo, rehearses and syntheses each player's input towards a harmonious collective outcome. The free-ranging nature of the security environment, however, requires the ability to manage the emergence arising from complex adaptive systems; this is more jazz than classical – Monk rather than Mozart.

---

[27] John Kania, Mark Kramer and Peter Senge (June 2018). *The Water of Systems Change*. FSG, 7.

Afterword

After this book was written, in February 2022 the Russian Federation illegally invaded Ukraine. As the book went to press, the conflict was ongoing but already thousands had been killed. Our thoughts are with the people of Ukraine.

Ukraine's National Security and Defence Council (NSDC) was at the centre of planning for and managing the response to the Russian invasion. Following the 2014 annexation of Crimea, the NSDC had prioritized countering aggression from the Russian Federation, and had worked to build relationships with supportive governments. However, when the Russian government's aggressive military posturing turned into war, it caught the people of Ukraine, and indeed many other countries (including many in the Russian military and general public) off guard. Consequently, not everything Ukraine aspired to or needed to protect its sovereignty was in place.

Ukraine's national security strategy prioritized membership of NATO and the European Union, but partly prompted by concerns among some members of those organizations about provoking Russian aggression, Ukraine had not joined. In making its strategy dependent on EU and NATO membership, however, Ukraine effectively ceded control of its strategy to the members of those organizations. While Ukraine had made progress towards satisfying the membership criteria, there was not enough time. And time is a critical resource in developing and implementing a national security strategy. Ukraine's government did build support short of membership. Ukraine received non-lethal military aid, weapons and training, which Ukraine's armed forces used bravely and effectively. However, Ukraine was slow to adopt a strategy that mobilized the whole nation. The National Resilience Concept was adopted in 2021 with the Territorial Defence Forces launched in January 2022. These added civilian components to Ukraine's defence system, akin to the Total Defence approaches in Finland or Sweden (and others), but late.

This book argues that effective design of a NSC requires: *congruence* with the threat, security system and NSC purpose; *capable* institutions and people, and; *credibility*. Considered as a single body, the NSDC had many positive features against these criteria. However, its relationship with other parts of the national security system was less developed. The reliance on informal mechanisms, such as the personal power of key individuals, was a constraint, and the NSDC also faced problems with other security actors over whom it lacked power. However, even if the NSDC had addressed these issues, it may not have been enough to prevent the February 2022 invasion. It faced an overwhelming threat that exceeded Ukraine's national capacity. But it would be inappropriate and unfair to criticise or blame Ukraine's government and NSDC for the Russian Federation's invasion or Ukraine's response, which showed remarkable courage and unity in the face of overwhelming firepower. Responsibility sits firmly at President Putin's door.

Military attack by powerful neighbouring states may not be the only overwhelming threat beyond the capacity of any single nation: climate change may well be another. Nations and NSCs will need to learn to coordinate their actions, not just nationally but internationally too, perhaps this is the evolution beyond National Security 3.0 that Lord Sedwill describes in his Foreword: National Security 4.0 perhaps. If so, congruence, capability and credibility will remain relevant but take on an international dimension. The greater actor complexity this will entail reinforces the need for institutions and people that can build and sustain effective partners and partnerships.

Author biographies

Manuel Almeida

Dr Manuel Almeida is the Head of Research at ARK Group, specializing in stabilization, development, and preventing and countering violent extremism (P/CVE) projects on behalf of governmental donors and international organizations, in support of vulnerable and hard-to-reach communities. He is also a Civilian Advisor to the UK's Stabilization Unit. He is an expert on mix-methods research in fragile and conflict affected states, post-conflict stabilization, and prevention of violent extremism, with a special focus on the Middle East and North Africa. He holds a PhD in International Relations from the London School of Economics and Political Science on the theme of top-down interventions in 'failed/fragile states'.

Kwesi Aning

Professor Kwesi Aning is Director of the Faculty of Academic Affairs and Research (FAAR) at the Kofi Annan International Peacekeeping Training Centre, and Clinical Professor of Peacekeeping Practice at Kennesaw State University, Atlanta. He served as the African Union's first continental expert on counterterrorism from 2005–2007. In 2006 and 2014, he wrote the independent mid-term in-depth evaluation of the Global Programme on Strengthening the Legal Regime against Terrorism and a UN Secretary General's report on the African Union relating to peace and security for the UN Security Council. Until January 2019, he served on the UN Secretary General's Advisory Group for the Peacebuilding Fund. He holds a BA(hons) in History from the University of Ghana and a doctorate in Political Science from the University of Copenhagen, Denmark. He specializes in peacekeeping economies, hybrid security/political orders and organized crime.

Patrick Chevallereau

Vice Admiral (ret'd) Patrick Chevallereau was the Defence Attaché of France to the United Kingdom between 2015 and 2018. He had a leading role in managing the defence bilateral relations between the two countries and served as the senior defence advisor to the French Ambassador to the UK. Previously, he served as Head of the Euro-Atlantic Division at France's Joint Headquarters, working as the senior advisor to the Chief of Defence for NATO, EU and bilateral defence relations policy with over fifty countries in the Euro-Atlantic sphere. He has worked with officials across the French administration, serving as the Deputy Secretary General for the Sea between 2011 and 2013, helping to manage inter-ministerial coordination and drive policy development for France's maritime strategy as well as maritime crisis management in the world's second largest exclusive economic zone. He also served in various positions at NATO's Allied Command Transformation. including as Executive Assistant to NATO's Supreme Allied Commander Transformation. As a naval aviator, he participated in joint operations in the Mediterranean, Africa and the Balkans.

Aaditya Dave

Aaditya Dave is a Research Analyst focusing on South Asia at the Royal United Services Institute (RUSI). His research interests include South Asian foreign policy, regional security and strategic dynamics, and Chinese engagement with South Asia. He is part of the Navigating the Indo-Pacific programme within ISS and works on India's role in the Indo-Pacific and maritime security in the Indian Ocean Region. Prior to joining RUSI, he worked using open-source intelligence to identify specific hotspots for militant activity in South Asia for both private and public sector clients. He has completed an MA in Conflict, Security and Development from King's College London.

Abel Esterhuyse

Professor Abel Esterhuyse is a member of the Department of Strategic Studies in the Faculty of Military Science, Stellenbosch University at the South African Military Academy. Holding a PhD from the University of Stellenbosch, he is also a graduate of the Senior Leadership Programme of the African Center for Strategic

Studies in Washington DC and the Programme on the Analysis of Military Operations and Strategy (SWAMOS) of Columbia University's Saltzman Institute of War and Peace Studies in New York. Before joining academia, he served as a lieutenant colonel in the South African Army. A rated scientist of the South African National Research Foundation, he specializes in South African security, military strategy and conflict processes. His most recent publication is a journal article titled 'The South African security predicament: making sense of the objective realities'.

Ann M. Fitz-Gerald

Professor Ann M. Fitz-Gerald is the Director of the Balsillie School of International Affairs and a Professor of International Security in Wilfrid Laurier University's Political Science Department. She has worked at both at the Centre for Defence Studies, King's College, London University, and at Cranfield University, where she was the Director, Defence and Security Leadership. She is widely published on issues concerning conflict, national security and security sector governance, with a particular focus on Africa. She is a Visiting Professor at Nkumba University (Uganda), Jimma University (Ethiopia), Njala University (Sierra Leone) and Queen's University (Canada). She has advised, and has been seconded to work with, a number of countries on issues relating to national security policy/strategy issues including Ukraine, Lebanon, Ethiopia, Afghanistan, Botswana, Jamaica, Sierra Leone, Albania, Montenegro and Nigeria. She is currently facilitating the development of the Gambian defence policy. She also supported H.E. Thabo Mbeki's AU High Implementation Panel during the post-referendum peace talks between North and South Sudan.

Charles (Chuck) Freilich

Professor Chuck Freilich, a former deputy national security adviser in Israel and long-time senior fellow at Harvard's Belfer Center, teaches political science at Columbia, NYU and Tel Aviv Universities. He is the author of *Zion's Dilemmas: How Israel Makes National Security Policy* (Cornell Press 2012); *Israeli National Security: A New Strategy for an Era of Change* (Oxford Press 2018); and *Israel and the Cyber Threat: How the Startup Nation Became a Global Cyber Power* (forthcoming 2021). He has published numerous academic articles and over 170 op-eds, and appears frequently on US, Israeli and international TV and radio stations.

Aram Habeeb Ahmed

Aram Habeeb Ahmed is an Iraq-based researcher and analyst specialized in security and development. He is currently the Iraq Research Officer at ARK Group, working on a project which focuses on strengthening social cohesion and community resilience in three governorates, including the liberated areas. He has significant experience in the humanitarian sector in Iraq, working with multiple international NGOs in Iraq, as well as the United States Agency for International Development (USAID) during and after the conflict with Islamic State. He obtained his bachelor's degree in English Language and Literature from Kirkuk University in Iraq in 2014.

Frank Hoffman

Dr Frank Hoffman has served as a Distinguished Research Fellow at the National Defense University, Washington DC, since 2011. A retired US Marine infantry officer, he has served over forty-two years in the US defense establishment, including thirty years with the Marines as an analyst and concept developer, and senior executive-level appointments at the Pentagon. In addition to his research portfolio in strategy and military innovation, he regularly teaches at NDU and the wider US joint education system. He also serves on the Board of Advisors at the Foreign Policy Research Institute, and as a Senior Associate Fellow at RUSI. He graduated from the Wharton Business School at the University of Pennsylvania in 1978 and holds Masters degrees from George Mason University and the US Naval War College. He earned his PhD in War Studies from King's College, London. His latest book is *Mars Adapting: Military Change During War*, Naval Institute Press (2021).

Yasuhiro Matsuda

Professor Yasuhiro Matsuda is Professor of International Politics at the Institute for Advanced Studies on Asia, University of Tokyo. He received his PhD in law from the Graduate School of Law at Keio University in Tokyo. He spent sixteen years in the National Institute for Defense Studies, Japan Defense Agency (later, Ministry of Defense) subsequently moving to the Institute for Advanced Studies on Asia. His research focuses on Japan's foreign and security policies and wider Asia, including politics and foreign relations in the PRC and Taiwan. He served on the Council on

Security and Defense Capability in the New Era, the Prime Minister's advisory group. In 2011, he won the seventh Yasuhiro Nakasone Award of Excellence. He has published numerous books and articles in Japanese, English and Chinese. Recent publications in English are: *China's UN Peacekeeping Operations Policy: Analysis of the Factors behind the Policy Shift toward Active Engagement* (2016); *The Taiwan Policy of the Xi Jinping Administration in its Second Term: An Outlook on Cross-Strait Relations in the 'New Era'*, Society of Security and Diplomatic Policy Studies (2018); Changes in the Dynamics of the Taiwan Strait due to Taiwan's Success in Controlling the Novel Coronavirus, *Asia-Pacific Review*, vol. 27 (2020).

Paul O'Neill

Paul O'Neill CBE is a Senior Research Fellow at RUSI with over thirty years' experience in strategy and human resources. He worked on the United Kingdom's Strategic Defence and Security Reviews in 2010 and 2015 and the National Security Capability Review 2018. He has advised the Afghan Ministry of Interior on strategy and policy. His research interests include national security strategy and organizational and people aspects of defence and security. He has masters degrees in laws, defence studies and international relations, and was a Chief of the Air Staff Fellow at the Universities of Cambridge and Oxford. He is a Companion of the Chartered Institute of Personnel and Development and visiting professor at the University of Winchester.

Oscar Palma

Dr Oscar Palma is an Assistant Professor at the Faculty of International, Political and Urban Studies, and former Director of the Observatory on Illicit Drugs and Weapons, at Universidad del Rosario, Colombia. He has a PhD in International Relations from the London School of Economics, and an MA in International Security Studies, University of Leicester, as a Chevening Scholar. He is a Visiting Lecturer at the George C. Marshall Center for European Security Studies in Germany, a Scholar at the William J. Perry Center for Hemispheric Security Studies, in Washington DC and a visiting lecturer at the Joint War College of Colombia and the Schools of Intelligence of the Colombian Navy and Army. Formerly a Colombian Army Intelligence Officer, he was a member of the Centre for Strategic Studies at the Joint War College in Bogota. He is also a Coordinator for the

International Federation of Committees for the Liberation of Hostages in Colombia (FICIB), a member of the Board of Directors for the PeaceStartup Foundation, and member of the International Board of Editors of the Journal *Politics*. His analysis of national security is sought for several national and international media outlets.

Jim Rolfe

Dr Jim Rolfe is a Senior Fellow at the New Zealand Centre for Security Studies, Victoria University of Wellington. He has spent his career working on aspects of national and international security both as a practitioner and as a scholar. He has worked in think tanks in New Zealand, Australia, the United States and Indonesia, for the UN in East Timor and Libya and as an officer in the New Zealand armed forces and an official within the New Zealand national security system. His research interests and publications have focused primarily on New Zealand's national security interests and on Asia-Pacific regional security issues.

Anders Romarheim

Dr Anders Romarheim is an Associate Professor at the Institute for Defence Studies (IFS), a part of the Norwegian Defence University College where he heads the Centre for International Security. Previously he was affiliated to the Norwegian Institute of International Affairs from 2003 to 2006. He was part of the writing team for Norway's National Security Law, adopted in 2019. He has also been a guest researcher with the Centre for Strategic and International Studies in Washington DC. His academic interest is national security in its broadest sense, specializing in terrorism, US security policy and digital influence operations. He holds a PhD in War studies from King's College, London and a master's degree in Political science from the University of Oslo. He briefs the Norwegian government at all levels, including parliament, comments to Norwegian media and regularly gives public lectures on security matters.

Nalia Salihu

Dr Naila Salihu is Research Fellow and Deputy Programme Head at the Faculty of Academic Affairs and Research (FAAR) at the Kofi Annan International

Peacekeeping Training Center (KAIPTC). She is also a faculty member and lecturer for post-graduate programmes at KAIPTC. Naila holds a PhD in Defence and Security, from Cranfield University UK, with a dissertation on Transforming Defence in Ghana's Fourth Republic. She obtained a Master of Philosophy Degree in International Affairs and Bachelor of Arts (Hons) in Political Science and Linguistics from University of Ghana. Her research interests include Peacebuilding, defence and security sector governance in Africa. She has published extensively, focusing on Ghana, Cote d'Ivoire, Burkina Faso and African regional institutions, specifically ECOWAS and African Union.

Hugh Segal

The Honourable Hugh Segal OC O.Ont CD is a Mathews Distinguished Fellow in Public Policy at the School of Policy Studies, Queen's University, Kingston and Senior Advisor at Aird & Berlis, LLP, Toronto. He served in the Canadian Senate from 2005 to 2014 and chaired the Foreign Relations and Special Anti-Terrorist Senate Committees. Previously Chief of Staff to the Canadian Prime Minister and Associate Cabinet Secretary in Ontario, he was President of the Institute for Research on Public Policy in Montreal, Chair of the NATO Association of Canada and former Co-Chair of the Democracy-10 Strategy Forum, a Track2 round table (CIGI, Atlantic Council). Principal Emeritus of Massey College at the University of Toronto he holds honorary doctorates from Royal Military College, Queen's University and the University of Ottawa. A recipient of both the Conference of Defence Associations Vimy Award for service to democracy and national security from the Conference and the Churchill Society's Award of Excellence, he has written several books on public, foreign and defence policy, conservative politics and income security. He is a former member of the Commonwealth Eminent Persons Group, which focused on modernization, human rights and the rule of law.

Natia Seskuria

Natia Seskuria is a Founder and an Executive Director of the Regional Institute for Security Studies (RISS), a Georgia-based think tank specializing in security in the Black Sea region. She has a broad experience in policy-making, strategic foresight and analysis on defence and security issues. A Black Sea Fellow at the Middle East Institute (MEI), she also holds an advisory role at Chatham House and is an Associate Fellow at RUSI. She is a lecturer in Politics at the Business and Technology University and the University of Georgia. Previously she served at the Office of the National Security Council and Ministry of Defence of Georgia. She has also worked for the Foreign Editor of *The Sunday Times* of London, and in the International Security Studies Department at RUSI. Her research focuses on conflicts and security in the South Caucasus and the Black Sea region. She holds an MA in Politics, Security and Integration and a BA (Hons) in Politics and East European Studies from University College London.

Hanna Shelest

Dr Hanna Shelest is the Head of Security Programmes at the Foreign Policy Council 'Ukrainian Prism' and Editor-in-chief at UA: Ukraine Analytica. Prior to this, she spent more than ten years as a Senior Researcher at the National Institute for Strategic Studies under the President of Ukraine, Odessa Branch. In 2014, she was a Visiting Research Fellow at the NATO Defence College, Rome. Previously she had experience in PR and lobbying for government and business, as well as teaching at Odessa National University. She was an adviser of the Working Group preparing Ukrainian Navy Strategy 2035. She is currently involved in working groups developing Foreign Policy Concept of Ukraine, Asian Strategy for MFA, and Ukraine's NATO Public Communication Strategy. Dr Shelest led different policy related projects, among others: Scorecards of the Ukrainian Foreign Policy (2016–2020); The Hybrid War Decade: Lessons Learned to Move Forward Successfully (2019), Foreign Policy Recommendations for the Parliament of Ukraine (2017–2020); Ukrainian Naval Forces Strategic Appraisal (2018); Ukrainian Peacebuilding School (2014–2017); Elaborating recommendations on the Ukrainian OSCE Chairmanship (2012–2013).

Singo S. Mwachofi

Singo S. Mwachofi teaches Comparative Politics and International Relations at the Department of Political Science and Public Administration, University of Nairobi, Kenya. He is also consulting Deputy Director at the Security Research and Information Centre (SRIC), a Kenyan civil society organization researching small arms and light weapons proliferation. From 2007–2014, he served as Director for the Peace and Security Programme at the International Conference on the Great Lakes Region (ICGLR) based in Burundi. A member of the Editorial Board of the Arms Trade Treaty Monitor (ATT), he is also an Associate Research Fellow at the Horn International Institute for Strategic Studies, where he co-chairs the Maritime Working Group. He has researched and published on Small Arms and Light Weapons proliferation, regional dimensions of conflict and peacebuilding, terrorism, and governance. He is a trainer and facilitator at the International Peace Support Training Centre (IPSTC) based in Nairobi. He is currently reading for his PhD in Public Policy at the University of Nairobi, focusing on Security Policy.

Catarina Thomson

Dr Catarina Thomson is Senior Lecturer in Security and Strategic Studies in the Politics Department of the University of Exeter. Her background is in clinical psychology and international relations. Her approach to security studies incorporates political psychology and domestic factors to understand the strategic behaviour of state and non-state actors in times of international conflict. Her recent work compares the foreign policy attitudes of security experts and the general public in the UK, Europe, and the United States, incorporating quantitative methods with qualitative interviews. Her work has been funded by the American National Science Foundation, the US Department of Defense's Minerva Research Initiative, and the Economic and Social Research Council among others. Catarina is a research affiliate at START (National Consortium for the Study of Terrorism and Responses to Terrorism) and is unreasonably proud to be the University of Exeter's 2019 Winner of the 'Whose Lecture is it Anyway' Comedy Improv trophy.

Martin Verrier

Martin Verrier is an international security specialist. He served as Argentina's Deputy Secretary of State for Drug Enforcement between 2015 and 2019. Previously, he worked as a senior consultant for international organizations (IADB, OAS, PADF), directing operations at a Buenos Aires security consulting firm and served as Head of the Security Committee Advisor's Board at the National Parliament. He is a former Professor of International Relations Theory at the International Relations Department and the Organised Crime Postgraduate course at Universidad de Belgrano, Buenos Aires and was a money-laundering prevention professor at the Universidad de Buenos Aires. He has a BA in International Relations from the Universidad de Belgrano in Buenos Aires, a MA in Strategy and Geopolitics from the Argentine Army War College, a Postgraduate Certificate in Countering Transnational Organised Crime from the George C. Marshall Centre European Centre for Security Studies, Garmisch-Partenkirchen, Germany. He completed a MA in Intelligence as a Chevening Scholar at Kings College London, and currently resides in London working as an independent consultant, an Associate Fellow of RUSI and an adjunct professor at the George C Marshall Center, Germany.

Selected further reading

National Security Coordination

Africa

Arthur Chan (2018). *Overcoming Challenges Arising from the Creation of National Security Councils: a Framework and Lessons from Sub-Saharan Africa*. RAND.

Paul Nantulya (February 2016). *More than a technocratic exercise: National Security Strategy Development in Africa*, Africa Centre for Strategic Studies.

Argentina

Guillermo O'Donnell and Philippe Schmitter (1986). *Transitions from Authoritarian Rule: Tentative Conclusions about Uncertain Democracies* (Baltimore, MD: John Hopkins University Press).

Canada

Minister of Supply and Services Canada (1979–1981). *Commission of Inquiry Into Certain Activities of the Royal Canadian Mounted Police*. First Report, *Security and Information*, 1979; Second Report, *Freedom and Security under the Law*, 1981; Third Report, *Certain RCMP Activities and the Question of Governmental Knowledge*, 1981.

Ghana

Kwesi Aning. 'Resurrecting the Police Council in Ghana' in Alan Bryden and Fairlie Chappuis eds. (2015). *Learning from West African Experiences in Security Sector Governance* (London: Ubiquity).

Emma Birikorang and Naila Salihu (Forthcoming). *The Securitization of Health and the Security Sector; Ghana and Covid-19*.

India

Harsh Pant ed. (2016). *The Routledge Handbook of Indian Defence Policy: Themes, Structures and Doctrines* (London: Routledge).

P.S. Raghavan (2019). 'The Evolution of India's National Security Architecture', *Journal of Defence Studies*, vol. 13(3).

Israel

Charles Freilich (2012). *Zion's Dilemmas: How Israel Makes National Security Policy* (New York: Cornell).
Charles Freilich (2013). 'National Security Decision-Making in Israel: Improving the Process', *Middle East Journal*, vol. 67(2).

Kenya

President of Kenya (2020). *Annual Report to Parliament on the State of National Security*.
Francis Omondi Ogolla (2014). *Determinants of Kenya's national security policy since independence*. Masters Dissertation, University of Nairobi.

Japan

Ministry of Foreign Affairs (27 October 2015). *Diplomatic Bluebook 2014 Summary*.

New Zealand

Department of the Prime Minster and Cabinet (August 2016). *National Security System Handbook*.
DPMC National Security Governance System at https://dpmc.govt.nz/our-programmes/national-security-and-intelligence/new-zealands-national-security-system/national-1.
Royal Commission of Inquiry (26 November 2020). *Report of the Royal Commission of Inquiry into the terrorist attack on Christchurch masjidain on 15 March 2019*.

Norway

Gjørv Commission Report (2012). *NOU 2012: 14, Rapport fra 22. juli-kommisjonen* at www.regjeringen.no/no/dokumenter/nou-2012-14/id697260/.

South Africa

Lindy Heinecken (2020). *South Africa's Post-Apartheid Military: Lost in Transition and Transformation* (Switzerland: Springer).
Jacques Pauw (2017). *The President's Keepers: Those Keeping Zuma in Power and Out of Prison* (Cape Town: NB Publishing).

South African Government (December 2018). *Report of the High-Level Review Panel on the State Security Agency*.

United Kingdom

Paddy Ashdown, George Robertson et al. (2009). 'Shared Responsibilities: A national security strategy for the United Kingdom. Final report of the IPPR Commission on national security in the 21st Century'. *Institute of Public Policy Research*.

Joe Devaney and Josh Harris (2014). *The National Security Council: National Security at the Centre of Government*, Institute for Government.

Joint Committee on the National Security Strategy (JCNSS) (13 September 2021). *The UK's National Security Machinery*. HC231/HL68.

United States

John Lewis Gaddis (2005). *Strategies of Containment: A Critical Appraisal of American National Security Policy During the Cold War* (New York: Oxford University Press).

Volker D. Franke and Robin Dorff eds. (2012). *Conflict Management and 'Whole of Government': Useful Tools for U.S. National Security Strategy?* (Carlisle, PA: Strategic Studies Institute).

Security sector reform

African Union (2014). *SSR Trends and Challenges in Africa: a Partners' Summary of the first Africa Forum on SSR*.

Laura R. Cleary and Roger Darby eds. (2021). *Managing Security: Concepts and Challenges* (Abingdon: Routledge).

Ann Fitz-Gerald (2012). *SSR and Peacebuilding: Thematic Review of SSR and Peacebuilding and the Role of the Peacebuilding Fund*. United Nations.

Ann Fitz-Gerald, Paula MacPhee and Ian Westerman, 'African Militaries, Security Sector Reform and Peace Dividends', in David Francis (2017) *African Peace Militaries* (London: Routledge).

Paul Jackson (2018). 'Second-Generation Security Sector Reform'. *Journal of Intervention and Statebuilding*, vol. 12(1).

OECD (2006). 'Whole of Government Approaches to Fragile States'. *DAC Guidelines and Reference Series*.

OECD (2007). *The OECD DAC Handbook on Security Sector Reform (SSR): Supporting Security and Justice*.

Geneva Centre for Security Sector Governance (DCAF) (November 2014). *SSR Trends and Challenges in Africa: A Partner's Summary of the First Africa Forum on SSR*.

Albrecht Schnabel and Vanessa Farr, eds. (2012). *Back to the Roots: Security Sector Reform and Development*, Geneva Centre for the Democratic Control of Armed Forces.

Management studies /organizational design

Chris Argyris (September–October 1977). Double-loop Learning in Organisations. *Harvard Business Review*.

Jay Galbraith (2014). *Designing Organizations: Strategy, Structure and Processes at the Business Unit and Enterprise Levels* (San Francisco: Jossey-Bass).

Charles Handy (1986). *Understanding Organisations*. 3rd Edition. (London: Penguin).

Rosabeth Moss Kanter (July-August 1994). 'Collaborative Advantage: The Art of Alliances'. *Harvard Business Review*.

Complex adaptive systems

John Kania, Mark Kramer and Peter Senge (June 2018). *The Water of Systems Change*. FSG.

Alexander Siegenfeld and Yaneer Bar-Yam (2020). 'An Introduction to Complex Systems Science and Its Applications'. *Complexity*, at https://necsi.edu/an-introduction-to-complex-systems-science-and-its-applications.

Risk management

Mikkel Vedby Rasmussen (2006). *The Risk Society at War: Terror, Technology and Strategy in the Twenty-First Century* (Cambridge: Cambridge University Press).

Paul Bracken, Ian Bremmer and David Gordon (2008). *Managing Strategic Surprise: Lessons from Risk Management and Risk Assessment* (Cambridge: Cambridge University Press).

Wicked problems

Jeff Conklin (2008). *Dialogue Mapping: Building Shared Understanding of Wicked Problems* (Chichester: Wiley).

Horst Rittel and Melvin Webber (1973). 'Dilemmas in a General Theory of Planning'. *Policy Sciences*, vol. 4.

Endorsements

'In this fascinating and methodical book, we get unique insight into an area of the security sector that is notoriously difficult to access, especially for researchers: national security. Through rigorous analysis and a wide range of case studies, we are given a view of how national security councils and coordination work, what it looks like when they do and do not, and why coordination of the security sector is crucial. Thank you to the editor and authors for this tour de force that is an excellent companion for practitioners and researchers alike.'

Peter Albrecht, Senior Researcher,
Danish Institute for International Studies

'A timely and much-needed comprehensive study of national security structures building upon the experiences of different countries, political systems and strategic cultures. An invaluable reference for academicians, political analysts, foreign policy experts and practitioners working in the field.'

Dr Yevgenia Gaber, former Foreign Policy
Advisor to the Prime Minister of Ukraine (2021)

'It is an excellent idea to review the different approaches countries have taken in building their security organizations. I regret that this sort of book was not around when we were designing New Zealand's system. Where we had largely to rely on our own circumstances, we can now compare and learn from the wider experience of many others from across the world.'

Gerald Hensley, New Zealand's first Co-ordinator of
Domestic and External Security (1987–1989)

'The book fills in an important gap in existing literature and will serve as an invaluable source for practitioners, academics and researchers to explore how different nations have developed coordinating security bodies in response to existing threats. The book provides a comprehensive comparative analysis of successes and shortcomings of respective bodies in different countries, including in dealing with the

COVID-19 crisis. Such literature would have served as an incredibly useful resource at the time when we were forming the new National Security Council of Georgia.'

Nino Iobashvili, Member of the Parliament of Georgia
Deputy Head of the Office of the National Security Council
of Georgia (2019 – 2021)

'An invaluable source for those interested in understanding how different states define their national security and organize their state institutions to address the challenges they face. The book provides a concise, yet comprehensive comparison of the national security structures of a diverse array of states. The go-to source for practitioners, scholars and students alike.'

Ilan Mizrahi, Former Head of Israel National Security Staff
and Deputy Head of Mossad

'This is an important and timely book – it enables practitioners and researchers to learn from a wider base of experience. I recognize from the UK experience, that any NSC must focus elite expertise to coordinate the essential Whole of Government approach to strategic challenges; but it must do so without creating an over-whelming burden of extra "process" (described as "meeting hell" by one UK MOD official during the Libya operation).'

Lieutenant General (Retd) Professor Sir Paul Newton KBE,
Chair in Security and Strategy, Director of Strategy And
Security Institute, University of Exeter

'This book is – simply – a great idea. Through such diverse examples it allows the reader to reflect on how different governments have sought to adapt to the network of threats and vulnerabilities in the modern world by developing new ways of organizing and co-ordinating thought and action. In most cases this adaption is still a work in progress, and that is precisely why the insights here will be so useful both for current practitioners and for all those in academia who study national security, international relations, politics and governance.'

Suzanne Raine. Visiting Professor at King's College London,
Affiliate Lecturer at the Centre for Geopolitics,
University of Cambridge. Former British Foreign and
Commonwealth Office specialist on foreign policy,
counter terrorism and national security issues.

'A ground-breaking book which makes the first broad comparative survey of an important issue: how governments are organizing to respond effectively to the ever-widening range of security threats. Full of fascinating insights and rigorous analysis, it's just the kind of guide to best practice I could have done with when I had to set up the UK's National Security Council!'

Lord Peter Ricketts, first UK National Security Advisor (2010–2012)

Index

In sorting Arabic names, the definitive article is ignored.
The letter *f* following an entry indicates a page that includes a figure.
The letter *t* following an entry indicates a page that includes a table